TREASURES OF THE BASEBALL HALL OF FAME

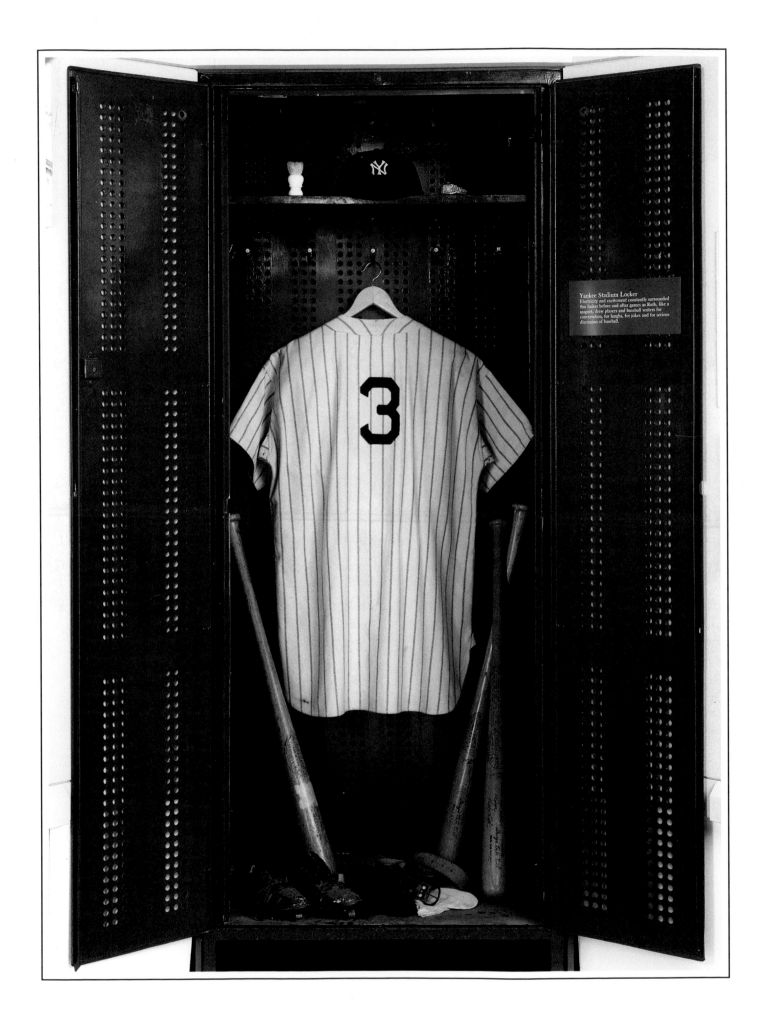

Yankee Stadium Locker

Electricity and excitement constantly surrounded this locker before and after games as Ruth, like a magnet, drew players and baseball writers for conversation, for laughs, for jokes and for serious discussion of baseball.

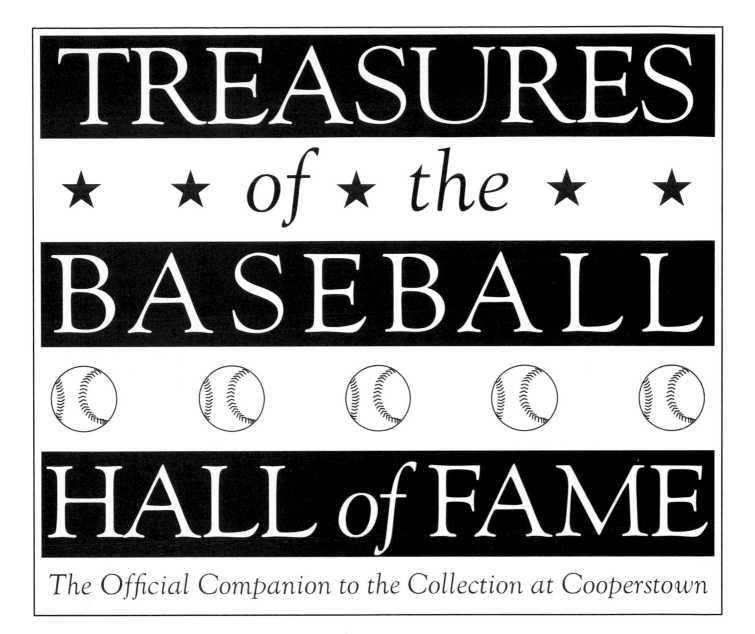

TREASURES ★ of ★ the ★ BASEBALL HALL of FAME

The Official Companion to the Collection at Cooperstown

JOHN THORN
and the
National Baseball Hall of Fame and Museum

PHOTOGRAPHS BY DAVID JORDANO

Foreword by Ted Williams
Introduction by Donald C. Marr, Jr.

VILLARD
NEW YORK

All rights reserved under International and Pan-American Copyright Conventions.
Published in the United States by Villard Books, a division of Random House, Inc., New
York, and simultaneously in Canada by Random House of Canada Limited, Toronto.

Villard Books is a registered trademark of Random House, Inc.

Library of Congress Cataloging-in-Publication Data

Thorn, John
Treasures of the Baseball Hall of Fame / John Thorn and the
National Baseball Hall of Fame and Museum; introduction by Donald
C. Marr, Jr.
p.   cm.
Includes index.
ISBN 0-375-50143-6
1. National Baseball Hall of Fame and Museum.   2. Baseball—United
States—History.   3. National Baseball Hall of Fame and Museum—
Catalogs.   4. Baseball—United States—Equipment and Supplies—
Catalogs.   I. National Baseball Hall of Fame and Museum.
II. Title.
GV863.A1T48   1998   796.357'074'74774—dc21   97-45740

Random House website address: www.randomhouse.com
Printed in the United States of America on acid-free paper

2 4 6 8 9 7 5 3

FIRST EDITION

Book design by Carole Lowenstein

For Jacquie, my treasure

July 25, 1966.

I remember it as if it were yesterday. Back then, the Hall of Fame ceremonies were held in a little park at the rear of the Hall. A beautiful place. Just beautiful. The crowd gathered on the slopes of a tree-shaded hillside. Gosh, there were an awful lot of people.

And there I was. Theodore Samuel Williams—a skinny kid from San Diego—being welcomed into Cooperstown. Well, maybe I wasn't skinny anymore—but you get the picture. Getting inducted with me was Casey Stengel. The Old Perfessor. And welcoming the two of us were those players and managers already in the Hall: Joe McCarthy. Joe Cronin. Bill Dickey. Bill Terry. So many greats. So many.

I gave a little speech that day. And part of it was about the greats who *weren't* there. The Negro Leaguers who didn't get a chance to play alongside us. Now many of those fine players, outstanding players, *are* enshrined in Cooperstown. I like to think I had a little to do with it. I hope I did.

It means a lot to be a member of the Hall of Fame. It's a great honor. To be named as one of baseball's greats, as one of the best ever at your profession—boy, you *can't* beat it. It's the culmination of a lot of hard work. A lot of practice. A tremendous lot of effort. That's what creates excellence. That's what creates a Hall of Famer.

But there's more to being a part of Cooperstown than being named as one of the game's immortals. It's also a privilege to be associated with a tremendous institution like the National Baseball Hall of Fame. The Hall is a lot more than plaques, you know—and you will certainly realize that after reading this fine book. You see, the full name of the operation in Cooperstown is the "National Baseball Hall of Fame *and Museum*." And it's a helluva museum, covering just about everything that has to do with this great game. It's baseball's Metropolitan Museum of Art, Library of Congress, and Louvre all rolled into one.

What's in Cooperstown? That's the wrong question. What isn't? The Hall of Fame traces baseball's history from the very beginning: trophies, bats, uniforms, gloves—from the immortals, from the great moments in the game's history. Photos and programs and advertisements. Films and sheet music. You name it. It's all there and presented in a way that will knock your eyes out. You learn something new—you see something new—every time you visit the place.

Every fan should visit Cooperstown. It's gorgeous—just gorgeous. But if you can't (or if you *have* visited and you want a spectacular memento of the place), you should have a copy of *Treasures of the Baseball Hall of Fame*. Author John Thorn (one of baseball's sharpest historians) and photographer David Jordano (a true artist) have combined to produce this wonderful book.

Treasures should more than satisfy your cravings for baseball history. It takes you inside Cooperstown like no book ever has. You'll enjoy it.

—TED WILLIAMS

ACKNOWLEDGMENTS

For the Baseball Hall of Fame and Museum, this volume represents more than sixty years of collecting, preserving, and displaying the treasures of our national game. For me, it culminates a lifetime romance with baseball and twenty-five years of writing about its glorious past.

My first research trip to Cooperstown was in 1973 and I have returned there every year since. The people at the Baseball Hall of Fame and the National Baseball Hall of Fame Library have been unfailingly helpful, offhandedly erudite, wondrously enthusiastic. While this book took "only" four years to construct and write, its inception as a project dates back ten years, and in truth *Treasures of the Baseball Hall of Fame* has been in the making ever since that first visit. In all the years since then, my understanding and appreciation of the game have been enriched by a large cast of Cooperstown characters, from Cliff Kachline, Jack Redding, and Tom Heitz, on through Howard Talbot and Bill Guilfoile, and up to the current leadership of Don Marr and Frank Simio. As the faces changed in the Museum and at the Library, Ed Stack and Bill Burdick were constant sources of support and friendship.

Other Baseball Hall of Fame friends who were more directly involved with *Treasures* in recent years include curator Ted Spencer, registrar Peter Clark, associate registrar Susan MacKay, registrar's assistant Mary Bellew, librarian Jim Gates, director of photography collections Pat Kelly, technical services librarian Corey Seaman, and research director Tim Wiles. Also helpful at many points along the way have been executive director of communications Jeff Idelson, Hall of Fame photographer Milo Stewart, director of film, video, and recorded sound Greg Harris, and executive assistant Kim Bennett. Research and fact-checking help also came from senior researchers Scot Mondore and Bruce Markusen and accessions associate Helen Stiles.

This book has been a true collaboration between author and institution, and a very happy working experience. My most happy collaboration of all was with nonpareil photographer Dave Jordano, whose sensitivity, technical excellence, and vision are evident throughout the book.

At Villard, thanks go to Peter Gethers, who championed this project; Diane Reverand, who signed it on; Ian Jackman, who brought it home brilliantly; Joanne Barracca, who oversaw production; and Carole Lowenstein, whose love of the game is reflected in its design. Literary agent Gerry McCauley earned his reward several times over as *Treasures* drifted from one year into the next; through it all, his friendship has been steadfast. My friend and fellow baseball author Paul Adomites played a vital role, getting the stories unstuck from my brain and, in the process, enhancing the book. Tom Shieber and David Pietrusza supplied some notable tidbits and corrections.

Finally, we must acknowledge the ghosts who have given us such great stories to tell, the donors of the artifacts that create the echoes at the Hall of Fame, and the baseball fans who will hear these tales of ancient exploits, and pass them on.

—JOHN THORN

CONTENTS

Foreword   *ix*

Acknowledgments   *xi*

List of Illustrations   *xv*

Introduction   *xvii*

CHAPTER ONE   Why Cooperstown?   3

CHAPTER TWO   The National Baseball Hall of Fame and Museum   10

CHAPTER THREE   The Spur to Memory   14

CHAPTER FOUR   The Time Line   17

    To 1901   17

    To 1920   37

    To 1941   53

    To 1960   70

    To Date   98

CHAPTER FIVE   Special Historical Exhibits   112

    Black Baseball   112

    Umpires   116

    Minor Leagues   119

    Women in Baseball   121

    Baseball Abroad and Tours   124

CHAPTER SIX   The Changing Game   132

    Bats   132

    Balls   134

    Gloves and Masks   140

    Caps   143

    Uniforms   144

CHAPTER SEVEN   Ballparks and Fans   149

CHAPTER EIGHT Special Achievements 155

CHAPTER NINE All-Star Games 167

CHAPTER TEN World Series 173

CHAPTER ELEVEN The Art Gallery 182

CHAPTER TWELVE Movies, Music, and Media 190

CHAPTER THIRTEEN Baseball Cards, Games, and Memorabilia 209

CHAPTER FOURTEEN The National Baseball Hall of Fame Library and Archive 220

CHAPTER FIFTEEN The Hidden Hall of Fame 228

Opening day, Baseball Hall of Fame, 9
Plaques of the First Five, 13
Gotham Base Ball Club pin, 15
"Lady Met" pins, 16
Elysian Fields of Hoboken, Panorama of New York, 17
Baseball belt worn by Knickerbocker Napoleon McLaughlin, 18
Silver ball presented to Knickerbocker Samuel H. Kissam, 19
Eckfords of Brooklyn, 20
Eckfords monogram, 22
The Wright Brothers, 23
Silk ribbons of the 1860s, 24
Cincinnati Red Stockings of 1869, 25
Cincinnati Red Stockings, 26
American Association Ball, manufactured by Reach, 28 (upper left)
Red Stockings ball, 1869, 28 (upper right)
Eagle Base Ball Club broadside, 1871, 28 (bottom)
National Association, 1871–1875, 30
Buck Ewing tribute bouquet, 31
New York Gotham uniform patch, 32 (left)
Stock Exchange medal, Buck Ewing, 1883, 32 (right)
King Kelly medal, 1887, 33 (left)
Field day trophy, Willie Keeler, 1895, 33 (right)
St. Louis Browns, 1888, 34
Hugh Duffy loving cup, 1901, 35
Trophy bat, George Van Haltren, 1894, 36 (top)
Charles Comiskey bat, Wagon Tongue model, 36 (center)
Bats of Willie Keeler and George Wright, 36 (bottom)
New York Giants "Championship" pin, Mike Donlin, 1908, 37
Christy Mathewson, 38
Christy Mathewson sweater, 39
Honus Wagner, 41
Ty Cobb, 43
Shoeless Joe Jackson's shoes, 45 (top)
Tris Speaker decal bat, 45 (bottom)
Frank Chance tribute, 46 (left)
Rube Waddell glove, 46 (right)
Federal League pins, 47
Chief Bender jersey and cap, 48 (left)

Tom Needham's Chicago Cubs jersey, 1908–1912, 48 (right)
Bats of Edd Roush and Nap Lajoie, 49 (top)
Miracle Braves' pennant-clinching ball, 1914, 49 (bottom)
Ball from Cy Young's five hundredth win, 50
Cy Young, 51
Cy Young license plate, 52 (top)
Cy Young portrait, 52 (bottom)
Rabbit Maranville glove, 53 (top)
Fiftieth anniversary of National League commemorative baseballs, 1926, 53 (bottom)
Fiftieth anniversary of National League commemorative pin, 54 (left)
Home Run Baker cap, 54 (right)
Johnny Neun triple-play ball, 55 (top left)
Carl Hubbell crown, 54 (top right)
Bill Terry sweater, 54 (bottom)
Pepper Martin cap, 56
Rogers Hornsby items, 57
John McGraw, 58
Lefty Grove jersey, 59
Jimmie Foxx, 60
Lou Gehrig, 63
Joe Medwick bat, 64 (top)
Dizzy Dean jersey, 64 (bottom)
Walter Johnson, 66
Night game ticket, Ebbets Field, 1938, 67
Bats of George Kelly and Pie Traynor, 68
Max Carey glove, 69 (top)
Burleigh Grimes glove, slippery elm bark, 69 (bottom)
Baseball and World War II, 71
Hank Greenberg's three hundredth home-run ball, 72
Warren Spahn jersey, 73 (right)
Eddie Gaedel jersey, 73 (left)
Robin Roberts jersey, 74 (left)
Luis Aparicio jersey, 74 (right)
Bob Feller, 76
Jackie Robinson, 78
Connie Mack, 81
Philadelphia Athletics jersey, 1954, 82
Walt Dropo and Enos Slaughter baseballs, 83 (top)
Phil Rizzuto helmet, 83 (bottom)
Joe DiMaggio, 85
The shot heard 'round the world, 86
Brooklyn Dodgers, 89

Stan Musial, 90
Bats of Ralph Kiner and George Kell, 92
Satchel Paige items, 93
Casey Stengel, 94
Phillies Phantom pin, 1964, 96
Willie Mays, 97
George Brett's "pine tar bat," 98
Ray Knight helmet, 1986 World Series, 99 (top)
Steve Carlton's Cy Young Awards, 99 (bottom)
Mike Schmidt bat, 100 (top)
Al Kaline three thousandth–hit bat, 100 (bottom)
Mickey Mantle, 102
Carl Yastrzemski jersey, 103
Reggie Jackson bat, 1977, 104 (top)
Johnny Bench jersey and mitt, 104 (bottom)
Gaylord Perry jersey, 105 (left)
Gil Hodges jersey, 105 (right)
Roberto Clemente and Ferguson Jenkins baseballs, 106
Roberto Clemente, 107
Brooks Robinson, 109
Bats of Billy Williams and Willie McGee, 110
Lou Brock stolen base, 111
Cool Papa Bell's shades, 112
The Negro Leagues, 113
Sol White guide, 115 (right)
World's Colored Championship program, 1924, 115
Frank Umont's glasses, 116 (left)
Jocko Conlan's whisk broom, 116 (right)
Ball-strike indicator, 1887, 117
The Three Umpires, Norman Rockwell, 118
Caps of Scott Bakkum and Andy Carter, 119
Minor League season passes, 120 (left)
Scout items, 120 (right)
AAGPBL baseballs, 121 (top)
AAGPBL yearbooks, 121 (bottom)
AAGPBL caps, uniforms, 122
All American Girls Professional Baseball League, 1943–1954, 123
Moe Berg Japan tour jacket, 1934, 124 (left)
Sam Crawford world tour jacket, 1913, 124 (right)
Harry Wolter Olympics jacket, 1936, 125
All-American Tourists lithograph, 126

Spalding's tour mementos, *127*
The World Tours, *128*
Baseball and Japan, *130*
Handmade bat, 1852, *132 (top)*
Pete Browning model Louisville Slugger, *132 (bottom)*
Mushroom-knob bat, *133*
Flat bat, 1885 model, *133*
Heinie Groh bottle bat, *134 (top)*
Evolution of baseballs, *134 (bottom)*
Shibe Centennial Exhibition case, 1876, *135 (top)*
Federal League baseball, *135 (bottom)*
William Hulbert National League baseball, *136*
The early game, *137*
Doubleday baseball, *138*
Infielder's glove, 1880s, *140 (left)*
Catcher's mitt, 1890s, *140 (right)*, *141 (top)*
Mickey Cochrane mitt, *141 (bottom)*
Catcher's masks, Thayer and Howland models, *142 (top)*
Bill Doak model glove, *142 (bottom)*
Cap assemblage, *143 (right)*
Pancho Snyder's New York Giants cap, 1922, *143 (left)*
Jim Turner's Boston Bees jersey, 1937, *144 (left)*
Baraboo, Wisconsin, uniform, 1866, *144 (right)*
Fred Snodgrass jersey, 1912, *145 (left)*
Red Murray's St. Louis Cardinals warm-up jacket, 1906, *145 (right)*
George Browne's New York Giants jersey, 1906, *146*
Expansion-era uniforms, *147*
Chicago trolley sign, *149*
Number 9, Forbes Field scoreboard, *150 (left)*
Cornerstone, Shibe Park, *150 (right)*
Season-pass assemblage, *151 (top)*
Royal Rooters pin, Boston, 1897, *151 (bottom)*
Comiskey Park blueprints, *152*
Kerchief, Boston Red Sox, 1912, *153 (left)*
Ticket assemblage, *153 (right)*
Season ticket, Philadelphia Athletics, 1874, *154*
Tom Browning, perfect-game ball, *155*
Babe Ruth, *157*
Babe Ruth's "King of Swat" crown, *158 (top)*
Babe Ruth's locker, *158 (bottom)*
Harvey Haddix perfect-game ball, *159*
Triple Play: Neal Ball pin and glove, Mickey Morandini jersey, *160*
Eight-game homer bats: Dale Long, Don Mattingly, Ken Griffey, Jr., *161 (top)*
Worcester 1880: H. H. Pollard sketchbook and Lee Richmond perfect-game score card, *161 (center and bottom)*
Roger Connor prize, 1889, *162 (left)*
Pete Rose's hit number 4192 game ticket, *162 (right)*
Rick Wise bat; two-homer, no-hit game, 1971, *163*
Hank Aaron, *164*
Roger Maris bat and ball, home run number 61, 1961, *165*

Twelve RBIs: Jim Bottomley bat, Mark Whiten cap, *166*
Tie clasp, American League All Stars, 1936, *167 (top)*
Ted Williams home-run ball; won 1941 All-Star Game, *167 (bottom)*
Ted Williams wooden sculpture, *168*
Ted Williams, *169*
Bo Jackson cap, 1989 All-Star Game, *170 (top)*
All-Star Game ticket assemblage, *170 (bottom)*
Addie Joss benefit game, 1911, *171 (right)*
Chick Hafey jersey, National League, 1933, *171 (left)*
1933 All-Star Game program, *172 (top)*
All-Star press-pin assemblage, *172 (bottom)*
New York Yankees World Series watch, 1928, *173 (left)*
1912 World Series press pin, *173 (right)*
Helen Dauvray pin for 1887, awarded to Sam Thompson, *174*
The Hall Championship Cup of 1888, *175 (left)*
The Temple Cup, 1894–1897, *175 (right)*
Agreement between Boston (AL) and Pittsburgh (NL) for World Series, *176 (top)*
First ball pitched, 1903 World Series, *176 (bottom)*
Scorecard, 1903 World Series, Game 2, *177 (right)*
Turnstile receipt, 1903 World Series, Game One, *177 (left)*
Ticket assemblage, World Series, *178 (top)*
Game ball, Gene Larkin's Series-winning hit, 1991, *178 (bottom)*
Al Gionfriddo glove, 1947 World Series, *179 (top)*
Don Larsen's perfect 1956 World Series game assemblage, *179 (bottom)*
Bill Mazeroski items, *180 (top)*
World Series press-pin assemblage, *180 (bottom)*
Little Base Ball Player, J. G. Brown, *182*
Grover Cleveland Alexander, J. F. Kernan, *183 (left)*
Kenesaw Mountain Landis, Dick Perez, *183 (right)*
Juan Marichal, Leroy Neiman, *184 (left)*
Joe Palooka at the Hall of Fame, M. Leff (and Ham Fisher), *184 (right)*
Base Ball at the Elysian Fields, Nathaniel Currier and James Merritt Ives, *185 (top)*
Pitcher and *Batter*, K. Muller & J. Deacon, *185 (bottom)*
The Second Great Match Game for the Championship, J. L. Magee, *186 (left)*
Mine Baseball, Mervin Jules, *186 (right)*
Joe Wood, anonymous, *187 (left)*
Ty Cobb, J. F. Kernan, *187 (right)*
Baseball Player, Douglas Tilden, *188*
Fugue of the Pepper Players, David G. Baldwin, *189*
Sporting Life pin, *190*
Early baseball publications, *191*
Five-cent story papers, *193*
Baseball Magazine, *195*
Early baseball books, *197*
1920 Series press pin, *198*

"The Marquard Glide," *199 (top)*
"Live Oak Polka," *199 (bottom)*
"Take Me Out to the Ball Game," *201*
Roy Hobbs jacket, *The Natural*, *202 (top)*
"Lou Gehrig Scrapbook," *Pride of the Yankees*, *202 (bottom)*
Posters, *The Winning Team* and *The Kid from Left Field*, *203 (left)*
Poster and "*Life* magazine" from *A League of Their Own*, *203 (top right and bottom)*
Film cans, *204*
"Casey at the Bat," *205*
Casey statue, *206*
The press and broadcast media, *207*
Goodwin round album, *209*
Quaker Puffed Wheat Babe Ruth premiums, *210*
Baseball cards to 1900, *211*
Baseball cards, 1900–1941, *212*
Baseball cards, 1950s forward, *215*
Cobb, Johnson, Mathewson advertisements, *216*
Three baseball games, *217*
Throwaway trinkets, *218*
Sterling silver season passes, *219*
Lou Gehrig letters, *220*, *221 (top)*
Play Ball: Stories of the Diamond Ball Field, King Kelly, *221 (bottom)*
Mort Rogers scorecard, 1871, Davey Force, *222 (left)*
The Krank: His Language and What It Means, Thomas W. Lawson, *222 (right)*
Baseball as Viewed by a Muffin, S. Van Campen, *223*
Sam Rice letter, opened posthumously, *224*
Hack Wilson photograph, *225 (top)*
1924 California tour scrapbook, Babe Ruth, *225 (bottom)*
Union of Morrisania: carte de visite, painting, ticket, *226*
Early scorecard assemblage, *227 (top)*
Scoresheets, Johnny Vander Meer no-hitters, 1938, *227 (bottom)*
Fan pin, 1914, *228 (left)*
Pin, Tecumseh team of London, Ontario, *228 (right)*
Mickey Owen mitt, 1941 World Series, *229 (left)*
Brooklyn Bum, Willard Mullin, *229 (right)*
Decal-mania bat, *230 (top)*
House of David broadside, *230 (bottom)*
Jesse Tannehill jacket, Boston Pilgrims, 1907, *231 (left)*
Hooks Wiltse jersey, New York Giants, 1905, *231 (right)*
Arlie Latham bat, *232*
"Red" Faber's world tour sweater, 1913, *233 (top)*
"Red" Murray's low-cut shoes, *233 (bottom)*
Harry Hooper mackinaw, *234 (top)*
Jim Gentile grand-slam bat, *234 (bottom)*
Maury Wills shoes, *235 (top)*
Babe Ruth letter to George Weiss, *235 (bottom)*
Sandy Koufax *Life* magazine, Murray Tinkelman, *236 (left)*
"Who's on First?" record, *236 (right)*
Casey Stengel's envoi, *237*

INTRODUCTION

On the surface, it's just a fifty-year-old baseball bat, distinguished neither by its size, nor its color. Yet it was responsible for one of the biggest home runs ever in the history of baseball. And to look at it, you'd never know.

On October 3, 1951, during the last playoff game with the crosstown Brooklyn Dodgers, the New York Giants' Bobby Thomson used that bat to homer in the bottom of the ninth, putting the Giants in the World Series. It's called the "shot heard round the world" because so many baseball fans were focused on that game, waiting earnestly to find out if this would be Brooklyn's year.

Like so many of the artifacts at the Hall of Fame, the value of Bobby Thomson's bat isn't derived from a decorative or ornate appearance, but from its unique place in baseball history. Since the Hall of Fame opened in 1939, we have collected millions of items that are part of baseball history, amassing the finest collection anywhere on the history of the game. Maybe it is a baseball from the first World Series, a sportswriter's score book, a uniform shirt worn during a hitting streak, a Hall of Famer's scrapbook, a pennant from a minor league champion, or a hat worn by a pitcher during a no-hitter. We continue to collect these items to preserve the legacy and the great moments of the game.

The Hall of Fame's role as baseball's premiere showcase comes through our efforts to preserve these artifacts and use them to help educate visitors on the history of the national pastime. The Registrar's and Library staffs serve as tremendous caretakers to this national legacy, providing the finest museum, library, and archival care to this irreplaceable collection. Through the efforts of the Curatorial and Education staffs, the stories of baseball are told, providing the visitors with the history of the game. Thus, the true value of these rare artifacts, their ability to bring baseball history to life, is fulfilled.

This is why the Hall of Fame is a special, if not magical, place. The artifacts that we use to tell the story about baseball history not only illustrate the game, but, more important, illuminate our memories and dreams. We might be reminded of our first baseball game when we see the baseball cards we collected as children. We might be reminded of stories that our grandfather told about seeing Satchel Paige pitch as we view his plaque. We might remember growing up in the Midwest when we see the Women in Baseball exhibit. And we might be reminded of our mother's undying love for the Brooklyn Dodgers when we see Bobby Thomson's bat. Maybe Ernie Harwell said it best when he called it the "game for all America," for we are all found in its history.

It is my pleasure to invite you to enjoy these treasures of the Hall of Fame. I hope that you will find yourself, your family, and your community in these pages as well.

And I hope that you will find your way to Cooperstown, where you can see many more treasures or our national pastime, and bask in the sunshine of the game's greatest glories.

—Donald C. Marr, Jr.

TREASURES OF THE BASEBALL HALL OF FAME

CHAPTER ONE

Why Cooperstown?

Baseball is at the core of our national life, and the Baseball Hall of Fame and Museum is the game's national shrine, the repository of its heritage. Dedicated souls make the pilgrimage to Cooperstown, New York, a picturesque village of 2,300 inhabitants that is served by no airport, no passenger train, no major highway. They don't get here by finding it on the way to there.

Yet 400,000 fans visit the institution each year, while millions of others, perhaps at the other end of the country or the globe, dream of making the trip. And we hope you will, too, if you haven't—or that you'll come again, if you have. Until then, let this volume be your virtual tour of baseball's hallowed ground.

If baseball is played everywhere today, and bat-and-ball games have been played everywhere for centuries, why do visitors come to Cooperstown with such a sense of reverence, even a belief that baseball started here? There are several answers rather than one, and they tell a wonderfully American tale, equal parts history and myth, which begins with Abner Doubleday and ends with him. Along the way his legend was created, enlarged, punctured, and in the end enriched.

While the precise origins of the game we call baseball can be debated, we can state with certainty that it did not spring full-blown from the fertile mind of Abner Doubleday, or anyone else, in Cooperstown, or anyplace else. There was never a historical moment when someone said, "Hey, let's use this stick to hit this round thing, and we'll put four bases ninety feet apart and after you hit the round thing you can run around the bases and stop on a base if you want but you don't get a point until you come all the way back to the base you started from." The origin of baseball was not even as compact as someone deciding that a particular game of bat and ball would be more fun if it were better organized, although if any one person is responsible, Alexander Cartwright came close.

But the selection of the remote hamlet of Cooperstown, New York, was based on just such a notion: that anything as glorious as baseball must have begun in one place, at one particular time, and must have been the brainstorm of some ingenious American lad. Given these premises, a creation myth was inevitable; all that remained was to determine its particulars. To the question "How did baseball come to be," evolution seemed an unsatisfactory answer—messy, purposeless, and undramatic. It is at this point that the interests of Albert Goodwill Spalding and the good people of Cooperstown intersect.

Before 1939, Cooperstown was a typical American village, although blessed by a spectacular setting. At one end of town lies the glorious Lake Otsego, the shimmering body of water that James Fenimore Cooper (for whose father the village was named) called "Glimmerglass" in his *Leatherstocking Tales*. All around the nine-mile lake were softly rolling hills and a democratic mixture of stately homes and sportsmen's cabins. The Susquehanna River has its origin here, at the south end of Lake Otsego, flowing from its height of 1,200 feet above sea level all the way through Pennsylvania and into the Chesapeake Bay. And here is the spot known as Council Rock, where the Iroquois nations met. And there is the spot known as Phinney's Pasture, where baseball is said to have begun.

In the late 1880s, when Albert Spalding's World Tourists—two teams of major-league players—attempted to spread the gospel of baseball to heathen lands, there was a widespread, goodwilled debate about the origins of baseball among such prominent figures as John Montgomery Ward, Henry Chadwick, and Spalding. Chadwick, sports journalist, hopeless egotist, inveterate rule tinkerer, and relentless proselytizer, had played rounders in England before coming to these shores. Ever since he commenced to write about baseball in 1856, he had always ascribed the origins of his adopted game to rounders. In the 1904 edition of *The Spalding Guide,* for which he had long been the editor, Chadwick once again made the case for baseball's debt to the British game.

Spalding had heard Chadwick's argument a hundred times before and had always been content to disagree, politely. But this time he either lost his patience, or saw his opening, or—as Chadwick believed—was merely having some fun at his old friend's expense. Rhetorically, Spalding took the position Ward had previously articulated: that something so typically American in every way could not have been of exotic origin. Those of a skeptical bent might add that Spalding's motivation for stirring the pot had more to do with commerce than sport, or history, or even patriotism. Through the promotion attendant to the "Great Debate," Spalding's company might be counted on to sell additional balls and bats.

Spalding published his rebuttal to Chadwick in the 1905 *Guide,* but he still wasn't satisfied. He encouraged the presidents of the two leagues, Harry Pulliam and Ban Johnson, to form a commission to settle the issue for once and for all. It eventually settled the question much as the Warren Commission alleviated doubts about JFK's assassination.

Baseball's genealogy can actually be described on the run in a couple of minutes. Cooperstown will not come up, nor will Doubleday.

There had been two ball games popular in Britain for over 150 years. One was rounders, the other was called "tip cat," or "cat," implying no reference to a household feline but instead to a catapult device that lay on the ground: step on a lever, pop the ball into the air, and whack it with a stick. The toy merchants continue to crank out new versions of this basic device every few years, appending some current star's name to the contraption. Another name for this sort of amusement, in Old England and Young America both, was the prosaic "catapult ball."

"One 'o' cat" used two bases, as in cricket. Sports-history tomes generally term it "one old cat," but again, no superannuated puss inspired the game. Think of how difficult it is to say "one hole cat," and you'll see instantly why the "h" was aspirated. The "hole" is that into which the ball had to be placed at one of the bases to stop the further scoring of runs—not totally unlike cricket and not unlike games many of us middle-aged gents played as boys.

More players, more bases, more 'oles. In England, when you gathered a lot of players and the game turned into four 'o' cat, rounders became the next step. Each side took its turn batting and then fielding, as in cricket, and every member of the side had to have his chance to bat before the boys in the field could come in and bat. If the last batter hit a "rounder" (home run), the whole side stayed in and went through its order again.

Rounders was also played in America, but the ultimate extension of cat-ball games was town ball, in which as many as fifty men per side—the whole young male population of a small town—could take the field to play each other in a kind of glorious mayhem of batting and running. Limiting the town-ball concept to just eleven players and four bases happened more or less simultaneously in Massachusetts and upstate New York, but not in New York City, where a bat-and-ball game called "shinny" or "shinty" was favored. The New York rules were codified by the Knickerbocker Base Ball Club in 1845, other variations died out, and the Massachusetts Game, with equally distinct rules, never made an inroad. The biggest differences between the two games were (1) the New York Game established boundaries to separate fair territory from foul, and (2) the Knickerbocker rules eliminated the practice of putting a runner out by "soaking," or hitting him with a thrown ball, when he was off base. With the new civility in place, a harder ball could be used, as in cricket, that manly sport which the Knickerbockers hoped to emulate. The harder, larger ball could be batted and thrown farther. Not exactly "Presto, baseball!" as in the Doubleday legend, but reasonably linear.

Spalding's commission set out to find an unknown genius because he simply had to exist, like the source of the Nile. It was not surprising that they found their man. The commission consisted of seven men: Morgan Bulkeley, the former governor of Connecticut and the original president of the National League; Arthur Pue Gorman, former U.S. senator from Maryland; Abraham G. Mills, another former National League president, who was named chairman of the commission; Nicholas Young, first National League treasurer and figurehead president of the league for seventeen years; Al Reach, one of the earliest professional ballplayers and later a sporting-goods tycoon; the estimable George Wright, a supremely talented athlete who switched from cricket to the new game and, like Spalding and Reach, created a sporting-goods empire; and James E. Sullivan, president of the Amateur Athletic Union.

The Mills Commission acquired numerous reports from people who offered testimony to the origins of baseball. But there is no indication that the aforementioned gentlemen worked really hard at studying them. (It has frequently been written that the commission did nothing for three years, then settled upon its designated genius, Doubleday. This is simply not so. The original reports that came into the commission were destroyed in a fire at Spalding's American Sports Publishing offices in lower Manhattan in 1916, but carbon copies have survived, tucked away all these years in archival storage in the Mills Collection at the Baseball Hall of Fame.)

The critical piece of evidence in the eyes of the commission was a letter from Abner Graves, a mining engineer living in Denver, Colorado. In the letter Graves said he remembered with unusual clarity an incident related to the discovery of baseball. One summer day in Cooperstown, in 1839 or so (Graves at first was uncertain as to the year), a group of boys had gathered for a day's play of town ball, in which the Cooperstown lads typically ran headlong into one another, injuring themselves in their enthusiasm. But on this day young Abner Doubleday drew a diagram of a baseball diamond in the dirt at Elihu Phinney's cow pasture, and from that point on the boys began to play this new, organized game. To Spalding this was glorious stuff—the game for all America invented by a great general of the Civil War. Doubleday was long dead, so no one could ask him whether Graves was telling the truth or not, but Robert Doubleday, Abner's nephew, claimed his uncle told him at length the story of how he invented baseball.

The commission asked Graves a few more questions, and its members were satisfied. They filed their report on the final day of 1907, fulfilling their three-year mandate. It was official: baseball came from America and nowhere else; Abner Doubleday made it happen, in a spark of boyhood genius reminiscent of the already legendary though still quite alive Tom Edison. The league presidents accepted the commission's findings in 1908. Chadwick was denied his chance at rebuttal, for he caught cold on Opening Day in Brooklyn and died before the month was out. The issue was settled . . . sort of.

In 1909 Bruce Cartwright and writer Will Irwin, in Collier's magazine, campaigned in the press for Alexander Cartwright. And decades later Robert Henderson, head librarian at the New York Public Library, wrote a scholarly paper showing the antiquity of ball games the world over, including games calling for bat, ball, and base.

Researchers have concluded that Abner Doubleday was not in Cooperstown in the summer of 1839; he was at West Point. Even if he had been, Abner Graves was only five then and Doubleday twenty. How many twenty-year-olds invite preschoolers to take part in their games? Doubleday's extensive journals make no mention of baseball. His claim to fame was returning fire at Fort Sumter, so if he deserves credit for starting something, it was the Civil War.

The official pronouncement, however, was what America, and Al Spalding, were ready to hear. The next step was the one that sparked the establishment of the Baseball Hall of Fame and Museum. In Ilion, New York, in the winter of 1917, five men sat around a hot stove at Michael Fogerty's cigar store and agreed that there should be a monument to

Doubleday in Cooperstown to honor his "creation." Besides Fogerty, the men were Hardy Richardson, who had a fourteen-year career in the majors in the nineteenth century; baseball enthusiasts George Oliver and Patrick Fitzpatrick; and former ballplayer and boys' coach George "Deke" White. They each pitched in the munificent sum of twenty-five cents and started the Doubleday Memorial Fund. But what they did next was more important. They enlisted the efforts of Sam Crane, former major-league second baseman and then sportswriter for the *New York Journal*. Crane promoted the idea.

Next, the citizens of Cooperstown got into the act. Dr. Ernest L. Pitcher (perfect name) was a local dentist who headed up the fund drive to buy Phinney's field and make it a baseball park. The folks of Cooperstown chipped in $3,772 and did just that. It took some further legal wrangling over the next few years and some help from outside sources to close the deal. Ground was broken on June 2, 1919, and the first game was played there September 6, 1920, with National League president John Heydler in attendance. Before the decade was done, people who wanted to see where baseball was born began to make trips to the hamlet on the lake.

The people of Cooperstown saw they had a good thing going. They approached Major League Baseball for its support of a celebration in 1939 to commemorate the hundredth anniversary of Doubleday's invention. The response from the leagues was encouraging, and the locals set to work. In a merger of national and local interests, federal funds from the Works Progress Administration were combined with Village of Cooperstown funds to expand Doubleday Field, add stands, and make it the gem that it is today. What other village of 2,300 inhabitants has a ball field that seats 10,000?

The concept of a baseball museum to go along with the field was the brainchild of Stephen C. Clark, Sr., whose grandfather, attorney Edward Clark, had represented inventor Isaac M. Singer in a patent-infringement suit. The elder Clark's association with Singer grew through the years, as they formed a partnership and Clark became the business head of I. M. Singer & Company. With the success of the Singer sewing machine and the thoughtful leadership of Clark, the company prospered, as did the fortunes of both men. Prior to the Civil War, Edward Clark began to spend summers at his wife's birthplace, Cooperstown. Over the next three generations the Clark family's wealth grew, and with it grew their love for the Village of Cooperstown. By the 1930s their philanthropy was evident throughout the village. They had funded numerous construction projects, including a hospital and a community gymnasium.

In 1935 Stephen C. Clark, Sr., was the vice president of the Otsego County Historical Society. The story goes that in that year a farmer in nearby Fly Creek discovered an old trunk in his attic that had belonged to the Mills Commission's star witness, Abner Graves. Graves had left New York in 1848 at the age of fourteen to find his fortune in the Gold Rush. In this trunk were the possessions he had left behind, including a homemade baseball, battered and beaten, the cover torn open. This was indeed a baseball of great antiquity, hand sewn and of a small diameter like the few others that survive from the town-ball era. Mr. Clark purchased the ball for five dollars and displayed it in the historical society's exhibition room, where it came to be called the Doubleday Ball (although there is no indication that Doubleday ever used it).

At this point one of Clark's New York City employees, Alexander Cleland, a man with a keen promotional sense, got behind the idea of a national baseball museum. It was formally incorporated as the National Baseball Museum, Inc., a not-for-profit educational institution, in September 1936. The five-member board of directors contained names familiar to all Cooperstown residents: Clark employee Waldo C. Johnston, Mayor Rowan D. Spraker, newspaper editor Walter L. Littell, writer James Fenimore Cooper (grandson of the novelist), and Stephen C. Clark. Cleland was retained as the organization's executive secretary and point man.

To the Doubleday Ball Clark added his own collection of baseballs and two of the game's most famous pieces of early art—a lithograph of Union prisoners playing ball at Salisbury, North Carolina, during the Civil War and the 1866 Currier & Ives print of a championship game at the Elysian Fields in Hoboken, New Jersey. National League president Ford Frick donated the 1889 championship trophy of the New York Giants, shown in this book.

The idea for a baseball hall of fame to salute the game's immortals was Frick's. It wasn't brand new: in 1901 New York University had opened a Hall of Fame for Great Americans, though it didn't include any sports figures. He suggested the concept of a baseball hall, and everyone loved it. Of course now we have Halls of Fame for everything from pediatricians to rock 'n' roll.

Many donations came in. One man gave a collection of old Spalding *Baseball Guides*. Clark Griffith, pitcher with the Chicago White Stockings and subsequently owner of the Washington Senators, presented Cooperstown with his collection of photographs, and Christy Mathewson's wife donated the pitcher's glove. (The Museum's collection was thus built by the generosity of a nation of fans, players, and executives who wanted to "make it to the Hall of Fame." This method endures as the sole path to acquisitions; while millions have been spent to display and preserve the collections, the Museum has spent not a penny to acquire them.)

But how to select those who deserved enshrinement in the Hall? After trying out the idea of somehow having the fans choose, Cleland decided instead to have the Baseball Writers Association of America make the determinations. The controversy over who goes in and who stays out began with the first voting procedure. There were two categories of players—those who played in the nineteenth century and those who played from 1900 to 1935. The plan was to elect ten men from the list of thirty-three nominees from the "modern" era, and five were to be selected from twenty-six nominees of the nineteenth century by a special panel. Instantly, the press began to bicker about the choices, so the list of nominees was dumped. All that was required to be elected, the new rules held, was for the player to receive votes on 75 percent of the ballots cast.

When the votes were tabulated, more howls went up. Only five modern players had received enough votes, and none of the old-timers did. Cy Young received votes in both categories, but not enough in either. The first Hall of Fame plaques—Ty Cobb, Babe Ruth, Walter Johnson, Honus Wagner, and Christy Mathewson—were displayed in December 1937. Although not without squabbles, the voters seemed to straighten things out by the formal opening of the Hall on June 12, 1939, when twenty-five greats of the game were inducted.

As the Doubleday myth unraveled over the years, much like the stitching on the Doubleday Ball, Hall of Fame officials felt concerned, as if the Cartwright advocates had been trying to move the Hall to Hoboken. But calm and reason prevailed, and after some agonizing about the unseemly implication that the Hall of Fame was tossing old Abner overboard, in the 1980s Hall executives settled upon this elegant official position:

> Whatever may or may not be proved in the future concerning Baseball's true origin is in many respects irrelevant at this time. If baseball was not actually first played here in Cooperstown by Doubleday in 1839, it undoubtedly originated about that time in a similar rural atmosphere. The Hall of Fame is in Cooperstown to stay; and at the very least, the village is certainly an acceptable symbolic site.

But that's severely understating the case. If baseball was not in fact invented in Cooperstown, it ought to have been. And by now the National Baseball Hall of Fame and Museum of Cooperstown, New York, is not merely a monument that commemorates a historical event, real or fanciful—it has a history of its own, in its own time, in its own place.

Oddly, the most recent research into baseball's origins has reversed field, angling back northwest from New York City and Hoboken to upstate New York and back in time from the mid-1840s to the 1820s. And Abner Doubleday has undergone a rehabilitation, too, from a figure of fun as the patron saint of baseball's flat-earth holdouts to a somewhat less cuddly equivalent of Santa Claus, tossed up with a wink and a nod. What's wrong with Abner Doubleday as a symbolic paterfamilias of baseball?

Even though Cooperstown was not truly the home base of baseball in 1939, it has been ever since. Like Mount Olympus, it is where the legends live.

—★—

It was a really big show—the official opening of the Hall of Fame on June 12, 1939. Trains full of baseball legends and dignitaries emptied into the town. The Delaware & Hudson line reopened a long-abandoned right of way and ran a special passenger service into Cooperstown. Comedian Joe Cook announced he had the rarest baseball artifact ever—"a baseball that isn't signed by Babe Ruth!" When the time came to tour the Museum, Carl Hubbell hesitated before entering, telling the person next to him, "I better not go in. They might want to keep this old left arm of mine as a relic." More than 15,000 spectators crowded into the street in front of the Museum for the presentations. Crowds that size and more are routine for Induction Day now, but nothing like this had ever been seen in Cooperstown before.

One of the highlights of the activities was the special commemorative stamp issued by the United States Post Office; Postmaster General James A. Farley was on hand to add his stature to the ceremonies. The three-cent purchase was a huge hit; Judge Kenesaw Mountain Landis himself, in his tight red-white-and-blue centennial baseball cap, bought the very first one. Out of 65 million of the stamps issued, one million were sent to Cooperstown. Nearly half were postmarked that very day. The stamp showed a group of boys playing ball in an all-American–style setting (heck, it might as well be Cooperstown).

Each of the sixteen major league teams (yes, there were only sixteen back then, representing only ten U.S. cities—none west or south of St. Louis) sent two representatives to the ceremony. Honus Wagner and Eddie Collins were honorary managers of the two teams that played at Doubleday Field. They tossed the bat to see who would choose first as they picked sides. Wagner's huge mitts outdid Eddie's. As the scorecard shows, future Hall of Fame members played that day—Charlie Gehringer, Lloyd Waner, Ducky Medwick, Billy Herman, Mel Ott, Lefty Grove, Arky Vaughan, Dizzy Dean, Carl Hubbell, and Hank Greenberg. Some of these men must have thought about whether they would one day join Babe Ruth and Ty Cobb and the nine other living inductees. Wagner announced, "I'm playing for keeps," and Vaughan, the other Pittsburgh shortstop now in the Hall, doubled and scored the tie-breaking run in the sixth inning as Honus's boys beat Collins's kids.

That day saw not only the induction of the five original electees of 1936—Cobb, Wagner, Ruth, Johnson, and Mathewson—but also twenty other electees who earned their fame either on the field or as one of the game's "Pioneers." Each of the living Hall of Famers was present that year, including Cobb, Wagner, Ruth, Johnson, Collins, Connie Mack, Cy Young, Grover Alexander, Tris Speaker, Nap Lajoie, and George Sisler.

Questions about baseball's true birthplace were on no one's mind that day. Fifty years later, again on June 12, the Doubleday dilemma was neatly sidestepped by celebrating not the sesquicentennial of baseball, but rather a historic event on very firm footing: the demicentennial of the Hall of Fame itself.

CHAPTER TWO

The National Baseball Hall of Fame and Museum

Just to the left of the entrance to the National Baseball Hall of Fame and Museum is a scoreboard, a simple, hand-tended list of the scores from the major-league games of the day before. The symbolic point is clear: once the game is over, it is history, and it belongs to Cooperstown.

For a first-time visitor, the walk down Main Street to the Museum is impossible to perform slowly; the undertow of the building is too hard to resist. But Main Street, Cooperstown, provides a complimentary experience of baseball in America, a living museum that provokes thought and wonder of a different sort. Along with the coffee shops and drugstores is a souvenir extravaganza, from trinkets and cards costing less than a dollar to autographed rarities that could be in the Museum itself. The tradition is long: curio sellers lined the path of the Crusaders on their way to the Holy Land; peddlers' shacks were a blight at Niagara Falls by the 1840s. In Cooperstown, however, the row of shops is pleasing: thanks to the foresight of the village fathers, even stores selling plastic coffee mugs, refrigerator magnets, and "authentic replicas" must hawk their dubious wares from attractive venues. A jewel like the Hall of Fame must have a proper setting.

Step inside the Museum, your heart racing, then pause to catch your breath and find your bearings. Relax—there is no wrong turn. The story of baseball may be approached from the beginning, or from the end, or from any of the thousands of entry points between. If you go straight ahead, you find yourself in the Hall of Fame Gallery, with its silent array of plaques. Do you like to save the best for last? I suggest that you go around the bases, then return here, to baseball's real-life home plate.

The Perez-Steele Art Gallery, a new addition, is a little gem, a museum of its own that celebrates play and art, twins defiant of time. In the welcoming area you can't help but notice the amazingly lifelike wooden sculptures of The Babe and The Kid. Go on, get up close. Try to find a flaw in Armand La Montagne's craftsmanship and verisimilitude (as the artist, maybe he can; you can't).

A cornucopian gift shop occupies one side of the welcoming area. It'll be hard to keep the kids (or the kid in you) from running in immediately, but as with the plaque gallery, take my word that you'll enjoy the time spent here all the more for having had a full experience of the Museum.

Take the escalator on the left, in the Fetzer-Yawkey Wing, and you can walk into a multimedia tribute to the pageant of baseball in the Grandstand Theater, brilliantly dressed up as Old Comiskey Park. While waiting for the next thirteen-minute show to start, look at the Today's Stars exhibit, including a locker-room display of uniforms and gear from each of the current major-league teams; or read the walls in the Record Room; or take in the enormity of effort and accomplishment represented in a long glass case of no-hit baseballs. So much life, such greatness, memorialized in these remains of the day.

After the Grandstand Theater presentation, embark upon a serpentine path through baseball history, beginning with bat-and-ball games in ancient Egypt. From bat, ball, and beer it's just a turn around a corner to the bibulous Knickerbocker boys, who liked their new game of baseball almost as well as the banquets that followed each game. The brilliantly compact time line hurtles us through the decades—the indubitably old though not Doubleday baseball, the undefeated tour of the Cincinnati Red Stockings, the tumultuous years of the American Association (often called the "beer-and-whisky league") and other rival circuits, the dead-ball geniuses, the sluggers of the Golden Age of Sport, the advent of African-Americans and Hispanics in the game, the Gotham-dominated midcentury seasons, the expansion era and beyond. But for the twentieth century, "modern baseball," the curators of the museum have lovingly organized displays by year, making it easy to linger and lose oneself in time, flooded with memories that leap across generations.

There are artifacts of shortstops from George Wright to Cal Ripken, tiny press pins from the early years of the World Series, large lumber used by Ruth and Greenberg, pristine flannels last worn a century ago. And there are radar guns and composite bats, and batting gloves and video displays, and special exhibits on the no-longer-forgotten heroes of the Negro Leagues and the newly discovered women baseball stars.

Up another level, there are All-Star and World Series exhibits, sheet music and trading card displays. (Want to see a T206 Honus Wagner? It's here.) There is a Ballparks Room, where you can sit yourself on a bench from a long-gone ballpark or touch the cornerstone from Brooklyn's Ebbets Field. And there is the minor-league exhibit, and the evolution of the uniform, and . . . better get those legs in shape before you come to Cooperstown.

The building itself keeps growing. New wings were added in 1959 and 1979, the Fetzer-Yawkey Wing in 1989, and the National Baseball Library and Archive, which moved into its own building in 1968, was vastly enlarged in 1993 and newly connected to the Hall of Fame. The Library features a new Baseball at the Movies exhibit, with continuous showings of classic bits of reel baseball. And underneath the Library, invisible to the visitor, is a state-of-the-art, climate-controlled archiving facility. (Also in this subterranean region is one of my favorite places, the storerooms in which are kept thousands of items—some glorious, some ridiculous—that for one reason or another have not been displayed in recent years. You can't visit down there during your next trip to Cooperstown, but if you'd like the thrill of poking around in the Hall of Fame's "basement," join me in Chapter 15.)

Until the 1970s, the Museum was a much less organized, more down-home sort of place—like a local historical society. Strange items long since consigned to the archive were then on display—a giant painting of Cy Young, an antique pitching machine, a display of baseball board games, a capitol building constructed from miniature wooden bats and balls, and an 1860s cigar-store baseball figure known as "Joe Wood." Horizontal display cases were filled with disparate items united by an indiscernible logic. It was a quirky place then, and navigating it was a challenge, like solving a puzzle, or taking up a scavenger hunt, or finding something on the Internet.

But make no mistake—the new museum is vastly better, and the proof of that is on display every day. Just watch the watchers. A child enraptured by an image of Frank Thomas will be gently pulled away by his father to see a statue and hear a story of Roberto Clemente. A grandfather will proudly regale his family with tales of seeing Josh and Satch, in the years before anyone thought there could be a Jackie. You can see people's eyes light up as they come across an artifact that holds special magic for them: a game ball ("I was there!") or a battered glove ("That's the kind of glove I used to wear—imagine Derek Jeter trying to make a play with *that*!").

Not so long ago—sometime in the 1980s, I figure, and it must have been for an Induction Weekend— I was walking through the Museum for the umpteenth time, revisiting my favorite exhibits and being surprised by what I had previously overlooked. Walking through the time-line section a few yards ahead was a little old man accompanied by a couple of men not much younger than he. The fellow paused at a photographic blowup of the unassisted triple play that Cleveland's Bill Wambsganss pulled off in Game 5 of the 1920 World Series. And as he started telling a story about the men portrayed in the panoramic photo, I realized who he was: Joe Sewell, the Indians' shortstop who had the best seat in the house to see that unprecedented play and who himself was portrayed in the photo, to the right of Wambsganss.

I kept a respectful distance behind Sewell and his party, but I hung on his every word, shaken to think that here I was, listening to the man who had been called up from the minors to replace Ray Chapman at shortstop a month after his fatal beaning in August 1920. And here was Joe Sewell, born in the previous century, standing in front of that grainy blowup, saying that Wamby could have tossed him the ball, it would have been so easy, but then it wouldn't have made history, would it?

For a delicious moment, I was a part of that extended history ("I was there!") with Joe Sewell on October 10, 1920, and some sixty years later. And I realized that the enormous pleasure of that moment—the reliving of history in a highly personal way—is what defines the Baseball Hall of Fame experience and gives purpose to this book.

——★——

The Hall of Fame Gallery is a shrine. Walk inside; people speak in hushed tones. The cool marble gives the feel of an ancient temple, and it is indeed a holy place for those of us whose religion is baseball. The plaques may be less interesting to the baseball scholar than items that relate to a man's life as he lived it; to fans, however, these bronze tablets are magical, like fragments from Mount Sinai.

The likenesses are uneven: some are brilliant, others less so. The words are prosaic and functional, never rising to the level of grandeur. But in the aggregate—the entire gallery, with its hundreds of plaques, or even a smaller grouping such as these First Five—the effect can only be described as poetry. No plaque praises its honoree at a decibel level that would diminish another Hall of Famer. The dignity and solemnity of the tablets is in keeping with the celebration of a life now over. Even for living Hall of Famers, what has ended is the endeavor that won a man his fame. A man elected to the Hall of Fame as a player, for example, may go on to manage in the big leagues or become a distinguished executive (Henry Aaron and Joe Cronin spring to mind), but I know of no case in which a man previously enshrined in the Hall has gone on to a career of equal stature in the game.

It is impossible to do justice, in forty words or less, to the achievements, much less the style, flair, and vigor of these men or how they changed our nation and every one of us. The art of these plaques lies in not trying to do too much, in trusting to the wind to keep these players' fame aloft. Here are the first baseball greats to be elected to the Hall of Fame, the five immortals who form the corners of Cooperstown's home plate, in the order of their votes received: Ty Cobb, Babe Ruth, Honus Wagner, Christy Mathewson, Walter Johnson. Today we look on these five with awe and reverence, baseball's equivalent of Mount Rushmore. What we forget is that their accomplishments were quite recent in the minds of those who voted for them in 1936; most of the electors had seen each of the men play, many times. And of course, of the five immortals, only one had actually gone on to his eternal reward—Mathewson, who died in 1925. (Another committee of "old-timers" wasn't able to achieve consensus on which long-retired veterans would be inducted at the first ceremony. Cap Anson and Buck Ewing got the most votes. Both were inducted by the grand opening in 1939, along with other worthies of the near and distant past.)

Ruth had retired as an active player just one year before his election. Cobb had played his final season in 1928, Johnson in 1927, Wagner 1917, Mathewson 1916. These were legends, all right, but they were as fresh in the minds of the voters then as the five men listed below—each of whom played his last game a similar number of years prior to his induction—would be to today's writers and fans: Mike Schmidt, Johnny Bench, Willie Stargell, Willie Mays, Eddie Mathews. Think about it.

CHAPTER THREE

The Spur to Memory

To see a world in a grain of sand
And a heaven in a wild flower,
Hold infinity in the palm of your hand
And eternity in an hour.
—WILLIAM BLAKE,
Auguries of Innocence

One picture is worth more than a thousand words.
—CHINESE PROVERB

Every picture tells a story.
—ROD STEWART

We have heard the stories all our lives, and we share them warmly with our children. But we come to the Baseball Hall of Fame to see, to see the instruments of glory, the stuff of legend, the tangible remains of departed heroes and forgotten fields. This is a museum like no other because it is about baseball, that singular American institution by which we mark our days. Not simply historical relics, these artifacts spur us to recall to life an image dormant in our brains for decades. They connect us not only to our own childhood and to our parents but also to a national, collective past, one whose presence we sense but whose details have been lost.

Time stops in the Museum in the same way it does at a baseball game. At the Museum it attaches itself to those things that make us halt in our tracks and reflect upon their essence and ours. Time doesn't truly stop, of course; we do. We imagine that we bend time and somehow elude it through the pleasure of play and remembrance. (The Latin root of "elude" is *ludere*, to play.) Like Proust's magical biscuit, the artifact recovers for us a lost bit of

time. Look at Babe Ruth's locker, forever open to display the Yankee uniform he last wore, and a shiver of unforeseen emotion comes over you.

This is the experience of the National Baseball Hall of Fame and Museum, an experience enriched by the stories embedded within the objects. But for many artifacts, it may have been so long since the tale was last told that hardly anyone remembers what it was. The descriptive lines that accompany each item on display at Cooperstown provide a key to its identity, but only rarely do they expand into a story. For that you had best be equipped with a life-long experience of the game or, better yet, have an old-timer as your personal tour guide.

Which is where I come in, with a "memory" of King Kelly, whom I never saw play, as vivid as my recollection of Mickey Mantle, whom I did. Let me take you on a tour of the Museum, Library, and Archive, pausing at various treasures to tell a story you may not know or simply to talk a little baseball. A picture may be worth a thousand words, but only if it speaks to you. The intent here is to provide an experience that will enrich your next visit to Cooperstown and entertain you until then; it is about walking and talking, you and I, and giving voice to the past.

There was a time, perhaps eighteen years ago, when during one of my frequent research trips to the National Baseball Library I held in my hand an object that had a story to tell, but I was not yet wise enough to hear it. Looking back, I believe this incident provided the germ of the idea for this book.

At that time, long before its 1993 enlargement, the Library was cramped for space and pressed for cataloging services. Some large boxes were filled with unrelated items of mixed provenance and scant documentation. In one such box, packed loosely among some truly notable curios (I recall Cy Young's rookie contract from 1890 and Christy Mathewson's from 1899) was a thin wooden stick, with irregular hand-hewn notches along part of its perhaps ten-inch length. With the unquestioning confidence that only comes with ignorance, I snorted at finding this insignificant piece of kindling, in a plastic bag without any indication that it had been cataloged as a gift to the Museum. "I know you'll take anything here," I laughingly announced to some library staffers, "but I thought at least it had to have something to do with baseball!"

All of us were puzzled by the stick, and none of us had an answer as to how it had entered into the collections or why it was being retained. I chalked this up to the early accessions policy of the Hall of Fame, which, like that of so many American museums and archives, was not overly discriminating. This endearing commitment, as baseball's attic, to accept even the most humble offerings from fans everywhere is the magic that brings the multitudes to Cooperstown. I thought no more about the stick for the next five years, until I was reading through Henry Chadwick's scrapbooks, on deposit at the New York Public Library . . . and then the stick became The Stick. There, in Volume 20, which was dominated by cricket stories, I came upon the following innocuous note:

> Previous to 1746, the score was kept by notches on a short lath: hence the term notches for runs. The notching-knife gradually gave way to the pen, and the thin stick to a sheet of foolscap.

The fool's cap should have been placed on my head. I had dismissed as inconsequential what was surely a scorer's stick from a very early game of baseball, an artifact earlier than Doubleday or Cartwright, perhaps the most resonant of all items relating to the prehistory of the game as we know it.

I offer this story to illustrate the difficulty of hearing the stories the artifacts have to tell, particularly the ancient ones. Large objects like statues and trophies and paintings may wag comparatively small tales, while small items like pins and ribbons and newsprint may speak volumes. Generally, the more removed the object is from the event that inspired or employed it, the less interesting it is to the historian and the less rich its associations with other events in baseball and the world. What is most fascinating and what moves us most deeply is seldom the stuff that was created in order to be treasured by future generations, although commemorative pieces (like the gifts for Lou Gehrig on his farewell day, July 4, 1939) can be beautiful and meaningful, too. But in my view, the best artifacts are the ones that were meant to be tossed aside yet improbably survived.

So in selecting the treasures for this volume, a disproportionate number of early pieces are included because it is distance that enables us to see the past clearly (in years to come Joe Carter's Series-ending home run bat, for instance, will loom larger than it does now). Also, there was the fear that if some of these stories were not liberated from the treasures that held them, they might not be told for generations to come.

To give an idea of how large a story one trinket may tell, and how rich in association it may prove, allow me to present a baseball pin no larger than a dime along with a common nursery tale: "Three wise men of Gotham went to sea in a bowl,"  went the Mother Goose rhyme; "if the bowl had been stronger, then my rhyme had been longer." Mother Goose, or *Songs for the Nursery*, was first published in London in 1760, based on English and French sources, including Charles Perrault's *Contes de ma mère l'oye* (1697). Not a propitious beginning for a baseball story, is it? But look at the accompanying photograph of a pin worn by members of the Gotham Base Ball Club of New York in the 1850s.

Let's track the story back even further, to 1460, when the "Foles of Gotham" were first mentioned in print, and a century later, when the absurd doings of the people of that village (seven miles from Nottingham, England) were collected in a book, *Merrie Tales of the Mad Men of Gotham*.

At that time the simplicity of the inhabitants was legendary. One absurdity attributed to them was the building of a thornbush round the cuckoo to secure eternal spring; another was an attempt to rid themselves of an eel by drowning it. But the archetypal tale of Gothamite behavior was when King John intended to establish a hunting lodge nearby. The villagers, fearful of the cost of supporting the court, feigned imbecility when the royal messengers arrived. Wherever the king's men went, they saw the fools of Gotham engaged in some lunatic endeavor. When King John selected another spot for his lodge elsewhere, the "wise men" boasted, "We ween there are more fools pass through Gotham than remain in it."

How did this tale come to resonate with the members of the Washington Base Ball Club, formed in 1850 as the second club after the Knickerbockers and two years later renamed after the proverbial wise fools? Gotham is understood today as Batman's hometown, but it is also a common synonym for New York and has been so since our English cousins began to refer to those "fools" who sailed from the mother country (three men in a tub) to make their fortunes in New York as residents of the "New Gotham." Washington Irving also applied the name of Gotham to New York in 1807, in some of his *Salmagundi* letters from Mustapha-Rub-a-Dub Keli Khan. ("Rub-a-dub-dub, three men in a tub . . .")

Proper businessmen scorned the young men who played baseball in the New York area around 1850 for acting like fools, trying to extend their youth beyond the time when men should give over childish things. So the Washington Base Ball Club, in a defiant stance against the British, cricket, and their elders' puritanical attitudes toward play, renamed themselves the Gotham Base Ball Club and made up this little badge of honor for its members. This example, the only one known to survive, was issued to charter member Henry Mortimer Platt and was donated to the Hall in 1939 by his daughter.

For me, this is one of the most splendid pieces in the Hall's altogether splendid collection. But if I had been charged with selecting these treasures a hundred years ago, I don't know if the Gotham pin would have made the cut. Who knows—a hundred years from now, the gloriously tacky Lady Met pins shown above, from about 1975, might hold a story as richly layered as that of the Gotham pin.

CHAPTER FOUR

The Time Line

TO 1901

This stunning panorama of "New York and Vicinity" has been labeled in the mount "Baseball in Jersey City in 1868." Not exactly.

What we see in the foreground is baseball at the Elysian Fields of Hoboken, a pleasure grounds for New Yorkers ever since the dawn of the century, when bearbaiting and bare-knuckle prizefighting competed for attention with buffalo hunts and cricket matches. Most visitors to the

site came for the cool breezes, soothing libations, and relief from the strains of city life. Ferries departed every fifteen minutes from the Barclay Street docks in Manhattan. The steamers were controlled by the John C. Stevens family, which also owned the resort grounds—a model of commerce that would mark baseball's development through the age of trolley cars, short-line rail, and subways: create a remote attraction, and control the access to it. The Stevens Castle is the large house to the right of the ball grounds.

The Elysian Fields became not only a place of rest but also recreation as the prospect of employment lured young bachelors from the farm to the city, only to leave them pining for rural bliss.

Cricket was played at the Hoboken grounds before baseball, but by 1845 the New York Knicker-bockers had taken heed of the northward push of industry in Manhattan and had taken their new game of "base ball" to Hoboken.

The lithograph, printed and published in Philadelphia in 1866, offers a bird's-eye view of extraordinarily intricate if untrustworthy detail. The artist is John Bachman, famous for such views of northeastern cities. Depicted are two quite different games of "base ball" being played within a few yards of each other, separated by the refreshment pavilion. At the left two teams are playing the Massachusetts Game, in which the batter stood between fourth base and first—a variant nearly dead in New England and never played in the New York area but perhaps still alive at the time in Philadelphia, where the Olympic Club had organized in 1833 to play town ball, from which the Massachusetts Game derived. To the right two other teams appear to be playing according to the rules of the New York Game, which has come down to us as the game we would recognize today. The codification of rules for the New York Game are attributed to Alexander Cartwright, Daniel Lucius "Doc" Adams, and other primal members of the famed Knickerbocker Base Ball Club of New York.

Among the critical innovations of the Knickerbockers was the concept of a boundaried playing field (cricket, town ball, and the Massachusetts Game had no prescribed bounds). The Knicks were constrained by their playing site (look at how close their field, the one at the right in this picture, was to the Hudson River). Accordingly, not only was a foul ball declared a non-event, but, as stated in Rule 20, the last of their original rules of 1845, "But one base allowed when a ball bounds out of the field when struck." Doc Adams made the leather-strapped balls himself, an exceedingly tedious task, and he wasn't going to stand for some young Hercules sending his handiwork into the drink.

The Elysian Fields, known as Turtle Grove in the 1780s, was gone by the end of the 1880s, over-taken by rail and industry. But you may still visit the Knickerbocker playing fields site by asking the friendly watchman at the abandoned Maxwell House Coffee plant to let you into the courtyard. You might even detect the site of the Sybil's Cave, a lovers' destination in the 1840s, now walled up within the rock abutment along the river road, once described as "romantic and beautiful . . . a narrow, circuitous path, overarched with oak branches." Today it is an industrial service road called Frank Sinatra Drive, after Hoboken's favorite son.

Every picture tells a story, but some offer a peephole to the past, in which the closer you get to the opening, the more you see. Like the tiny Gotham Base Ball Club pin shown in Chapter 3, and, for the same reasons, this is one of my favorites.

—★—

The relationship between baseball and cricket is a tangled one, epitomized in this peculiar belt, found in the Hall of Fame's basement archive in the course of research for this book. The web belt belonged to Napoleon Bonaparte McLaughlin, who frequently wore it in the 1860s while playing cricket. The brass buckle refers not only to the

eleven-man game brought over from England, but particularly to the visiting All-England Eleven, led by the celebrated John Wisden and John Lillywhite, against whom a twenty-two-man Young America competed in 1859 at the Elysian Fields before 24,000 spectators. The Americans offered puny opposition, even with twice as many batsmen on their side. The native press at the time, well aware of baseball's growing popularity, referred to the two games as "our national pastimes."

This contest of 1859 marked the high point of cricket in the United States. Six years later, as America came out of its Civil War still intact, cricket had become merely an anglophilic affectation. The tramping soldiers had taken a bat and a ball on their marches, and wherever they stopped they played. The manicured pitch required for cricket was out of the question. They played baseball. And when they came home to their various communities, baseball was firmly, undisputedly the national pastime.

Back to that belt: its owner was not only a cricket devotee who played regularly at Hoboken—he was a dedicated baseball player. Napoleon Bonaparte McLaughlin's daughter, when she gave the belt to the Hall of Fame in 1955, wrote in the note accompanying the donation that he often wore it while playing baseball with his fellow Knickerbockers. This humble article of clothing thus becomes the only surviving item ever used by a Knick on the field of play.

—★—

The inscription reads: "Presented to Samuel H. Kissam by a fellow member to commemorate his twenty-fifth anniversary of membership in the Knickerbocker Base Ball Club. And as a remembrance of an unbroken and warm friendship in 1854, the green fields of Hoboken 1879. And also attesting his many sacrifices and kindnesses which will be cherished forever, by your loving and grateful friends. God be with you." This fond farewell to member Kissam was followed three years later by the dissolution of the Knickerbockers themselves, who had pretty much stopped playing ball anyway. The professional game was all the rage, and industry was encroaching on their Elysian Fields site as it had in 1843–44, when they moved from Madison Square (near 27th Street) to Murray Hill (near 34th), and finally across the Hudson in the fall of 1845.

An Old-timers' Game in 1875 brought back such Knickerbocker luminaries as Doc Adams and James Whyte Davis (who, twenty years later, would be buried in the Knickerbocker flag that had flown from the roof of their clubhouse). But the age of gentlemen playing a gentle game, requiring great camaraderie and little skill, was over.

—★—

By the mid-1850s there were two different types of organized teams. There were the "gentlemen's clubs," like the pioneer Knickerbockers of New York, which were made up not of aristocratic bluebloods but simply the period's equivalent of white-collar workers—bank clerks, doctors, lawyers, merchants, brokers. And there were the workingmen's teams, usually groups that were united by (1) their trade or their employer, such as Henry Eckford's Brooklyn shipbuilders/mechanics and the Pocahontas nine of Brooklyn dairymen, or (2) their avocation, such as the Mutuals of New York, who were municipal employees, and the Atlantics of Brooklyn, outdoor laborers, both of which groups liked to languish in fire stations, ball grounds, and banquet halls.

The Eckfords of Brooklyn were dockworkers, so they could practice only once a week, and they engaged in no matches with other clubs in the year of their founding, 1855. But in the next year they showed their mettle when they played and defeated the Unions of Morrisania, a community then located in southern Westchester County, but now redistricted within the Bronx. Before the 1850s had run their course the New York area had nine strong teams: the Knickerbockers, Gothams, Eagles, and Empires of New York, the Unions of Morrisania, and the Eckfords, Atlantics, Excelsiors, and Putnams of Brooklyn.

On July 29, 1857, the Eckfords defeated the Empires, 35–33, using the lively rubber-core ball common at the time (the score is testament); here it is, sitting on top of the red morocco-bound scorebook of the Eckfords, which in turn rests upon a gloriously tattered flag with its shipwrights' symbol of a winged mule, Pegasus taken down a peg. The custom of the day was for the winning nine to claim the ball used in the game, repair to their clubhouse, gild the ball, and record on it the score of the game, the date, and the contestants.

From July 20, 1858, when admission was first charged for a Brooklyn–New York All-Star match, the line between gentlemen's clubs and laborers' teams was blurred: winning was what counted. In rapid succession over the next seven years came the first enclosed ball field, secret payments to supposed amateurs like the Excelsiors' Jim Creighton and the Eckfords' Al Reach, large-scale gambling and pool selling, an undefeated season (1863), and the first game-fixing scandal.

On September 28, 1865, the Eckfords were unwitting beneficiaries of gifts from three Mutual players—catcher William Wansley, third baseman Ed Duffy, and shortstop Thomas Devyr—as the Mutuals kicked the game away to the Eckfords, 28–11. Two weeks later the "muffin nine" (soft, inept players) of the Eckfords defeated the second-raters of the Empire club, 46–43, a lighthearted match nonetheless memorialized with a golden ball no less grand than that accorded a victory by the first nine.

On March 17, 1871, the Eckfords became a member of the new National Association of Professional Base Ball Players, thus marking an end to the amateur competition that had begun in the fifties when clubs like the Knickerbockers and the Gothams blazed the path. But the Eckfords and Washington Nationals, who also enlisted in the new association, declined to pay ten dollars toward the purchase of a "whip pennant" that would be awarded to the champion club. The Eckfords, uniformed in white flannel trimmed with orange, played almost sixty games in 1871, most of them against other association clubs, but their record will not be found in the encyclopedias, for want of ten dollars.

However, in the 1872 campaign, the Eckfords' first in fully professional ranks, the team won only three of twenty-nine games and then resumed its semipro status, which in fact it had not abandoned even in the National Association. Like four other "cooperative" clubs (Atlantics, Nationals, Washington Olympics, and Middletown Mansfields), their players split gate receipts rather than re-

ceiving salary. The Eckfords disappeared from the record books once again—this time for good, as they formally disbanded before the 1873 campaign—but one player from that final-curtain nine, infielder Jack "Candy" Nelson, was still playing ball in the major leagues in 1890. The club that grew from the docks of Brooklyn survived as a social club into the twentieth century, and this wealth of Eckfordiana, which includes a great many more gilded trophy balls and the dazzlingly preserved silk monogram ("EBBC" for Eckford Base Ball Club), came to the Hall when the social club at last closed its doors.

—★—

More than thirty years before a pair of brothers named Wright made aviation history, another Wright duo was instrumental in changing baseball from a social-club pastime to a professional game. Baseball's Wright brothers were George and Harry, cricket players who saw the future in the American game. The artful disarray of this photo composition is a sort of archaeological cross section, embracing more than seventy years of ballplaying history. Let's poke around a bit in this "Wright brothers' attic."

The opened book opens our story. It is *Felix on the Bat*, a classic cricket instructional manual written and illustrated by the great Kent and All-England batsman of the 1840s, "N. Felix," which was the pen name for Nicholas Wanostrocht. It was presented to Samuel Wright, father of Harry and George in 1858, on his Benefit Day at the St. George Cricket Club, Elysian Fields, Hoboken, where the English-born Sam was the cricket professional and Harry and George two of the key players (Harry by 1854, George beginning in 1861). George was eleven at the time his father received the book, and it is not clear when Sam passed it on to George, who wrote on the flyleaf: "This book I prize very highly as it was given to me by my Father in the year 1865. Often I have viewed its contents when a boy looking forward to some day to play the game of cricket well. G.W."

Of course, by 1865 young George was not only adept at cricket, he was well on his way to becoming the best baseball player in the land. Harry had begun to divide his time between cricket and baseball in the late 1850s, when he joined the Knickerbocker Base Ball Club, whose grounds adjoined those of the St. George Cricket Club. Mirroring the divided loyalties of pre–Civil War America, both continued to play cricket for at least two more years, Harry with the Cincinnati

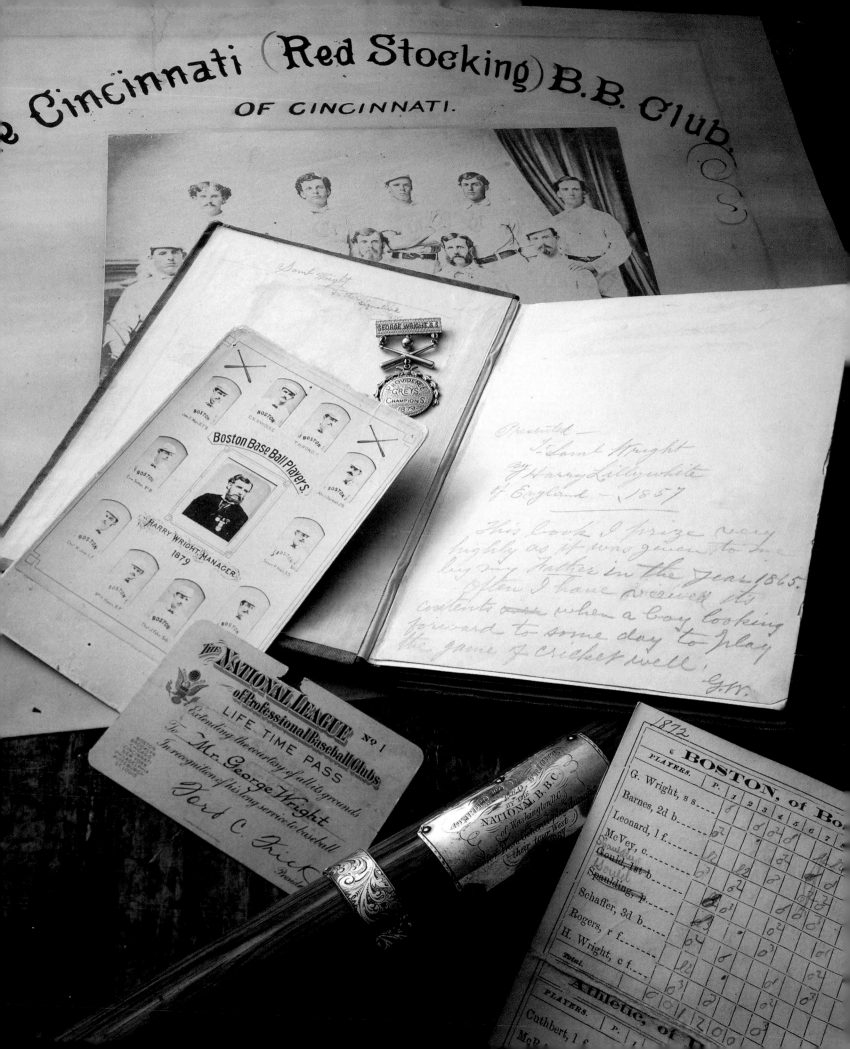

Cricket Club, which had lured him west with the position of cricket professional and an invitation to organize a first-class baseball club. George left the champion Union of Morrisania team after the 1866 campaign to join the covertly professional Washington Nationals as they toured the west. George was supposedly earning his living as a government clerk, but the address of his "employer" as listed in the City Directory was just a public park. They traveled as far as Illinois, where the Nationals were upset by the Forest City of Rockford and their boy pitcher, Al Spalding. George received this handsome rosewood trophy bat for "best general play."

By 1869 both were members of baseball's first openly all-professional team, the celebrated Cincinnati Red Stockings. George was the greatest player of his time, with wonderful batting and fielding skills and an acrobat's flair. In 1869 George hit .518 with fifty-nine home runs in fifty-two games. Harry, twelve years older, was a fading player, but he was the organizer, promoter, and father figure of the Red Stockings and professional baseball itself. In the photo of the Reds, George stands in the top row, second from the left, and captain Harry is seated beneath him. And, following a tradition far older than baseball, both left for a new opportunity when the money beckoned. When the Reds collapsed and the National Association of Professional Base Ball Players formed, Harry moved to Boston as manager and took brother George and other Red Stockings along with him to join former Rockford stars Al Spalding and Ross Barnes and Cleveland's Deacon White. The Wrights and Boston rolled over the competition in the National Association, winning four straight pennants by increasingly grotesque margins, thus hastening the demise of the league. In the new National League, Boston continued its winning ways, but after championships in 1877 and 1878, George went to Providence as a playing manager in 1879 and defeated Harry's Bostons in a close race. Both brothers' tokens of that 1879 season are on display here. In the mid-1930s, National League president Ford Frick gave George Wright, nearing the age of ninety, a lifetime pass to all National League grounds (note that it is #1, the first ever given).

———— ★ ————

From the personal collection of George Wright: an incredible array of silk ribbons from long-gone teams (okay, Harvard and Yale are still around). Some of these are from Wright's early years with such teams as the Gothams of New York, the Nationals of Washington, and the Unions of Morrisania, when he was not only the new national pastime's star player but also an emblem of the public's passage from cricket to baseball. Like his English-born brother Harry, native-born George had played cricket at the Elysian Fields in the 1850s before trying his hand at baseball.

Represented here are some of the teams that the Wright brothers' pioneering professionals, the Cincinnati Red Stockings, played in their tours of 1869 and 1870, when they won eighty-four consecutive games. Harvard gave them one of their toughest games, losing a 17–12 lead in the ninth inning. The Atlantics of Brooklyn was the team that ended Cincinnati's winning streak, in a fabulous eleven-inning 8–7 battle that I, for one, believe is still the greatest game ever played (more on this soon, I promise).

These ribbons, sometimes referred to as "silks," are exceedingly rare, and in twenty-five years of scouring private and institutional collections, I have come across only a handful, most of them in frightfully deteriorated condition (the New York Public Library has some). What were these silk tokens for? In an odd extension of chivalric tradition, the teams wore their own ribbon while they played, generally on their sleeve, and each losing player gave his to a member of the victorious team.

—★—

Baseball's great team of 1869, the Cincinnati Red Stockings, captured by America's great photographer of the day, Mathew Brady, in his studio in Washington, D.C. This photo is interesting not only because of the subject but also because it is the only baseball-related shot Brady ever took.

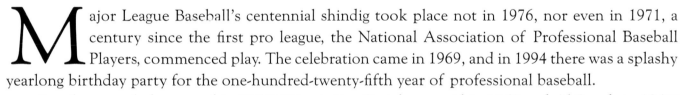

—★—

Major League Baseball's centennial shindig took place not in 1976, nor even in 1971, a century since the first pro league, the National Association of Professional Baseball Players, commenced play. The celebration came in 1969, and in 1994 there was a splashy yearlong birthday party for the one-hundred-twenty-fifth year of professional baseball.

So what exactly happened in 1869? Wasn't Jim Creighton paid in 1859 and Al Reach in 1863? Between 1865 and 1869, weren't there such professional teams as the Atlantics of Brooklyn, the Mutuals of New York, the Athletics of Philadelphia, and more? Sure. But there was something special about 1869: the manly admission of Harry Wright to the press that his Cincinnati Red Stockings were salaried and proud of it. The Reds were thus the first avowedly professional team in baseball history, a distinction that scholars insist on using to separate this mighty team from the under-the-table schemers and gate-receipt communards who had preceded them. Besides, the Reds were the best team ever assembled to that point, and they came from all over.

Harry Wright had come to the banks of the Ohio in 1865 at the behest of the Union Cricket Club. By 1867 he had organized a Red Stockings baseball club, too, though it wasn't yet strong enough to compete against the best. The arrival of pitcher Asa Brainard, former Brooklyn Excelsior, in 1868, followed by the advent of Harry's brother George for the 1869 season, made the team literally unbeatable.

The Red Stockings took on all comers, from Maine to California, in 1869, and never tasted de-

feat. They won eighty-four consecutive games in 1869–1870 before getting their comeuppance from the venerable Atlantics of Brooklyn, the champions of several earlier 1860s campaigns. Note the silk ribbons of not only the Reds but also the Atlantics. In addition there are the silks of Harvard, the Forest City of Rockford, and the Nationals of Washington. The Forest City of Rockford was accounted as one of the strongest nines following their 1867 upset of the touring Washington Nationals, then led by George Wright; those Nationals in turn had defeated Harry's developing Red Stockings, 53–10. Rockford's stars included Albert Spalding, Bob Addy, and Ross Barnes, and in 1870 they welcomed a young third baseman from Marshalltown, Iowa, named Adrian Anson. In that year Spalding's heady pitching led to a 12–5 victory over Cincinnati, avenging their 34–13 drubbing at the hands of the Reds in '69.

But that was not the Reds' first loss. On June 14, 1870, at the Capitoline Grounds in Brooklyn, the Reds jumped off to a 2–0 lead in the first, but the Atlantics held a lead of 4–3 after six frames. The Reds regained the lead with two tallies in the seventh, but the Atlantics knotted the contest at 5–5 in the eighth, and there things stood at the conclusion of nine innings. Captain Bob Ferguson of the Atlantics agreed to a draw, as was the custom, but Harry Wright of the Reds insisted that the game be played to a conclusion, "if it took all summer." Backed up by Reds president Aaron B. Champion, he ordered his men back on the field. Ferguson then did the same for his Atlantics.

After a scoreless tenth, the Reds appeared to settle the issue with two runs in the top of the eleventh. But Brainard's nerve was wearing thin, according to the *New York Clipper* report. He allowed a leadoff single to Charlie Smith, then followed with a wild pitch that sent Smith all the way to third. "Old Reliable," first baseman Joe Start, drove a long fly to right field, where Cal McVey had difficulty extricating the ball from the standing-room-only crowd. Smith scored, and now Start was on third. At this point Ferguson came to the plate and, seeing how his men had been foiled by George Wright's brilliant plays time and again, the right-handed hitter turned around to bat from the left side, simply to keep the ball away from the Reds' shortstop.

Ferguson drove the ball past the second baseman. Tie game! When George Zettlein drove a liner toward first base, Charlie Gould blocked it, but threw hurriedly and wildly to second base in an attempt to force Ferguson. The ball skittered into left field, and Ferguson scampered home with the winning run. Additional batters came to the plate, for the rules did not yet call for the game to end until three outs were registered in the final half inning, but no further scoring ensued. After the contest, Champion telegraphed the following message back to Cincinnati: "Atlantics 8, Cincinnatis 7. The finest game ever played. Our boys did nobly, but fortune was against us. Eleven innings played. Though beaten, not disgraced."

Other archaeological delights associated with the Reds on display in this tableau are a ticket to Cincinnati's Union Grounds for the game of July 1, 1869; a ball used in several games by the Reds of '69; and a menu from the banquet of June 29, 1870, welcoming the Reds back home. The *Clipper*, in background with woodcuts of captains Ferguson and Wright, contained sporting and theatrical news from its debut in 1853 until its demise in 1924, at which point it dropped its sports coverage and changed its name to become the entertainment business publication still with us today, *Variety*.

Al Reach, who along with Jim Creighton was one of the first men to earn a living playing baseball, had an eye for business. Following his playing days with the Philadelphia Athletics, he hooked up with Ben Shibe, the man who invented the cork-center ball and machines for making balls cost-effectively, thereby turning himself into a sporting-goods magnate, like his entrepreneurial pals George Wright (Wright & Ditson) and Albert Spalding (the Spalding Company, which went on to buy out Reach).

The Spalding ball became the official choice of the National League, as Spalding joined the Chicago team headed by William Hulbert, who founded the league itself. Reach was instrumental in the creation of the American Association and its strongest franchise, the Philadelphia Athletics; his reward was to have his ball made official. And Wright's ball was similarly honored by the one-year major league, the Union Association, in 1884.

This Reach ball is a very great rarity, and it came into the Hall's possession through a donation only a few years ago. (Don't think that all the great finds are over and done with. There's a whole nation of attics out there!)

———★———

Unattractive as an object but revered for its associations, this ball came from George Wright's brother in 1939, just two years after the old shortstop died. Painted over for no compelling reason, the venerable orb just barely reveals its secrets. The faint inscription reads "Red Stockings, 1869–1870," and one must struggle to make out "Cincinnati" and George Wright's name. Think of the hands that tossed this ball! For a baseball fan, looking upon this ball is like locating the silver dollar that Washington threw across the Potomac.

———★———

By 1871 the Eagle Base Ball Club was already celebrating eighteen years of existence. This club traced its origins as a ball club back to 1840, when it was playing a variant of rounders or shinny on a diamond-shaped field with two obtuse and two oblique angles. But it wasn't baseball. When the Eagles determined to play baseball, they reorganized in 1852 and soon became formidable rivals to the Knickerbockers. Their star shortstop, Marvin E. Gelston, went out west in the late fifties and created the Eagle Base Ball Club of San Francisco, the first ever in those parts.

The sharp-eyed and historically minded will note some interesting names among the organizers of the musical and sporting levee. There are Andrew Peck and Irving Snyder, whose sporting-goods business dwarfed all others until the advent of the ex-ballplayers Spalding, Wright, and Reach. And there's Andrew McCarty, whose banquet rooms hosted many a Knickerbocker soiree in the 1840s.

T he National Association was the first professional baseball league; it was not an organization of clubs, like the National League, which succeeded it in 1876, but rather a gathering of players. As organizations go, it was pretty ragtag. The National Association was founded in just one meeting on March 17, 1871, in Collier's saloon at 840 Broadway (near Tenth Street) in Manhattan. There was neither league constitution, charter, nor rules (the organizers simply adopted the rules of the amateur National Association, the "National Association of Ball Players" from which they had just broken off). The league provided no schedule of games, but instead left it to the clubs to schedule five games with each competitor with three victories ending the series—so the teams played varying numbers of games. But the major innovation of the National Association, besides its very existence, was the establishment of a pennant race. Any club that paid a ten-dollar fee by May 1 (toward the purchase of a "whip pennant" that would fly atop the champion's clubhouse) was able to challenge the others, and the championship team was to be determined by the best record overall.

Although the Eckfords of Brooklyn failed to come up with the ten dollars, and thus are invisible in the league standings, they played complete series against most of the other association's clubs. The scorecard shown here is from a notable game of July 4, 1871, when they shut out the favored Mutuals (Boss Tweed's team) 7–0 before 6,000 at Brooklyn's Union Grounds, providing an epic betting coup for their admirers and their own players and perhaps the Mutuals, too.

The Philadelphia Athletics were the champions in that inaugural season, by virtue of a defeat on October 30 of the demoralized Chicago White Stockings, playing in borrowed uniforms of various hues and styles because their equipment (and their ballpark) had been destroyed in the Great Fire three weeks earlier. The A's leading player, "Long Levi" Meyerle, was the league batting champion at .492, for which he was awarded the trophy bat on display here. The other decorative bat was given to Sam Jackson by his admiring fans back home in Rochester, where his exploits had brought him to the attention of Harry Wright, who hired him as a substitute for the Boston team of 1871.

Fan interest in Harry's Cincinnati club had disappeared in the second half of the 1870 season as the Reds, unbeaten in 1869, had the temerity to lose six of their seventy-four contests. The directors withdrew their support, the club disbanded, and the ballpark was razed, with the lumber and the Red Stocking trophy bats and balls selling at auction. Harry moved on to form the Boston Red Stockings, bringing along fellow Cincinnati alumni Cal McVey, Charlie Gould, Charlie Sweasy, and brother George. To this nucleus he added Rockford stars Al Spalding and Ross Barnes. The rest of the Reds—Asa Brainard, Fred Waterman, Andy Leonard, and Doug Allison—went to Washington as the Olympics, where they failed to scale the heights.

Spalding, whom we think of today as an entrepreneur rather than an athlete, posted a won-lost mark of 204–53 in his five years with Boston, while Barnes batted over .400 in each of his first three seasons there and averaged .390 in a Boston uniform. It is reasonable to think that Boston would have won the flag in that inaugural season of 1871, too, if George Wright had not injured himself, which forced Barnes to play shortstop half the year while Jackson filled in at second base. Boston

won handily in each of the remaining four years of the National Association, culminating in a record of 71–8 in 1875 while going undefeated at home.

The 1872 team is immortalized in this fabulous autographed folding fan. Sam Jackson was not part of Boston's championship years, as he moved on to the Atlantics in 1872, but his family kindly gave the Hall such treasures as his bat, his Red Stocking pin (each 1871 team member received one), and his complimentary season pass, the earliest known. The baseball, which came to the Hall from the family of George Wright, won its scuff marks of honor in an 1871 Boston Red Stockings game, and as such it is the only National Association ball to have survived.

—★—

The crossed bats, the horseshoe, even the sensitively arranged flowers speak a language understood by everyone in the nineteenth century. We may only guess at their full meanings today, just as we are puzzled by an old graveyard's symbol-laden signposts to the life beyond. But in this tribute bouquet, delicately painted on glass, there is no mistaking the warmth the Cincinnati fans held for their hometown favorite, William "Buck" Ewing.

Hometown? Wasn't Buck Ewing the famous catcher of the New York Giants? And wasn't he a New York laddie before that, with the Troy team that sent to the Hall of Fame not only Ewing but also Roger Connor, Tim Keefe, and Smiling Mickey Welch?

Sure. But if all politics is local, as Speaker of the House Tip O'Neill was fond of saying, then fandom is no less so. Once a ballplayer signs on with your club, he is instantly one of you and champions all your hopes for glory. But don't forget that he comes from somewhere else, and neither he nor his earliest supporters forget it (think of Paul Molitor closing out his career in Minnesota). Ewing was born in rural Ohio in 1859, played his first professional ball with the aptly named Buckeyes, and returned to Ohio to play with and manage the Reds in the 1890s.

In fact, in a story little noted today, he'd returned there in 1883. Ewing found himself suddenly without a home when the Troy franchise collapsed, so he signed with the Cincinnati Reds of the American Association. However, the great Harmony Conference (also known as the Tripartite Agreement) of the National League, the Northwestern League, and the American Association yielded a settlement by which Ewing (and fellow Trojans Mickey Welch and

Pete Gillespie) were turned over to the newly formed New York Gothams.

With New York he became a legend for his audacity, pluck, and field generalship. Intangibles went a long way with fans and sportswriters back then, more so than today when stats seem to be the sole measure of the man. But Ewing could hit: once he led in homers, another time in triples, and he hit as high as .344. He could throw: the snap throw to second from a crouch position started with Buck Ewing, not Pudge Rodriguez. And he could run, too, stealing fifty-three bases in the Giants' championship year of 1888.

So how great was he, really? Twenty years after his last game, veteran sportswriters compared him to Cobb and Wagner and pronounced him their peer. And when the Hall of Fame was opened in 1939, Buck Ewing, long gone but still revered in all his hometowns, became its first catcher.

—★—

When the National League abandoned Troy and Worcester after the 1882 season, it reestablished franchises in New York and Philadelphia for the first time since its inaugural campaign of 1876. Grumbling can still be heard in Troy and Worcester today, but their loss was baseball's gain, giving the shaky National League the two key eastern markets it had lacked.

The original Giants of 1883 wore the emblem of the city on their breasts, binding the team to the body politic and making baseball seem as much a part of old Gotham as Indians and beaver pelts, Knickerbockers and coopers. The uniform patch shown here is the original, worn by Buck Ewing. Other members of this team were future Hall of Famers: pitcher Mickey Welch, who in 1885 posted an imposing record of 44–11, and John Montgomery Ward, the perfect-game pitcher turned shortstop whose career home run record was finally surpassed by a guy named Ruth.

—★—

This medal is no sentimental tribute to a player past his prime. The Buck Ewing of 1883 was a pistol, new to Gotham as was his whole team, largely transplants from the expelled Troy franchise. (In fact, New York's National League team was known as the Gothams until manager Jim Mutrie, some years hence, exclaimed that his brawny lads were "Giants.") Ewing scored more than a run per game and played at second, short, third, and the outfield when the catching grind wore him down.

Also new to major-league baseball and New York that season was an American Association franchise called the Metropolitans. John B. Day had the good fortune to own both teams, so he parceled out some of his Trojan warriors to the Mets and some to the Gothams.

Following the regular season, the two new teams played each other in a four-game exhibition series won by the Mets. Ewing, however, was the leading run-gatherer of the series and so won this bright bauble as his consolation prize. The Stock Exchange Medal is interesting because it calls to mind that, in New York, ball games began at four o'clock to permit stockbrokers to get uptown for the opening pitch after the market's closing bell. Games seldom ran to two hours, but this accommodating precedent makes today's nighttime scheduling of World Series games a bit less venal, doesn't it?

—★—

Buck Ewing and King Kelly were quite a pair, though they never played on the same club. Ewing was Cincinnati's hometown hero who made his mark in the big leagues with Troy; Michael Joseph Kelly left his birthplace of Troy to become the toast (alas, too frequently, for he drank his way out of the league) of Cincinnati and several other venues, notably Chicago and Boston. Ewing was a catcher who in later years played increasingly at other positions; Kelly began as an outfielder but wound up catching nearly as many games as he played in the garden. Ewing was a model citizen and the model for all right-thinking individuals; Kelly was a reprobate and perhaps an idol for the rest of us.

They were different in all these regards, Kelly and Ewing, but they had this in common: ordinary speed on the base paths but cleverness and breathtaking daring. "Ewing's Famous Slide" was the title of a popular litho of the day, memorializing an apocryphal tale of his announced intent (and ultimate success) in stealing home after he had already stolen second base and third. Kelly's sliding wizardry was more scientific. He developed the hook

slide, whereby he encouraged his opponent to try to tag the front leg that was away from the base while his back leg landed him safe. His exploits were celebrated not only in a *Harper's Weekly* print from his Chicago White Stocking days but also in a Tin Pan Alley tune, "Slide, Kelly, Slide," that gently mocked his vanity: "Slide, Kelly, slide! Your running's a disgrace! Slide, Kelly, slide! Stay there, hold your base!"

There are a hundred great stories about the King, but let me share with you this almost certainly fictitious classic, a story that's so often told and so illustrative of his genius that it's better than merely true. Once, in the days when a substitution took effect upon a captain's announcing it, an opposing batsman lifted a low foul ball toward the Boston dugout, where Kelly was taking a day off to recover from a bruise of the day before or the booze of the

night before. Kelly saw his catcher would never get there in time, so he leapt from the bench, shouted, "Kelly now catching for Boston!" and snagged the fly. Not surprisingly, the rules makers changed things not long after that. No matter—rules were not made to constrain a King.

Sober or not, he was the best player in baseball in the mid-1880s. But Kelly's high-living, fun-loving lifestyle had him in constant hot water with his Chicago manager, Cap Anson. When Kelly was sold to Boston in 1887, at the height of his career, it was for $10,000, the largest amount of money ever paid for a ballplayer. The medal given him by his Boston fans in that year was for his eighty-four stolen bases, the most on the club and the third best total in the league.

Out of baseball after a few games with New York in 1893, he sought a new career on the boards. He was on his way to Boston to perform *Casey at the Bat* at the Palace Theatre in November 1894 when he was stricken with pneumonia. As they carried his stretcher into the hospital, it is said, the attendants tripped and dumped Kelly on the floor. "That's me last slide," he said. A few days later the "$10,000 Beauty" died.

Another story so good it must be true . . . right?

The only current baseball vestige of the former custom of the "field day" is the home run contest held before the All-Star Game each year. In professional basketball and hockey, such isolated skills as dunking and three-point shooting and speed skating and penalty shots are displayed to universal approbation.

Baseball field days were common throughout the latter part of the nineteenth century and well into the twentieth, occurring in stadiums before scheduled ball games or in place of them. Players would take part in throwing, hitting, and base-running contests. And as you can see, the winners earned some nifty trophies, like this gorgeous pitcher given Willie Keeler for his base-running exploits on October 14, 1895.

Win a trophy, lose a trophy. Less than a week be-

fore, Keeler's Orioles had had a chance to take home the Temple Cup, denoting major-league supremacy, by winning the postseason series with Cleveland. However, Cy Young, Jesse Burkett, and their fellow Spiders upset the Baltimore boys, four games to one.

—★—

"The Famous World Beaters!" This elephantine photograph of the champion St. Louis Browns of 1888, four-time pennant winners of the American Association, was replicated and sold in cabinet-card size throughout the land. In those cabinet cards the numbering system indicated on the cardboard mount corresponded to numbers scrawled on the players' chests, but in this full-size version the numbers provide no clue to the Browns' identities. So, for the record here is the elegantly frocked cast of characters (and the Browns had more than their share of strange ones, from obnoxious, foul-mouthed third baseman Arlie Latham—"the freshest man on earth"—to ambidextrous pitcher Icebox Chamberlain, who won his nickname for the cool composure with which he ate flies, presumably with either hand).

Top row (left to right, as in all identifications to follow): Latham, team mascot, and Tip O'Neill (who had batted a league-high .492 in 1887, the year when walks were registered as hits; not counting the walks, he merely hit .435 while leading the league in runs, hits, doubles, triples, home runs, and runs batted in). *Second row from top:* shortstop Bill White; pitcher Jim Devlin; second baseman Yank Robinson; Hall of Fame outfielder Tommy McCarthy, later to win fame with Hugh Duffy as one of the "Heavenly Twins" in the Boston outfield; pitcher Silver King, who won forty-five games in 1888; and utility man Ed Herr. *Third row from top:* principal catcher Jack Boyle; pitcher Nat Hudson, a twenty-five-game winner in 1888; captain and first baseman Charles Comiskey, another Hall of Famer; and reserve catchers Jocko Milligan and Tom Dolan. *In the front*, each holding one of owner Chris Von Der Ahe's prize greyhounds, are the aforementioned Chamberlain and outfielder Harry Lyons; one dog is named Fly and the other Prince, and it would be nice to report that Chamberlain was holding the pooch named Fly, but this cannot be confirmed.

Other notables who contributed to the Browns' success but who were no longer with the team in 1888 included Curt Welch, famous for the "$15,000 slide" with which he stole home in the tenth inning of the final game of the winner-take-all World Series of 1886, and pitchers Bob Caruthers and Dave Foutz, each of whom won ninety-nine games for the teams of 1885–1887.

—★—

In Hugh Duffy's first five big-league seasons he played for four different teams. It wasn't that he was a bad guy or a poor player. In fact, he was one of the nicest guys around and a pretty good hitter at that. Cap Anson, his first manager, with Chicago in 1888, thought he was too small. "Where's the rest of you?" the tactless Anson asked. This little guy stayed in the game long enough to become the Boston Red Sox batting instructor with a star pupil named Ted Williams.

After two years with Chicago, Duffy jumped to the Players League, which he led in runs and hits, but that league folded after the 1890 season. He then signed with Boston in the American Association, but the National League finally put that league out of business after that year. Joining Boston in the National League, he won the Triple Crown in 1894 (the fourth big leaguer ever to accomplish that) when he batted an amazing .440, with eighteen homers and 145 RBIs. He tacked on fifty-one doubles for good measure. That was the year after they moved the pitcher's distance back five feet, to the current 60'6". A lot of guys had banner batting years, but no one else has *ever* batted .440.

Little Hughie was playing manager for the Milwaukee American League team in 1901 (the next year they moved to St. Louis to become the Browns) and was awarded this loving cup by friends he had made in Boston. It was not that long ago that we held special "days" for our favorite players, giving them trophies, washing machines, cars. But Duffy had no long-term multimillion-dollar guaranteed deal. Back in 1895, after batting higher than anyone before or since, he was given a raise of $12.50 a month.

This remarkably ornate silver trophy bat—look at the engraved panorama of the Polo Grounds—was presented to Giants center fielder George Van Haltren by the *New York Mercury* in September 1894. George was on his way to a fine campaign for the Giants, who would go on to sweep all four games of the Temple Cup from the Baltimore Orioles. But this award was just for being a popular guy; indeed, he was declared the most popular league player in New York or Brooklyn (then a separate city, remember).

Like Babe Ruth, Van Haltren started out as a pitcher of the left-handed variety, winning as many as fifteen games in a big-league season. But he made his fame as a slashing hitter with a penchant for triples and stolen bases. Some modern observers, examining Van Haltren's record, see Cooperstown credentials, but he received only one official vote during the years he was eligible for consideration by the Base Ball Writers Association of America.

——— ★ ———

The Spalding Company's most popular bat in the 1880s and '90s was its Wagon Tongue model. Hearkening to the game's rural beginnings, this long, heavy bat gave promise of long balls like the ones the farm boys could recall hitting off Uncle Joe's friendly pitches back home. This wish-fulfillment model belonged to Charlie Comiskey,

who in the 1880s was the light-hitting first baseman of the rollicking St. Louis Browns, champions of the American Association four years running. Comiskey seemed to find better use for the Wagon Tongue in Chicago, where as a baseball magnate much like Spalding, he delivered a mighty licking to his opponents on the field and off.

——— ★ ———

The long and the short of it. The longer bat is a trophy given to vagabond "amateur" George Wright, who toured the west with the Washington team in 1867 and typically displayed the "best general play," the rather prosaic description of his remarkable talents. The billy club of a bat is much like the eighteen-inch "dellil" used for one-arm batting in town ball, which endured in George Wright's Cincinnati even after the Red Stockings' collapse.

But this thirty-inch stub of a bat is no relic of a

game whose rules no one remembers. It belonged to "Wee Willie" Keeler, the man who really did say, "Hit 'em where they ain't." Keeler was not even 5'5", but he used that bat (the smallest ever used in the majors) like Picasso used a brush. If an infielder played him in, Willie would slap the ball over the guy's head. If the infielder played back, Keeler would drop down a bunt. He batted .341 over a nineteen-year career, and he didn't do it with extra-base hits. As one of the stars on the sensational Baltimore Orioles teams of the 1890s, Keeler batted

.371, .377, .386, .424, .385, and .379 in consecutive years. He hardly ever struck out, either: in over 630 plate appearances in 1894, he fanned an astounding 6 times. When the hot sun baked the Baltimore infield to rocklike hardness, Keeler found he could slap down at the ball and beat out the high hop.

They still call those kind of hits "Baltimore chops." Under the tutelage of Hall of Fame manager Ned Hanlon, Keeler and McGraw perfected the hit and run. The Baltimore style became the "scientific game" that ruled baseball until Ruth.

TO 1920

No, the New York Giants weren't champions of anything in 1908. But a pin like this one, given to Mike Donlin, was awarded to each Giant player, and therein lies a tale.

As of September 23, 1908, when they squared off at New York's Polo Grounds, the Giants and Cubs were in a virtual tie for first. The game was tied 1–1 in the last of the ninth. With the Giants' Moose Mc-Cormick on first and one out, rookie Fred Merkle shot a single to right that moved the runner to third. After another out, Al Bridwell sin-gled to center, the winning run crossed the plate, and the Giants had extended their slim lead. Or had they?

Merkle, in the excitement, never bothered to touch second, instead running off the field to avoid the rush of fans storming out to celebrate. Somehow Cub second baseman Johnny Evers got the ball (or *some* ball, at any rate) and stepped on second, showing the ump he had forced Merkle and the run didn't count. Less than three weeks earlier the Cubs had tried to win a ruling on a similar force-out against the Pirates and were overruled.

Not this time. The umpires, Hank O'Day and Bob Emslie, declared the game a tie, as there was no way to clear the joyously cascading fans from the field. League president Harry Pulliam backed them up. The game was to be replayed if necessary to determine a pennant winner.

When the two teams ended the season in a dead heat, the Cubs won the replayed game as Mordecai Peter Centennial "Three-Finger" Brown defeated Christy Mathewson, 4–2, in a duel of future Hall of Famers. Merkle was dubbed "Bonehead" by the press and fans, even though teammates regarded him as one of the smarter players around (McGraw gave him a raise after the season), and he lasted for sixteen years in the bigs. The Cubs went to the World Series, where they drubbed Ty Cobb's Detroit Tigers.

Would it please Fred Merkle and the Giants of '08 to know that, nearing the end of the century, the Cubs have never won another?

———★———

Frank Merriwell, the "All-American Boy" of the dime novels, was not modeled on Christy Mathewson, although many believe this is the case. (Merriwell was a national sensation in 1896, when Matty was still in high school.) On the contrary, the future star twirler of the New York Giants, he of the disdainful glance at the opposing batsman before tossing up his inscrutable fadeaway, might well have modeled himself on Merriwell.

No matter—chicken or egg, Matty was the real-life embodiment of all the dime-novel improb-

abilities. He had indefatigable verve, nerve, pluck . . . even, for a while, luck. An early nickname for him was "Big Six," conferring upon him the combination of power and reliability of New York's most famous fire engine, the Americus No. 6, a double-deck steamer that was a true New York Giant, tipping the scale at over two tons. (Forget that stuff you often read about Matty being named "Big Six" on account of his six-foot height.) In an era when most ballplayers were rough-and-tumble characters from the wrong side of the tracks who believed that fists were the best way to settle any dispute, Mathewson stood out as "the Christian Gentleman." Tall, blond, aristocratic in looks and bearing, and college-educated, he earned a reputation for fairness and honesty that made him one of the game's first role models for boys of whom middle-class parents could approve. This was no King Kelly or Rube Waddell, no flouter of convention and target of the law, no saloon crawler or base-path brawler.

He was "no goody-goody," his wife, Jane, hastened to add whenever someone would expound upon his virtues, and that was probably true, but his press clippings declared him a paragon of virtue. He was known to cuss a bit, liked to gamble (though mostly on his own checker-playing skill), and there are a few recorded instances of his being involved in a scuffle. Some folks found him standoffish, even aloof, and accused him of having "a swelled head." But his teammates, his manager, and even those most skeptical of creatures, the writers who traveled with the team, simply adored "the Christian Gentleman." Like Kelly and Waddell, who had courted death through drink, Matty died not long after his playing days were over, though in his case from the aftereffects of poison gas inhaled during a wartime training exercise.

Mathewson began his professional career with Taunton of the New England League, in the summer after his sophomore year at Bucknell College, where he drew All-America attention as a fullback and drop kicker. During the following season, 1900, he went 20–2 for Norfolk in the Virginia League (contract shown here) and in midseason was purchased conditionally by the Giants, who were unimpressed by his pitching and tried to convert him to first base. After the season, they returned him to Norfolk, whence he was drafted by the Cincinnati Reds. (Isn't it amazing how a talent of this magnitude can escape the gaze of professional baseball people? It gives hope to every struggling rookie at every level of play.)

Fortunately for the Giants, Cincinnati proved to be no smarter than they had been. The Reds allowed themselves to be hoodwinked into an exchange of worn-out superstar Amos Rusie, whose career total of 246 major league wins were all behind him, for Mathewson, whose 373 wins were all ahead.

These artifacts recall Mathewson and his peculiar blend of piety and perspicacity. The small photos were bound into a flip book in 1907 by the Winston Film Company ("See Christy Mathewson Pitch!") and issued commercially. The ingenious Matty used them to augment his own pitches to prospective clients for his off-season insurance business. Now that's a calling card!

He was never without his Bible and his checkers. When traveling with the team, he would typically go to the local YMCA to play checkers in the evening, sometimes against a gaggle of opponents, whom he would play simultaneously, moving around the room from checkerboard to checkerboard. He was a Christian in upbringing and demeanor, but unlike Branch Rickey and other devout youths who had made promises to their mothers before embarking upon careers in professional baseball, he was not above playing exhibition baseball games on Sundays. He was one of the guys, and he liked his extra money just as the other Giants did.

As a pitcher he was at his best when the going was tough; his three shutouts in the 1905 World Series have never been equaled. His ghosted autobiography, *Pitching in a Pinch*, explained how he would take it easy unless the situation were tight, i.e., "the pinch." (Of course, that strategy was fine for the dead-ball era when weak batters were unlikely to drive the ball for an extra-base hit; today the six-inning "quality start" followed by two or three relievers is the preferred modus operandi.) Interestingly, Mathewson also took some of the toughest losses in history. In 1908 he would have been the winning pitcher on September 23, when Fred Merkle failed to touch second and turned a Giant victory into a tie game. When that tie forced a one-game play-off for the pennant, he lost to "Three-Finger" Brown. In the 1912 World Series he lost the final game in the last of the tenth inning when Fred Snodgrass muffed a fly ball and Merkle and the catcher, Chief Meyers, couldn't agree on who should catch Tris Speaker's foul pop.

—★—

There was something endearing—yes, winning—about Honus Wagner. It wasn't just that he was big and ungainly, with a blacksmith's forearms, a cowboy's bowed legs, and the huge hands of a stevedore. It wasn't just that he was quiet and unassuming, though not exactly shy. And it wasn't just that he was good, very good, some said better than Cobb. It was all of these things together, his utter unlikeliness and his utter likability, his clumsiness and his speed, his power and his modesty, that made him a workingman's hero.

His nickname, "Honus," was short for Johannes—German for John—and was pronounced HAH-nus. The Paterson jersey shown here is no replica—in a brilliant state of preservation, it is the one Honus wore for the Atlantic League team of 1896, against the backdrop of a monochromatic painting of Wagner by Tim Swartz and a fine bronze by W. Clark Noble. At Paterson, Wagner played for Ed Barrow, later to become Yankee general manager, who, even after working with Ruth, Gehrig, and DiMaggio, would always say that Wagner was the greatest player he ever saw. Looking at Honus, it was hard to believe. He was huge for his time, a barrel-chested two hundred pounds. But he was a sensationally fast base runner, five times leading the league in stolen bases, and a superb shortstop in the days when fields were rutted and rocky and errors were handed out by scorers less softhearted than today's. And what a hitter. Eight batting titles, six slugging titles, and he ranks among the top twenty batters in six different categories lifetime. He used his bludgeon of a bat with his hands spread (only someone with hands that huge could even hold the thing) to slug and spray balls around the field. His batting philosophy: "See something you can hit, and swat it."

Wagner was the first player to have his name engraved on his Louisville Slugger bat. He may also have been the first to insist that his baseball card be withdrawn from distribution because he

disapproved of the product whose sales it was designed to promote. The Wagner T206 baseball card shown here (the "T" is for tobacco) is the most valuable card in existence; a pristine example recently sold for over half a million dollars. Legend has it that Honus felt kids shouldn't be encouraged to smoke, so he sent back his royalty check and asked that the cards be destroyed; today fewer than a hundred such cards are known to exist.

Wagner began his major-league career with the Louisville Colonels but came home to his native Pittsburgh in 1900 when Colonels owner Barney Dreyfuss bought a share in the Pirates and swapped them fourteen members of his team, including future Hall of Famers Fred Clarke and Rube Waddell. Led by Wagner, Pittsburgh rose from seventh to second in 1900 and won three straight pennants, from 1901 to 1903. In 1903 the Pirates faced the Boston Pilgrims in the first modern World Series and lost, as Wagner managed only a .222 average. But in 1909 the Pirates returned to the postseason, where Wagner matched up with his American League rival for the title of "baseball's best player," Detroit's Ty Cobb.

Wagner won the face-to-face confrontation with a .333 average and six RBIs. Cobb hit just .231, and the Pirates won. The Pirates never reached the postseason again during Wagner's career. But after years of being a coach in baseball and basketball (always a love of his) and an unsuccessful businessman, Wagner returned to the Pirates as a coach in 1933 and stayed there till 1951. Always genial, he loved to tell tall tales, and when someone disputed the "accuracy" of one of his stories, Wagner's comment was "Maybe they ain't all true. But there ain't one of them you couldn't tell your grandmother."

One of the most famous Wagner myths came to be known as the "Krauthead story." Allegedly, during that 1909 Series, Cobb snarled down to Honus, "I'm coming down on the next pitch, Krauthead," at which time Wagner took the throw and loosened several of Cobb's teeth with the vicious tag. The story isn't true, though it's so good it ought to be. Cobb himself, when asked about it, said, "No man but a fool would mess with Honus Wagner. And I am not a fool." The Pirates erected a statue of this giant of a ballplayer outside Forbes Field in 1955; it resides outside Three Rivers Stadium now.

—★—

For Ty Cobb every game was a war; here are his weapons—bat, spikes, and sliding pads. He may never have really sharpened his spikes—he always maintained that he didn't—but taking a file to them while sitting in the dugout before a game had a certain, well, *effect* on the opposition. And Cobb was a consummate psychologist on the baseball field, though erratic and impulsive off it.

Cobb was totally consumed by a passion to excel. His father had named him for the city of Tyre, which had successfully withstood the onslaught of Alexander the Great despite being outnumbered. The elder Cobb, a respected teacher and school official in Royston, Georgia, had opposed his son's choice of career and sent him off with these weighty words: "Don't come home a failure." When young Tyrus returned home, however, it was to bury his father, who had been shot to death by his mother. Everything Ty Cobb attempted in life thereafter, he said, was to prove his mettle to his father.

In his first spring training with Detroit he was assigned to room with rookie catcher Boss Schmidt. When he returned from the ball field one day to find Schmidt in the bathtub, the fists flew. Schmidt, the bigger man, administered a fearful pounding to Cobb, then asked him what the heck had set him off. Cobb, blind with frustration and fury, cried, "You don't understand! I gotta be first."

Cobb held his bat with his hands apart (the prevailing style of the nineteenth century), which made it easier to adjust to breaking balls and trick pitches. For an easy pitch to handle, he would slide his top hand down and slug away; for tough pitches he would content himself with a slash through the infield or a poke over it. The key was to get on base, where he could assault the battery and dictate the tempo of the game.

Cobb was Babe Ruth's opposite in every possible way, and Cobb hated the unscientific slugging style he brought to the game. Not blessed with Ruth's natural ability, Cobb also reportedly hated Ruth for the seeming ease of his accomplishments (although it must be said there weren't many people Cobb liked). Before a game in 1925, a reporter asked Cobb about Ruth's home run feats. Cobb replied there was nothing to it; just bring your hands together on the bottom of the bat and swing for the fences. To prove it he belted three homers that day and added a double and two singles, thereby setting the American League record for total bases in a game (which still stands). Then he belted two more homers the next day to make five in two games, another mark still on the books.

Cobb's spiritual heirs form an odd couple indeed: Pete Rose, for the driven quality of his play and the full extraction of his physical gifts, and Jackie Robinson, for using anger as a spur to excellence. Rose would one day surpass Cobb's phenomenal hit total and end his career with the taint of scandal. Cobb also had a gambling-related run-in with the Commissioner's Office in 1926, having to do with an incident from the previous decade. Judge Landis's investigation resulted in Cobb's departure from the Tigers, followed by exoneration and a final two years of play with the Athletics. Cobb's link to Jackie Robinson, while less obvious, is more profound. Both had to fight for everything they got, and both excelled through anger yet were drained by it. Cobb was a virulent racist who, had he been an active player in 1947, would probably have been Robinson's most outspoken enemy and physical threat. Yet Cobb lived long enough to see Robinson overcome all the obstacles placed before him and intimidate his opponents more than they could hope to intimidate him. Surely Cobb held a grudging admiration for this fellow son of Georgia who played the game more like him than anyone before or since.

Herewith an oxymoron: Shoeless Joe's shoes. What might have been? That's the question fans still ask, even on the Internet, about Joseph Jefferson Jackson, the hayseed who hit a mere .356 in thirteen big-league seasons before his expulsion from organized baseball. What might have been? Heck, what *was* was pretty astounding and surely would place Joe Jackson in the Hall of Fame even if he had never played another day, were it not for the ineradicable stain of guilt. Oh, there are those who say Joe was an innocent, a rube who didn't understand what he was doing when he conspired with seven other White Sox players to throw the 1919 World Series. And there are those who point to his .375 batting average and twelve hits in the Series to *prove* that, while he may have accepted the gamblers' money, he never really sold out on the field of play.

But he sold out all right, as his confession before the Cook County grand jury in the fall of 1920 revealed (lost for seven decades, it turned up just a few years ago in the offices of the attorney for Chicago White Sox owner Charles Comiskey). Whether it was lack of sophistication, or guile, or greed that led him to do it, Joe Jackson's involvement in the 1919 Black Sox truncated and tarnished what might have been one of the greatest hitting careers of all, on a par with Ruth, Cobb, Williams, and Hornsby.

——★——

Louisville Slugger, the company named in reference to the major leaguer to whom it first supplied bats, Pete Browning of the Louisville Grays, knew the value of an endorsement. In the 1910s Hillerich and Bradsby issued a line of decal bats honoring the greatest players in the game—Cobb and Wagner were the tops in each league, by general acclaim, but not far behind was the "Grey Eagle," Tris Speaker. No outfielder ever got a quicker jump on the ball than Speaker, which is why he could play so shallow. His 448 outfield assists are nearly a hundred more than

the next best. He took part in 135 double plays, also the highest total for an outfielder, and turned four of them by himself. And he could hit enough to warrant an autograph model bat: .345 lifetime, an all-time high 792 doubles, and the only batting title not won by Ty Cobb in the thirteen-year span 1907–1919.

What accounts for the labelmania—the beer, wine, and whiskey labels in addition to the Speaker pictorial label—is lost to the ages.

——★——

The "Peerless Leader"? Wasn't Frank Chance simply the guy on the receiving end of all those twin-killing tosses from Joe Tinker or Johnny Evers? Not exactly. He was a revered figure in baseball in his day, and his Hall of Fame stature is conveyed more by an artifact like this than a mere statistical evaluation or a passing mention in Franklin P. Adams's now threadbare ditty. Once familiar to all fans, the poem now requires quotation:

These are the saddest of possible words:
  "Tinker to Evers to Chance."
Trio of Bear Cubs and fleeter than birds,

"Tinker to Evers to Chance."
Ruthlessly pricking our gonfalon bubble,
Making a Giant hit into a double,
Words that are weighty with nothing but trouble:
  "Tinker to Evers to Chance."

As further gloss, let it be said that "a double" here means a double play, and that "our gonfalon bubble" is the Giants fans' fantasy that, in 1908, when this was printed in the New York *Globe*, a pennant would be theirs.

Frank Chance was attending college in California, planning to become a dentist, when Chicago

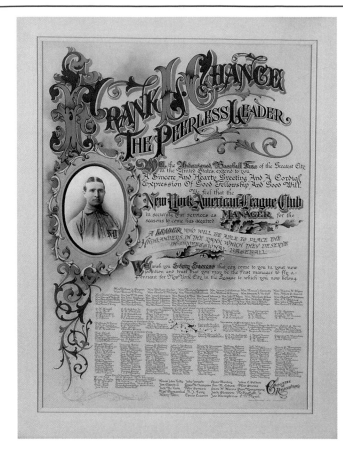

White Stockings star Bill Lange spotted him playing in a summer league and recommended that the team sign him. Originally a catcher and fill-in outfielder, he became a star when he took over at first base in 1903. Two years later he became the Cubs' manager, and under his leadership they captured National League flags in 1906, 1907, 1908, and 1910. As a player Chance was rugged, but leaning too close to the plate cost him frequent beanings, which led to hearing impairment and terrible headaches.

After a disagreement with the team's owner, he was let go after the 1912 season. The New York Highlanders snatched him up. This remarkable lithograph, which officially welcomes Chance to "the greatest city in the United States," has a list of names redolent with the history of the city and the nation. There are politicians from Teddy Roosevelt and William Gaynor to Dick Croker; Tammany Hall operatives and baseball magnates like James Gaffney, Charles Murphy, and Bill Devery. The list of entertainment giants reads like a clipping from *Variety*: George M. Cohan, Flo Ziegfeld, Al Jolson, Honey Boy Evans, David Belasco, DeWolf Hopper, and Harry Frazee (the man who sold Babe Ruth).

John McGraw added his name, as did John Montgomery Ward and former world heavyweight champion Gentleman Jim Corbett—and there, among those names, some still famous and others only dimly remembered, is a name that fairly leaps to the inquiring eye: Arnold Rothstein.

How could this professional gambler, the evil genius who masterminded the fixing of the 1919 World Series, be so openly linked to men at the apex of celebrity? Because that's the way the country was back then—politics, sports, theater, and gambling were inextricably intertwined. That was how the Peerless Leader came to be honored by the Peerless Swindler, and such was the soil from which the Black Sox Scandal sprouted.

———★———

Baseball has been blessed with a pantheon of colorful characters, from Casey and the Babe to the Bird and the Spaceman, but Rube Waddell is in a class by himself. The quintessential bad boy, Rube was a hero in counterpoint to the other league's Christy Mathewson, the equally gifted pitcher who played by the rules.

The wacky stories about him are hard to believe, but indications are that most of them are true. (Indeed, this could be the glove that Waddell tossed aside when he called the fielders in and proceeded to fan the side!) You didn't have to make anything up to add to Waddell's luster. For example, he began the year of 1903 sleeping in a firehouse in Camden, New Jersey, and ended it tending bar in Wheeling, West Virginia. "In between," as historian Lee Allen wrote, "he won twenty-two games for the Philadelphia Athletics, played left end for the Business Man's Rugby Football Club of Grand Rapids,

Michigan, toured the nation in a melodrama called 'The Stain of Guilt,' courted, married, and separated from Mae Wynn Skinner of Lynn, Massachusetts, saved a woman from drowning, accidentally shot a friend through the hand, and was bitten by a lion."

This relic, scarcely larger than a brakeman's glove, still glows with the luster of disuse. Maybe that's because it was rarely called into action, for its owner, the fabulous "sousepaw," led the American League in strikeouts six years in a row, from 1902 through 1907. His 349 strikeouts in 1904 stood as the major-league record for sixty-one years, until Sandy Koufax topped it, and it remains the highwater mark for an American League left-hander.

—★—

Wasn't the Federal League an invention of Robert Coover for that novel about dice baseball? No, the Feds were no fantasy, and they in fact became a nightmare for the National and American leagues, only recently at peace between themselves. The last real challenge to the two-league structure, the Federal League gasped its last after three short years in 1915. Its first year it played as an independent minor league and didn't seduce any big-league players to join, though such former stars as Cy Young and Deacon Phillippe took a turn at managing. The league struggled to stay afloat, as all clubs lost money.

But in mid-1913 a man named James Gilmore, a hard-driving Chicago businessman, took over the reins and guided the league to complete its inaugural season. For 1914, moreover, he declared the Federal to be a major league, and he declared war on his rivals. Baseball was thriving at the time, and Gilmore and his wealthy pals saw a chance to make some dough. Before long, name players such as Joe Tinker and Mordecai Brown had jumped. Walter Johnson did, too, then changed his mind. But the pockets of the Federal League

team owners weren't deep enough, and the established leagues kept winning court cases that kept many players with them.

The Feds did have a substantial impact on salaries overall. According to baseball scholar Harold Seymour, twenty important players received an average salary of $3,817 in 1913. By 1915 those same twenty were earning an average of $7,327—a whopping 92 percent increase. Even more important historically was the antitrust suit filed by Gilmore. First, an obliging judge in Chicago named Landis pleased the owners by refusing to rule. The leagues were then able to negotiate a settlement without fear of later legal reprisal. When the agreement left the Baltimore owners, who had refused to settle, high and dry they sued organized baseball. The case was ultimately decided in the U.S. Supreme Court in 1922, and it established that baseball is not engaged in interstate commerce and is therefore not subject to antitrust legislation. The owners of baseball have wielded that particular sword very effectively for a long time.

This is the principal legacy of the short-lived Federal League, of which barely these trinkets survive. But the Feds left behind one rather more substantial bauble, executed in concrete and steel rather than celluloid or electroplate. Its name was Weeghman Park, named for the owner of the long-since-harpooned Chicago Whales. We revere it today as Wrigley Field.

—★—

When the Pittsburgh Pirates and a few other clubs of the 1970s introduced an imitation of this old-style cap, the result was detested throughout baseball. But the original looks mighty stylish—even new—doesn't it? Under wraps for half a century, the cap and jersey of Charles Albert "Chief" Bender glisten in a way that words fail to capture. The creamy texture of the flannel, the crispness of the detailing, the precisely blocked cap—this combination could not have looked any better when Chief Bender last wore it, sometime around 1911. On display in the Baseball Hall of Fame time line, this item never fails to elicit admiration.

institute of higher learning which Jim Thorpe later attended). He didn't seem to mind the racism of the war whoops or the "Chief" handle. He signed autographs "Charles," and his manager, Connie Mack, called him by his middle name, Albert. Bender was used as a starter and in relief by Mack; wherever he was used, he excelled. Three times he led the league in winning percentage.

Bender was a highly stylish pitcher and a formidable competitor. Ty Cobb, who made studying pitchers an art form, called him the "brainiest pitcher I ever faced." Late in his life, Mack said, "If I had all the men I've ever handled and they were all in their prime and there was one game I wanted to win above all others—Albert would be my man."

The easygoing Bender was one-quarter Chippewa and educated at Native American schools (including Carlisle, a Pennsylvania

—★—

This classic shirt, seen in so many vintage photos, was worn by the Chicago Cubs from 1908 to 1912, the teams of "Three-Finger" Brown, Joe Tinker, Johnny Evers, and Frank Chance. But the man who wore this shirt is not a Hall of Fame player. He's not even close. But the fact that Tom Needham held a job at all tells what the game was like in the dead-ball era, when runs were hard to come by. In 1909, for example, the year Needham joined the team, the Cubs' ERA was a microscopic 1.75. Needham was nicknamed "Deerfoot," a funny name for a catcher. We're not sure if it was in jest or not because he stole only twenty bases in his eleven years as a backup catcher for three teams.

Anyway, you can't steal first base, and that was Needham's dilemma. From 1904 through 1914, he topped the .200 mark in batting average only four times. But defense was paramount for a catcher then (today, too), and if you could handle a pitching staff and throw a little, you had yourself a job you could

hang on to, even if you had a Johnny Kling and a Jimmy Archer ahead of you for playing time.

Needham was positively Ruthian compared to another catcher of the time, Bill Bergen, who broke the .200 mark only once in his eleven-year career in the bigs. His lifetime average of .170 is a full forty points below the next-lowest player in baseball history to have batted at least 2,500 times.

—★—

Here are battered bats from two great dead-ball-era hitters whose careers echoed each other in curious ways. The skinnier one belonged to Nap Lajoie (pronounced *la-JOEY* by some contemporaries, *LA-zho-ay* by others; neither is the way Nap's parents pronounced their name, which was *la-ZHWA*). In the first half of the first decade of the

century, before Ty Cobb entered the argument, Lajoie and Honus Wagner were considered the two best all-around players. Nap won the batting title, slugging title, and doubles title four times each and three times led his league in hits and RBIs. But he had his own hardheaded ideas about the game and frequently had difficulty with his managers. After

five years of slugging exploits with the Philadelphia Phillies (one year he hit .378), he jumped across town to the A's of the upstart American League in 1901. As much as any man, Lajoie made the American League a major league by winning its Triple Crown, batting .426 and leading in home runs and RBIs. He led the new league in hitting the next three years as well and was still posting prodigious averages a decade later, with the Cleveland Naps (now Indians), to whom he lent his name.

The other bat belonged to Edd Roush (pronounced *ROOSH*), who also jumped for the money in 1914 when he joined the Federal League. Roush, too, was not a managerial favorite. He kept himself in shape, so he always held out, not signing until spring training was nearly over. He thought the grapefruit league was a waste of time. In 1930 he was so perturbed with the Giants and John McGraw that he sat out the entire year, returning to play only when he was traded to Cincinnati the following season.

In the ten years between 1917 and 1926, Roush never batted less than .321. That forty-eight-ounce bludgeon of his was the heaviest any man ever used on a regular basis, though legend has it that Babe Ruth sometimes swung a fifty-two-ounce bat. In this age of batting gloves and pine tar, fans may look at this bat and say, "What's the tape for?" But those of us who are of a certain vintage recall the boyhood rite of taping the bat just so, to get a major league grip.

———★———

Before the "Amazing Mets" or the "Impossible Dream" Red Sox, there were the "Miracle Braves." The boys from Boston turned the baseball world upside down in 1914 by turning the standings upside down after July 4: in other words, they went from last place on that day to first place at the end of the season, and thence to an astounding four-game sweep of Connie Mack's A's.

In 1913, under new manager George Stallings, the Braves had ended the season in fifth place, their best finish in eleven years. But by mid-1914 they were in last place, fifteen games back. They even lost an exhibition game against employees of a soap company. But with an unlikely double play combination of young, fun-loving Rabbit Maranville and old, irascible Johnny Evers and a red-hot pitching staff anchored by new acquisitions Bill James and Dick Rudolph, they won fifty-two of their last sixty-six games. In fact, they swept past the defending National League champion New York Giants so fast that they clinched in early September (this ball was from that contest, at the Polo Grounds) and went on to win the flag by ten and a half games.

Then they did something really amazing; they toppled the world champion Athletics (the team with the $100,000 infield and pitchers like Chief Bender, Eddie Plank, and Joe Bush) in four straight games in the World Series. Connie Mack complained that his players were being wooed with big bucks to join the Federal League and as such didn't have their minds on the game. He reacted by getting rid of three quarters of his infield and Bender and Plank. The A's finished last in 1915. The Braves finished second in 1915, but their miracle was over; they wouldn't finish that high again for thirty-three years.

Ho-hum. Another win, just like the 499 before it and the eleven more to come. There—now you know who pitched this ball for his five hundredth victory, defeating Washington 5–2 on a four-hitter in eleven innings on July 11, 1910. Denton True "Cy" Young, fat and forty-three but still pitching effectively, was in his final full year in the American League with Cleveland, the city with which he had broken into baseball in the National League twenty years before. In mid-1911 he would return to the league with which he had started, the National, and to Boston, the city which had made him famous in 1901–1908 and whose Red Sox he had in turn made the main baseball attraction in town.

Cy thought he could go on forever because it was his control, not his speed, that was key to his success. He had seen a phenom arise in mid-decade, Irv Young of the Boston Braves, heard him called "Young Cy"—which immediately made Denton True into "Old Cy"—and kept on pitching after Young Cy was belted out of the league.

Old Cy went to spring training with the Braves in 1912, fully expecting to pitch another year, but quit before heading north because he realized that he could no longer move off the mound or bend down for bunts, and he didn't want to go out by embarrassing himself. Who will equal his record in the future? No one. In all discussion about the career record that will stand for all time, 511 victories tops the list. Win twenty-five games a year for twenty years and you're still looking up at Denton True Young.

——★——

In recent years, since the advent of free agency and the fabulous sums paid to aging stars, it has become commonplace for star players to hang on into their forties; advances in training and conditioning techniques have even enabled some of them to defy the ravages of time and enjoy some of their greatest seasons in their relative dotages. But a hundred years earlier, the playing career of a professional baseball player very seldom extended to twenty years and a graybeard like Jim O'Rourke or Cap Anson was considered a marvel not only for physical endurance but also for sustained enthusiasm. Remember, until the years following the Civil War serious people thought baseball was not a fit pastime for grown men, let alone a profession.

Denton True Young's twenty-two seasons of pitching in the big leagues seem a puny mark compared with those of such modern masters as Jim Kaat, Tommy John, Don Sutton, Steve Carlton, Phil Niekro, and Nolan Ryan. But Old Cy's longevity is legendary because his tenure spanned the two centuries of baseball and because he posted marks that are, uniquely in baseball's lifetime records, eternally beyond challenge. Before the year 1900 dawned, which was to be his career dividing line, Cy had already won 241 major league games. He pitched in the days when the distance from the mound to home was just fifty feet. He pitched the last ball of the last game of the last World Series of the nineteenth century, in 1892, for the Cleveland Spiders against the Beaneaters of Boston, both of them National League teams because the rival American Association had folded. And he

"CY" YOUNG STILL THE COCK OF THE WALK.

NIGHT MESSAGE.
THE WESTERN UNION TELEGRAPH COMPANY.
INCORPORATED
21,000 OFFICES IN AMERICA.   CABLE SERVICE TO ALL THE WORLD.

THOS. T. ECKERT, President and General Manager.

RECEIVED at

Cy Young

Mercer University Athletic
rejoices in your great success
for your practise here next season

MERCER BALL TEAM
TO BE THE BEST

MODEST CY. YOUNG

Not Only as a Ball Player but as a
Man He Becomes a Subject of
Editorial Approval.

THE GREAT MAN RISES TO THE OCCASION.

THE WESTERN UNION TELEGRAPH COMPANY.
INCORPORATED
23,000 OFFICES IN AMERICA.   CABLE SERVICE TO ALL THE WORLD.
ROBERT C. CLOWRY, President and General Manager.

RECEIVED at

Oct 14 1903
Dated St Louis Mo 14
To Young & Cruger Co
& Base Ball.

We salute the Champions

THE WESTERN UNION TELEGRAPH COMPANY.
INCORPORATED
23,000 OFFICES IN AMERICA.   CABLE SERVICE TO ALL THE WORLD.
ROBERT C. CLOWRY, President and General Manager.

RECEIVED at 249 5th Ave., near Wood St., Pittsburgh, Pa

New Comerstown O
Denton Young
c/o Monongahela House
Pittsburg Pa

Accept hearty congratulations
let us know day you come
home will have band out.
S. L. Douglass & R. H. Smith

D.T.Y.
R.E. HEIDRICK

pitched the first ball of the first game of the first "modern" World Series in 1903, this time as the star performer of the new American League (yup, that's the ball, square in the middle of the composition).

Cy Young won more than thirty games five times; twenty-five or more a dozen times, twenty or more fifteen times. Only Walter Johnson, with 417, is within a hundred lifetime wins of Young's record of 511. Tops among pitchers who began their careers after World War II, Steve Carlton at

329 wins is almost as far behind Johnson as Johnson is behind Young. It's no wonder that Cy Young is honored every year when each league names its best pitcher. He possessed fabulous control (in 1904 he walked twenty-nine men in 380 innings!) and a fastball so hot it earned him his nickname ("He throws like a cyclone"); it is said that he and Amos Rusie were personally responsible for moving the pitching distance back to its current 60'6" in 1893. Young's long-lived success was attributable to his enormous physical stamina and the fact that he never had a sore arm in his life. Young grew up a farm boy, and he stayed strong in the off season chopping wood and doing other heavy-duty farm work.

That 511 number joins a handful of others (4,191; 714; 2,130—all surpassed now) as the first ones kids of my generation memorized when they began to fall in love with the glorious world of baseball stats. Baseball may have seen better pitchers than Cy Young. (Lefty Grove? Walter Johnson? Bob Feller? Sandy Koufax? Greg Maddux? You pick.) But no pitcher will ever win that many again. Cy's legend is largely a function of time. In the nineteenth century pitchers were expected to start

forty or more games a year and finish most of them. They were taught how to conserve their strength, let the batters hit the dirty and battered ball at the fielders, and save the extra for "the pinch." That Cy Young relied on a fastball and changes of speed, with only an occasional breaking ball, serves to explain not only his win total but his loss total, for he holds the all-time record, there, too, with 313.

The scrapbook shows the congratulatory telegrams Young received after winning two games over the Pirates in the 1903 World Series. The license plate, dated one year before his death at age eighty-eight, shows that he was Ohio's favorite son. The heroic portrait by A. H. Thayer from 1907 shows that Cy was larger than life for Boston fans. But as you can see from the uniform in the foreground, Cy Young's memory was not yet a sacred thing while he was with Cleveland. When he tired of this jersey, it was not put away for posterity but handed down to a rookie call-up. Below the "D.T.Y." (Denton True Young) initials sewn into the collar you can see that R. Emmett Heidrick was next in line.

This is the glove that made the basket catch famous; forget what you hear about Willie Mays inventing it. It belonged to Walter "Rabbit" Maranville. Some modern fans who fancy themselves experts attempt to leap upon the shoulders of a Hall of Fame member and elevate themselves by declaring this man or that one to be unworthy of inclusion. One who has suffered such indignity more often than most is the Rabbit, whose shoulders may have been particularly inviting because he stood only five-feet-five inches and his record seemed paltry: a .258 average and only twenty-eight home runs over a twenty-three-year career.

But get your arms around this litany of achievement. Maranville's all-around fielding in 1914 is the greatest single season performance by any shortstop in the history of the game, according to *Total Baseball*. And Maranville played his original position well past the age when shortstops are usually eased over to another spot, and that tells you something about how he could play. In fact, he led the National League in fielding percentage as a thirty-eight-year-old shortstop in 1930 and when finally, at age forty, he was moved over to second base, he played 149 games there and led the league again. Maranville set major-league career records at shortstop in putouts and assists. Longevity is part of the reason, but you don't get to play shortstop for *that* long a time unless you're the best.

Maranville tried the patience of many a manager over the years, but in 1925 he got his chance to see how the other half lived when he was appointed to lead the Cubs. He proved no disciplinarian and lasted only fifty-three games. After the Dodgers released him in 1926 the Cards picked him up but sent him to the minors. Upon his return to the majors the next year he spoke these immortal words: "The national consumption of alcoholic beverages took a sharp downturn after May 24, 1927. That's the day I quit drinking."

TO 1941

When was the last time you saw a commemorative baseball with pictures of baseball potentates on it? This special sphere was created to honor the fiftieth anniversary of the founding of the National League, the league that put the owners, not the players, in charge. Here are the august visages of: Morgan Bulkeley, head of the short-lived Hartford club and the National League's first president; William Hulbert, the power behind Bulkeley's throne and, more than anyone, the man who invented major-league baseball (he has only recently been named to the Hall of Fame); A. G. Mills, who became National League president after Hulbert's sudden death in 1882 and oversaw the important Tripartite Agreement (National League, American Association, and Northwestern League) of 1883—he also implemented the universal application of

the reserve clause in that same year, binding players to their teams in perpetuity (he is better known to some as the eponymous head of the Mills Commission, which investigated the origins of baseball, the three-year labor that produced a new and heretofore unsuspected Father of Baseball, General Abner Doubleday); Nicholas Young, veteran baseball man and original treasurer of the National League, who ascended to the presidency after Mills resigned in protest of the amnesty that had been granted to blacklisted players; Harry Pulliam, a decent man whose frail constitution cost him and who committed suicide in 1909 because of the pressures of the league presidency (and the merciless hounding by New York baseball figures in the wake of the Merkle incident of 1908 that deprived the Giants of a pennant); and, on the side of the ball not visible in this photograph, succeeding presidents John Heydler, an early statistical analyst of the game; Tom Lynch, a onetime umpire; and John Tener, a former pitcher with the Chicago White Stockings as well as Pittsburgh of the Players League and Baltimore of the American Association (how's that for amnesty!).

The souvenir balls were handed out at a huge banquet celebrating the anniversary. Also handed out were golden jubilee pins like the one shown here, given to charter league player George Wright of the 1876 Boston Red Stockings, successors to the fabled Cincinnati franchise where George had first enjoyed national fame. The banquet had a poignant side, too, as elderly veterans of '76 such as Tommy Bond, Chick Fulmer, and Tommy York enjoyed their last hurrah and other pioneers down on

their health or their luck, such as John Day and Jim Mutrie, were invited.

The game always offers up celebratory occasions: the fiftieth anniversary of the Hall of Fame in 1989, the one-hundred-twenty-fifth anniversary of professional baseball in 1994; the one-hundred-fiftieth anniversary of the Knickerbockers' founding in 1995; the fiftieth anniversary of Jackie Robinson's breaking the color line in 1997, and so on. As author Larry Ritter has said, the best part of baseball today is its yesterdays.

————★————

You know how thousands of left-handed pitchers fill the baseball record books but only a few are named "Lefty"— and of these only four, Lefty Williams, Lefty Gomez, Lefty Grove, and Steve Carlton—achieved prominence? Well, even though many thousands of home runs are hit each season, the man who wore this gaily pinstriped cap is the only one modern fans think of as "Home Run." Third baseman Frank Baker led the American League in homers four times, but he never hit as many as a Baker's dozen in any season of his career, which ran from 1908 through 1922. His nickname derived from two clutch shots he banged in the 1911 World Series to lead his Philadelphia A's to victory over the favored Giants.

It's interesting that while he came to stardom as part of Connie Mack's "$100,000 Infield," he finished his career with the Yankees, a team that boasted another individual with a fairly plausible claim to the name. But George Herman Ruth was content to be called "Babe," and John Franklin Baker stayed with "Home Run."

————★————

The unassisted triple play—it's the rarest single event in baseball, accomplished only nine times this century. What makes Johnny Neun's feat doubly remarkable is that:

1. The trick had been turned just the day before, by Jimmy Cooney of the Cubs against the Pirates, and

2. Neun was Detroit's first baseman (nearly every other unassisted triple killing was performed by a middle infielder).

The story goes that Neun, who had read about Cooney's feat in that morning's newspaper, was waiting for his turn when Cleveland's Homer Summa lined into his glove with men on first and second and no outs on May 31, 1927. It was no problem to tag out the runner trying to retreat to first for out number 2. Then, with Glenn Myatt lumbering back toward second base and the shortstop screaming for the ball, Neun raced for second to touch the bag himself. He is said to have been hollering, "I'm running into the Hall of Fame!" Given his prior premonition that an unassisted triple play was coming his way, this scenario makes Neun the greatest seer since Nostradamus, for the Baseball Hall of Fame was announced nine years later, with the doors opening three years after that.

———— ★ ————

Of course it would be unbecoming for a player today to accept an award from a whiskey company, but the feat that this Seagram crown honors was worth remembering. When Carl Hubbell won his eighth straight start to begin the 1937 season, he had completed twenty-four consecutive wins over two seasons. It's no wonder that Giants fans referred to him as "The Meal Ticket." Hubbell's out pitch was the devastating screwball, thrown like a curve but with an opposite twist of the wrist. King Carl threw it so often that his arm wound up permanently bent backward.

Hubbell's screwball was never better than in the All-Star Game of 1934, when he used it to perfection, striking out—in succession—future Hall of Famers Babe Ruth, Lou Gehrig, Jimmie Foxx, Al Simmons, and Joe Cronin. "I figured those guys had

hit better fastballs than mine and better curves," he said. "If they were going to hit me, it would have to be my best."

Hubbell was actually signed by the Tigers, but manager Ty Cobb didn't like that screwball thing and refused to let Hubbell throw it. Three years later the released Hubbell was picked up out of Texas League ball by the Giants. Christy Mathewson's famous screwball (known then as a "fadeaway") was more of a change-up, and he threw it seldom, spotting it only in crucial situations because of the wear and tear on his arm. Since then the true followers of the Hubbell-style (fast and deadly) screwball are Warren Spahn, Tug Mc-Graw, and Fernando Valenzuela.

———— ★ ————

Before warm-up jackets became the vogue in the 1930s, there were warm-up coats, like dusters, down to the knees, and warm-up sweaters—rolled-collar turtlenecks in the 1890s and the 1900s, then heavyweight cardigans in the teens and twenties, like this one.

Strangely, such talk about the twists and turns of baseball fashion has unusual relevance to the man whose sweater it was, Bill Terry of the New York

Giants. Terry hit .401 in 1930; no National Leaguer has attained that lofty figure since, and only Ted Williams in the other league has surpassed it, and that was nearly sixty years ago. But to modern fans who never saw Terry play and who pore over the record books and analyze the statistics, the question still remains: Just how good was this guy? Does he deserve to be in the Hall of Fame? Everyone knows that 1930 was the most offensively potent year in major-league history, so maybe Terry's record means less. Of course there were thirty other future Hall of Famers playing that year, and none of them hit .400.

Terry's personality didn't win him many friends. Early in life he had struggled financially and quit baseball as a career. He was working for Standard Oil and playing first base for the company when John McGraw offered him a job. Terry's first question was "How much?" He knew from the start he was playing the game for the dough. No windy paeans to the glory of the national pastime for Bill Terry. The writers of the time were distressed that he wouldn't give them his home phone number. Terry was McGraw's choice to replace him as manager in 1932, and he kept playing first base until 1936 while winning three pennants and one World Series in ten years.

He shot off his mouth once, and it cost him. During a preseason interview evaluating the talent of the various National League teams, a reporter asked him about the Dodgers.

"Brooklyn?" Terry said. "Are they still in the league?"

With two games left in the season and the Giants in a tight race, the Dodgers knocked them off twice, and they had to settle for second.

When Terry retired he answered a question about the future of the game with characteristic bluntness. "I'm not worried about baseball. No business in the world ever made more money with poorer management. It can survive anything."

And so can Bill Terry's plaque.

———★———

In the 1931 World Series Pepper Martin ran out from under this cap and scared the dickens out of the powerful Athletics of Philadelphia. In the first five games of that Series Martin was twelve for eighteen, with four stolen bases, five RBIs, five runs scored, and four doubles. The A's pitched around him after that, although he still managed to swipe another base that led to a run in the Cards' Game 7 victory.

When a reporter asked him where he got his speed, Pepper replied, "Well, where I come from in Oklahoma, once a boy starts running, there ain't much to stop him." Martin was a throwback to the "rubes" of baseball history, a fun-loving natural talent who was always in the middle of the silly antics and practical pranks. And with the Cardinals of the 1930s he found kindred spirits galore, especially the Dean brothers. The rough, rugged, and often ragged Cardinals endeared themselves not only to St. Louis, the Ozarks, and the Dust Bowl, but to all of downtrodden America, which was struggling to get along in the Great Depression. These gritty Gashouse Gangsters were working-class heroes.

———★———

It looks as if Rogers Hornsby is wearing a halo on this medal that he was awarded for winning the MVP title in 1925. Believe me, no halo ever graced the Rajah's pate. Someone once said Hornsby thought diplomacy was a respiratory disease. In the 1920s, when he only once batted less than .361, he was traded three times. But he was without a doubt the greatest right-handed hitter the game has ever seen. Like Joe Jackson before him, Hornsby feared for his eyesight and refused to read newspapers or go to the movies lest it damage his eyes.

Maybe there was something to his superstitions:

only Ted Williams also won two Triple Crowns; nobody but Babe Ruth ever had more total bases in a season than Hornsby's 450 in 1922; he led the league in slugging ten times; his .424 batting average in 1924 is the highest since 1901. From 1920 through 1925 he was at his peak, averaging .397 for that span, winning the batting, slugging, and (mythical, since it wasn't calculated) on-base titles every season, twice leading the league in homers, four times in RBIs and doubles and once in triples. Whew. Hornsby's only vice (outside of terrifying pitchers) was playing the ponies. Allegedly, he won more than $300,000 doing it, which indicates he approached it with the same passion he took to the batter's box.

———★———

Has baseball ever seen a man who was a bigger tangle of contradictions than John McGraw? He tried to sign African-American second baseman Charlie Grant to a Giants contract, artfully changing Grant's background to Native American and dubbing him "Charlie Tokahoma." He hired Rube Foster and "Smokey Joe" Williams, also African-Americans, to work with his Giants' pitching staff. He pined openly for the dark-skinned Cuban star José Mendez. Yet at the same time McGraw carried around with him as a talisman a piece of rope that had been used by a Southern lynch mob.

He was a hardheaded advocate of scientific baseball—the hit-and-run, the bunt, the sacrifice. He once fined one of his players, Sammy Strang, for hitting a game-winning home run—because he had missed a bunt sign. Yet he let a strange good-luck charm of a man named Charles Victor "Victory" Faust warm up in his unique double-windmill style before every game for three years, and sit on the bench throughout the game, and even let him pitch in a couple of games, all to placate the fates for his team.

As a manager he was known for being a fierce umpire baiter and a strategic battler for every inch. Casey Stengel said he was glad the batting helmet hadn't been invented in his time or McGraw would have demanded he go up there and take a pitch in the head. He was in total control of his players (they didn't call him "Little Napoleon" just because of his height), and he didn't mind being verbally nasty or physically abusive if that was what it took to win. He was surely thrown out of more ball games and engaged in more on-field fisticuffs and suspended more times than any manager before or since. At the same time McGraw had plenty of friends in baseball, show business, and politics and a long, loving marriage. Perhaps because he and Blanche had no children of their own, and because he had experienced such a wretched childhood himself (he was beaten to the point that he ran away from home at age twelve), McGraw always had a player he treated like a son; it was as if

he needed an outlet for decency because he was so chronically a hard guy. Christy Mathewson was the first one; Ross Youngs, Fred Lindstrom, Bill Terry, and Mel Ott followed, each to become a Hall of Fame member, like their mentor.

As a player McGraw is remembered as the most vicious of the Baltimore Orioles, a great team that bent the rules and broke the spirits (and, often enough, bones) of their opponents. What isn't remembered is how great he was. His lifetime batting average was an impressive .334. His 1899 on-base percentage of .547 is the second-highest ever, and in the whole history of baseball only two men—Ted Williams and Babe Ruth—ever reached base more often. But it is as the consummate on-field manager of the New York Giants—with the longest continuous employment of any man be-sides Connie Mack, who owned his club—that we honor him. He took the tricky, strategic style of Hall of Fame manager Ned Hanlon and the Orioles and shaped it to the new century, handing it on to Casey Stengel, Billy Martin, and Earl Weaver.

———★———

If Rogers Hornsby has no rival as a right-handed batter in all of baseball history, Lefty Grove may have none among left-handed pitchers. (Spahn? Koufax? Ford? Great, sure. But I'll take Grove.)

In Grove's day, minor-league teams weren't wholly owned farm clubs of big-league organizations. The minors were independent, and they made what money they could by selling their best players to the majors. That fact may have cost Lefty Grove a chance to post win totals like Walter Johnson, Christy Mathewson, and Grover Cleveland Alexander (Cy Young is off the charts). Grove spent five years pitching for Baltimore (under Jack Dunn, who had helped along another young pitcher named Ruth) in the International League. Dunn's teams were winning, he was making money, and the idea of selling his superstar lefty to anyone for less than $100,000 was something he would not abide. Connie Mack had to come up with $100,600 to get Grove in 1925, but he was ready for major league hitters at least three or four years earlier.

The intensity that Ty Cobb and Pete Rose brought to the game was matched by Grove; a fierce competitor, he hated losing with a passion. As the ace of Connie Mack's superb Athletics squads of the late 1920s, Grove was nothing less than sensa-

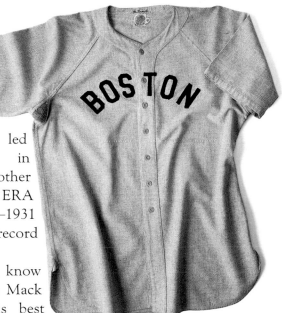

tional. He won twenty games or more seven times, led the league in strikeouts another seven, and in ERA five. In 1929–1931 his won-lost record was 79–15.

But we all know what Connie Mack did with his best players; he sold them off. Grove went to the Red Sox in December of 1933. There, his fastball wasn't what it had been, but his attitude hadn't lost an inch. He won four more ERA titles with the Sox and, despite the Green Monster in left field, went 18–0 at Fenway over a three-year period, disproving the notion that lefties can't pitch in Boston. He hung on, as Early Wynn would a generation later, to compile exactly three hundred wins. They had to rip the shirt off him to get him to quit.

"JIMMIE" FOXX

A friend has a surefire way to gain points in trivia contests. When the question involves old-time hitters, always guess Jimmie Foxx. It's true; Foxx is the forgotten man among baseball's all-time super sluggers. "Double X" was poison to pitchers, the first man to challenge Ruth as the home run king. The Bambino led the American League in home runs in every full season he played from 1918 to 1931, hitting sixty along the way in 1927. Foxx, too, hit sixty home runs—in 1932, when he wrenched the title from Ruth, but two were washed off the books by rain-outs. Still, his fifty-eight stand on the books as the most any right-handed hitter has ever struck (tied with Hank Greenberg and Mark McGwire). And he was noted for banging balls off the high wire fence in St. Louis, which might have been homers anywhere else.

When Foxx retired he was second to Ruth in all-time homers, and he stayed there until 1966. And Jimmie was more than a long-ball threat. He won the Triple Crown in 1933 after missing it by just three percentage points the season before, and he averaged .325 over his twenty years in big-league ball. His glory years came with the A's, especially in the pennant years of 1929–1931. But as a player Foxx reached his peak over the next four years, and he enjoyed some of his finest seasons with the Boston Red Sox, to whom he was sold/traded by a financially desperate Connie Mack after the 1935 season. In 1938 Foxx smacked fifty home runs, drove in 175 runs, batted .349, and slugged .704. No wonder that on June 16 of that year he was walked each of the six times he came to bat, a mark of respect without equal in modern baseball history.

Foxx's career parallels that of another Hall of Fame slugger, Mel Ott. Both attracted major-league scouts as sixteen-year-old catchers, though only Foxx played the position in professional ball. Both were personal favorites of their managers: Foxx was Mack's fair-haired boy when he came to the A's at age seventeen; Ott was especially close to John McGraw, who also kept him close beside him on the bench at that age.

Foxx was a true muscleman—"The Beast," they called him. The apocryphal tale of how he was signed says that he was plowing a field when a scout asked him directions to the ballpark and the youngster pointed—with his plow. Foxx once hit a homer off Lefty Gomez in Yankee Stadium so hard that it broke a seat in the upper deck. Gomez told the story later of Foxx coming to bat with the bases loaded. Lefty shrugged off every sign the catcher gave, then shook them all off again. The catcher came to the mound and said, "Well, what do you want to do?" Gomez responded, "Let's just wait around a while, maybe he'll get a long-distance phone call."

Except for intimidated pitchers (one marveled, "Even his hair has muscles"), everyone liked Foxx. He was quiet and friendly, but loved a good time. Foxx managed in the minors for several seasons and even for the Fort Wayne Daisies of the All-American Girls Professional Baseball League.

Lou Gehrig . . . disease . . . death . . . sadness. Yes, those are the connections we make automatically now, more than half a century since he withered away from amyotrophic lateral sclerosis. We look at this trophy, which his Yankee pals presented to him, this trophy that only two months after his last game was too heavy for him to hold during the farewell ceremonies of July 4, 1939. We think of the sympathetic portrayal by Gary Cooper in *The Pride of the Yankees* and how Lou loved his wife, Eleanor. It's hard to get past the Hollywood version and the sadness, beyond the black-bordered memorial, to reflect upon the powerful young man who filled out this white warm-up sweater when he played for Columbia University. Let's remember that fans loved Lou Gehrig not only because he was modest and kind, attributes that even today may be found in abundance; they loved him because he was extraordinary, a baseball player so relentlessly dependable that scribes likened him to a locomotive, "The Iron Horse."

Today few fans will offer his name when prodded for the greatest players of all time, no matter that his place in the Hall of Fame was secure even before there was a Hall of Fame. Gehrig was not flashy, not even graceful, but by many measures he was the second-best hitter the game had seen. That the only man whose exploits exceeded his also happened to play for the Yankees was not a tragedy; it suited Lou's character perfectly. When his friend, baseball writer Fred Lieb, asked him what it felt like to play in the shadow of Babe Ruth, Lou cheerfully replied, "It's a big shadow; there's plenty of room for me."

So permit me to do for Lou what he would never have done for himself: step forward to recite a few of his routinely astonishing feats. Not only did he play every game for fourteen years, amassing the total of 2,130 that will be identified with him always, even now that Cal Ripken has surpassed his mark; he broke the previous record for consistency by 823 games, or roughly five seasons. In the period 1926–1938 he *averaged* 147 RBIs, a figure many power-hitting Hall of Famers never equaled once. In 1931 Gehrig drove in 184 runs, still the American League record. But consider that in the previous season he drove in 117 runs in his road games alone (he was not a pure pull hitter and benefited little from the short right-field porch at Yankee Stadium). No one has come close to his record of twenty-three grand slams.

Gehrig was the man who never made any noise; he was in truth what he seemed to be: quiet, sturdy, strong, perfectly sure of his talents yet without an ounce of boast in him. Even when he did something great, he took a backseat. For example, the day he became the first American Leaguer to hit four home runs in a game (and barely missed a fifth), his feat was scarcely noticed. It was the same day John McGraw announced his retirement. Even after Gehrig's amazing performance in the Yanks' four-game sweep of the 1932 World Series—three homers, eight RBIs, a .529 batting average, and a 1.118 slugging mark—Ruth got all the press for his "called shot" (which Gehrig, incidentally, followed with a homer of his own).

His team, of course, was a dynasty, and Gehrig appeared in seven World Series (the pins he received, to which he added his MVP and All-Star jewelry, he made into a bracelet for Eleanor). He was the constant, the only man from the Series contestants of 1926–1928 to play with the world champs of 1936–1939. Even today, after all the stars of all the years since his passing, a look at the top lifetime marks in on-base percentage plus slugging average—that most elegant combined measure of batting proficiency, now called Production—offers this triad: Ruth, Williams, Gehrig.

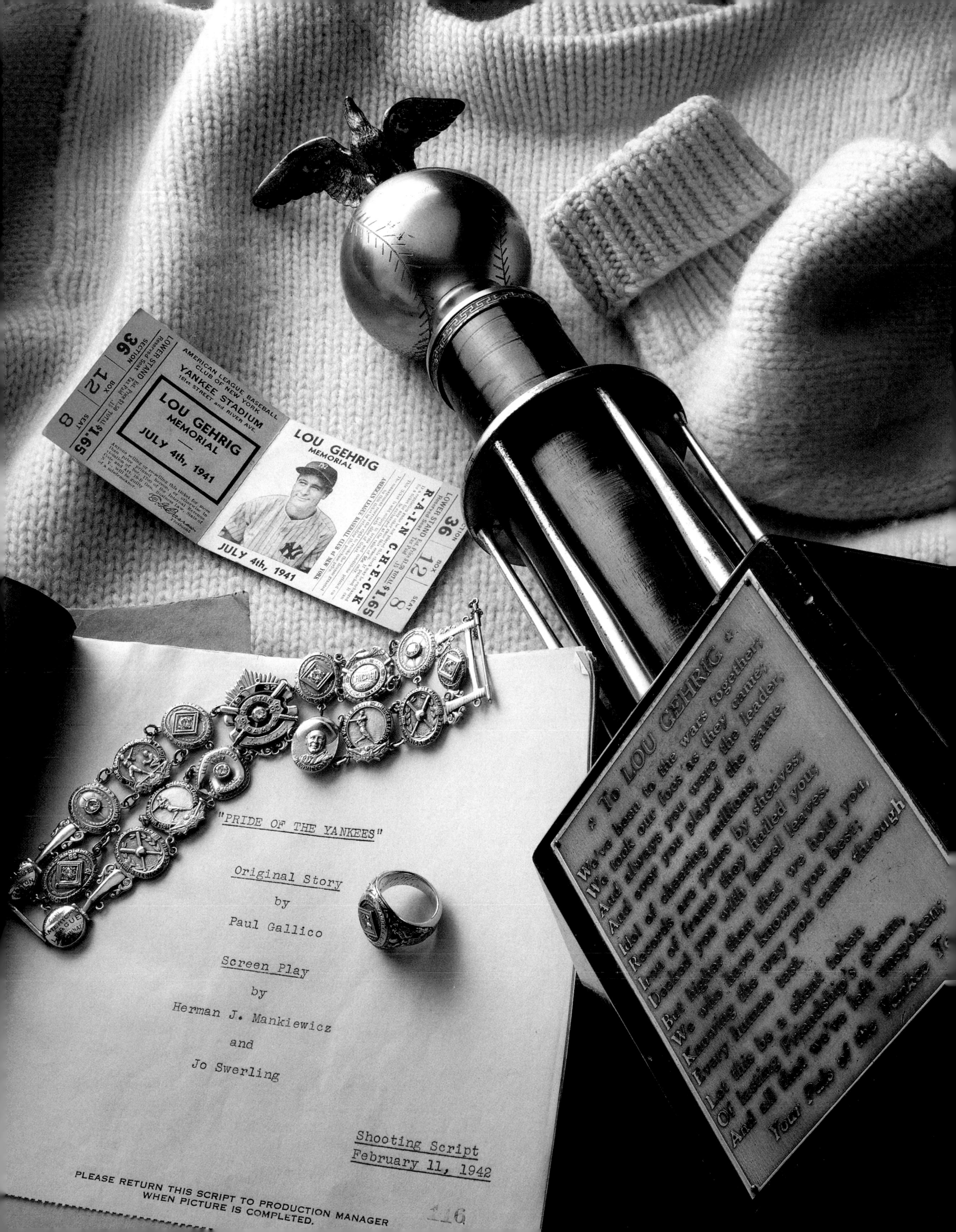

LOU GEHRIG
MEMORIAL

YANKEE STADIUM
161st STREET and RIVER AVE.

AMERICAN LEAGUE BASEBALL
CLUB OF NEW YORK

LOU GEHRIG
MEMORIAL

JULY 4th, 1941

JULY 4th, 1941

"PRIDE OF THE YANKEES"

Original Story

by

Paul Gallico

Screen Play

by

Herman J. Mankiewicz

and

Jo Swerling

Shooting Script
February 11, 1942

* To LOU GEHRIG *

We've been to the wars together;
We took our foes as they came;
And always you were the leader,
And ever you played the game.

Idol of cheering millions,
Records are yours by sheaves;
Iron of frame they hailed you,
Decked you with laurel leaves.

But higher than that we hold you,
We who have known you best;
Knowing the way you came through,
Every human test.

Let this be a silent token
Of lasting friendship's gleam,
And all that we've left unspoken—
Your Pals of the Yankee Team.

With this bat, Joe Medwick became the last Triple Crown winner in the National League, in 1937. And he didn't exactly luck into his crown, either: a .374 average, 154 RBIs, 31 homers, and 56 doubles for good measure (the previous year he had hit 64!). So now Medwick and Bill Terry (with his .401 batting average) are the National League's equivalent of the last of the Romanovs.

Medwick was called "Ducky Wucky" (later abbreviated to just "Ducky") by some wag in the minors who thought he walked funny. But calling Joe Medwick names was a bad idea. Joe didn't find social graces easy. He would say something nasty and then back it up with his fists, before the recipient of his comment had a chance to do anything. Though he came from New Jersey, Joe was born to be a member of the Gashouse Gang.

His most famous brawl came during the 1934 World Series. His team, the Cardinals, was handily beating the Tigers 7–0 in the final game when Medwick tripled to right to drive in the game's eighth run. Medwick felt that third baseman Marv Owen had deliberately tried to spike him. Medwick began kicking Owen, the two swung at each other, and umpire Bill Klem had to pull them apart. Medwick offered to apologize after the inning was over. When he went to take his place in left field, the Tiger fans went bonkers—throwing everything they had, which was mostly food, at him. The garbage had to be cleaned up several times. Finally, Commissioner Landis removed Medwick from the game, for his safety, and so they could finish the one-sided contest.

But where tomatoes and pop bottles had failed, in 1940 a baseball thrown at his head by a pitcher he had insulted succeeded; after the beaning, Ducky was never the same. He continued to play big-league ball until 1948, but his power was gone.

———— ★ ————

When Dizzy Dean was broadcasting games nationally on radio and television in the 1950s, he was subjected to a constant stream of letters from schoolteachers around the country claiming that his fractured brand of English was corrupting the linguistic standards of American youth (yes, it was a simpler time). Some of the Dizzy-isms were genuinely atrocious English ("he slud into third," "the players returned to their respectable bases"), but others were gems of Zen-like insight. For example, after being hit in the head by a ball he was asked what the doctors had said. "The doctors X-rayed my head and found nothing," he replied. Of a slow-moving Card teammate, Diz said, "He runs too long in one place. He's got a lot of up and down, but not much forward." "The good Lord was good to me. He gave me a strong body, a good right arm, and a weak mind." And the legendary "It ain't bragging if you can do it."

Dean's big toe was broken by a line drive off the bat of Earl Averill in the 1937 All-Star Game ("Fractured, hell!" Dizzy said. "The damn thing's broke!"). He tried to come back too soon and altered his pitching motion, which damaged his arm, and his career was all but over. He would win just sixteen more games after that season. One was a clutch 1938 performance that helped the Cubs nose out the Pirates for the National League pennant.

Another was a legendary return to the mound after a six-year absence. Calling the St. Louis Browns' games on the radio in 1947, Dean declared that, old and worn out though he was, he could do better than some of the team's pitchers. Told to put up or shut up, he put up, starting a game for the Browns and hurling four shutout innings before fatigue forced him back to the broadcasting booth.

Dean's numbers for the five seasons he was healthy are stupendous. No National Leaguer has won thirty games since he did in 1934. His five-year average of twenty-four wins a season, plus four league-leading seasons in strikeouts and three in complete games and innings pitched, give some idea of how great he might have been. Of course, with Dizzy, there's no sense moping about lost opportunities. He slud home, safe, in 1974, and in baseball's Valhalla, he'll live forever.

—★—

One of the many joys of Ken Burns's documentary film *Baseball* was the chance to see archival footage of Walter Johnson pitching. We all grew up knowing he threw the ball at remarkable speed; the testimonials and anecdotes are legion, and the evidence is in the record books. His lifetime strikeout mark lasted almost sixty years, longer than Ruth's "unbeatable" home run total. His twelve seasons of leading the league in strikeouts are without parallel—starting at age twenty-two and concluding in the "miracle year" of 1924 at age thirty-six.

What the film revealed was how low Johnson's sidearm delivery was and how economical of effort. Opposing batters used to describe the effect of a Johnson fastball crossing the plate in auditory terms: *"Whoosh!"* No wonder they called him "The Big Train." Viewing the film inclines me to believe that Johnson was, in fact, not as fast as some who followed him, such as Bob Feller, Sam McDowell, and Nolan Ryan, nor as fast as some who preceded him, like Amos Rusie (whom Connie Mack always said was the fastest ever). Johnson himself said in 1912, "No man alive is faster than Smoky Joe Wood," although some have ascribed the remark to his self-effacing, gentlemanly air. Seeing Johnson in action at last, I know why he didn't bother to develop a curve until his later years—obviously his fastball was enough for him to excel, but a curve thrown from that low sidearm release point couldn't have been too deceptive.

Johnson's fastball probably topped out at about ninety miles per hour. But, oh, what a terrifying fastball it must have been—darting, sailing, rising, exploding in the strike zone. He was simply one of the greatest pitchers who ever lived, no matter that Rob Dibble and John D'Acquisto threw faster. For the first seventeen seasons of his career he averaged about twenty-one wins a year for a team that seldom reached as high as fourth place. Through all the suffering with Washington ("first in war, first in peace, last in the American League," in sportswriter Charlie Dryden's jab), Johnson maintained his composure and resigned himself to never pitching in a World Series.

The placement of the Capitol behind Johnson in the clothing-ad portrait shows the extent to which he had become a Washington institution himself. The statue is a personal tribute, a papier-mâché creation given to the pitcher by an admirer. By 1920 Johnson was starting to slip: he lost a bit off his fastball, and his strikeout ratio and ERA began to slip, even though he did manage a no-hitter (the ball shown here is the one used for the final out). Great as he was—and I can't name a pitcher who was greater—Walter Johnson threw only this one no-hitter. The date was July 1, 1920, the opponent was the suddenly Ruthless Red Sox, and the score was, classically, 1–0.

"Old Barney"—a neat nickname, for it hinted at Johnson's speed by reference to the greatest race-car driver of the day, Barney Oldfield—appeared in more 1–0 games than any other pitcher. That was because he held the opponents down, and his team, the Washington Senators, restrained itself from scoring. By 1923 Walter's luck had begun to turn: Clark Griffith brought in some fresh

talent—Goose Goslin, Bucky Harris, Ossie Bluege, Earl McNeely—that, when added to Joe Judge and Sam Rice, made the Senators a contender. Allen Russell and Firpo Marberry became bull-pen fixtures. The Senators shocked the baseball world by going to the Series two years in a row.

In 1924 "poor old Walter" lost his two World Series starts, in Games 1 and 5, and fans everywhere were disappointed when manager Harris bypassed him for the start in the finale. But when the seventh game headed into the ninth inning tied at three, Walter came on in relief. He allowed just three hits and no runs in his four innings of work and was the winner when a ground ball struck a pebble and hopped over Giant third baseman Freddie Lindstrom's head in the twelfth inning. Washington went berserk, and Johnson had capped his career with a Series victory at last.

In the 1925 Series he won his first two starts, allowing only one run in the two complete-game victories. And as Game 7 began he appeared to continue his mastery of Pittsburgh, taking a 4–0 lead into the third inning. But the pesky Bucs, aided by two crucial errors by shortstop Roger Peckinpaugh, came back to win the game in the last of the eighth, 9–7. Two years after that Johnson retired; at a special celebration of the twentieth anniversary of his debut against Detroit on August 2, 1907, those at Griffith Stadium who purportedly saw him pitch his first big-league game wore this silk ribbon.

—★—

The legend reads "Night Game 1," a bright idea commemorated by this special ticket. Nowadays, when World Series games start at nearly nine o'clock at night, it's hard to imagine that baseball was a day game for all the years it was played by Ruth, Cobb, Wagner, Mathewson, and Johnson—the original five Hall of Fame electees.

Interestingly, it was men of vision in the minors and black baseball—those seedbeds of daring and innovation—who led the way to night games. Arc lights had been used by black barnstorming teams in the first decade of the century; the Kansas City Monarchs traveled with a sophisticated arc-light system; and an official minor league game had been played at night between Lynn and Salem in 1927. But the first permanent installation debuted on May 2, 1930, when Lee Keyser, president of the Des Moines Demons in the Class A Western League, fired up his permanent lights, which cost $19,000, for the first time. Trivia note: three days earlier a Class C club in Kansas played a game under temporary lights, but Keyser got the hoopla he deserved. No less than Judge Landis himself was there. Keyser's men topped the opposition, 13–6.

The majors, however, remained cool to the idea. Judge Landis said night ball would never happen in the bigs. The National League even put a rule in ef-

fect against it. But Larry MacPhail, general manager of the Cincinnati Reds, and owner Powel Crosley formulated a seventy-page proposal to have the rule rescinded. They won out, and on May 24, 1935, the Reds played the first major league night game. It was cold that night, but more than 20,000 fans were there. MacPhail's experiment was a huge success. Within thirteen years every major league club (except the Cubs, who held out for another forty years) had lights.

MacPhail was the man behind this ticket, too. He had joined the Dodgers in 1938 and put up lights in Brooklyn. But the real story evoked by this ticket is not the fact of a night game in Brooklyn but what happened that night. Johnny Vander Meer of the Reds pitched his second consecutive no-hitter. Was it because the brand-new lights weren't quite right? We'll never know. Also, because of a host of pregame activities,

ENTER GATES
22 TO 26 ROTUNDA
LOWER STAND
13 12 32
SEC. ROW SEAT
EBBETS FIELD
BROOKLYN
EST. PRICE $1.50
FED. TAX .15
TOTAL $1.65
NIGHT GAME
1

the first pitch wasn't thrown till 9:45 P.M. Maybe the Dodgers were just sleepy.

In Major League Baseball history, only six pitchers have come close to Vander Meer's mark. Ed Cushman (Milwaukee, Union Association, 1884), Howard Ehmke (Red Sox, 1923), and Ewell Black-well (Cincinnati, 1947) all threw no-hitters and then allowed just one hit in their next starts. Pud Galvin (Buffalo, National League, 1884), Dazzy Vance (Brooklyn, 1925), and Jim Tobin (Boston Braves, 1944) tossed one-hitters and then improved on those performances the next time out.

—★—

Crossed bats from two Hall of Famers, first baseman George Kelly and third sacker Pie Traynor, both of whose stock has declined with the years and the entrance into the Hall of superior players of more recent vintage. George "Highpockets" Kelly was a raw kid whom John McGraw took under his wing and taught the finer points of the game, keeping him on the bench for years before Kelly became a regular for the Giants. This was McGraw's typical finishing school for fine prospects whom he preferred not to expose to minor-league instruction. McGraw's "boys" included not only Kelly but such other stars as Ross Youngs, Mel Ott, Waite Hoyt (briefly), and Fred Merkle.

Kelly replaced Hal Chase as the New York first baseman because McGraw knew that Chase had been throwing games, just as he had done with other clubs. Kelly was the typical first-base slugger: big and strong, a little slow afoot, but an excellent fielder. (Despite his 6′4″ frame, he moved over to play second base for the Giants in 1926 to permit Bill Terry to play every day at first.) He knocked in more than one hundred runs four times and led the league twice in RBIs. He batted over .300 seven times. When Highpockets hit seven homers in the month of April in 1921, the New York papers ran comparisons to Ruth. Babe finished with fifty-nine that year. Kelly's twenty-three were still enough to lead the National League.

If you had asked a serious baseball fan in 1950 to name the all-time greatest third baseman, he probably would have named Pie Traynor. At that time and for decades to come, third basemen were scarcely represented within the Hall of Fame. There were Jimmy Collins and Home Run Baker—and Traynor could play with them, for sure. He hit .320 for his career and played an aggressive defense at third that stymied many bunters. Traynor had power, too, but he played in the mammoth Forbes Field, so he settled for doubles and triples. Only twice in his thirteen full seasons did he knock fewer than ten three-baggers.

Traynor's position is now represented in the Hall by the likes of Mike Schmidt, Eddie Mathews, and Brooks Robinson, among others, so he has had to surrender the top rung to others. Kelly's numbers pale before those of Willie McCovey and Harmon Killebrew, not to mention Gehrig and Foxx. But both Kelly and Traynor hold secure places in the hearts of baseball fans, and they have earned their eternal home in Cooperstown.

—★—

You might look at Max Carey's record and see a lifetime batting average of .285 with only seventy home runs in twenty seasons and wonder how this guy ever got his plaque. Carey is a perfect reminder, to those who need reminding, that there is more to baseball greatness than walloping the ball a long way.

"The place where triples go to die." This line was first applied to the glove of Willie Mays, but it is equally well suited to describe Max Carey's, despite its tiny webbing, unlaced fingers, and un-formed pocket. In fact, when it came to com-bined catching and throwing ability, the only Hall of Fame outfielders who may be mentioned in the same breath with Carey were Mays and Tris Speaker. Nicknamed "Scoops" for his ability to dash in and turn line drives into outs, Carey trails only Mays and Speaker in career putouts by an outfielder, and among twentieth-century center fielders only Speaker and Ty Cobb exceed his assist total.

Not shown here are his shoes, though they might have been. For while Maximil-ian Carnarius (his birth name) was a better-than-average hitter, he truly excelled on the base paths. In the thirteen-year period of 1913–1925 he led the National League in stolen bases ten times, and his rate of success was staggering. Today the league stolen-base average hovers around 67 percent year after year. In Carey's time the average was closer to 50 percent. For example, in 1922, when the league success rate was 54 per-cent, Carey's was 96 percent, as he stole fifty-one bases and was caught stealing only *twice*. In the whole his-tory of baseball, no one has stolen so many bases at such a rate of success.

———★———

Burleigh Grimes, whose leather hassock of a glove this is, was a durable right-handed pitcher with a bulldog determination to win. And win he did, 270 times over his nineteen-year career, several times posting twenty or more victories or leading the National League in complete games or innings pitched. He won Game 7 of the 1931 World Series, he managed the Dodgers, he coached for the Kansas City A's, he was named to the Hall of Fame in 1964, and he lived until the age of ninety-two. A great ca-reer, without a doubt, but his story is best embod-ied by this humble strip of slippery elm bark.

For Burleigh Grimes was a spitball pitcher in the days when that was an open and proud vocation. The spitball has a long and damply lovely history. First used in 1868 but not a factor until the turn of the century, it was not only legal but became the out pitch for great hurlers like Ed Walsh and Jack Ches-bro, the only two men to win forty games in one season in the twentieth century. Red Faber, Stan Coveleski, and Burleigh Grimes—Hall of Famers all—used it to excellent effect as well. Perry's sali-vary glands never came into play; he preferred the hypoallergenic properties of K-Y lubricant, hidden adroitly on his person. Slippery elm was Grimes's lubricant of choice ever since he started pitching professionally in 1912 with Eau Claire of the Class D Minnesota-Wisconsin League. He reached the Pittsburgh Pirates for a handful of games in 1916 but gained prominence with Brooklyn, especially in the memorable baseball season of 1920.

Over in the American League Babe Ruth come to the Yankees, the Black Sox scandal of the previous World Series was revealed, and Ray Chapman, shortstop of the Cleveland Indians, was fatally beaned in August. Anger over his death prompted a ruling to remove defaced or dirty balls from play, and the spitball and other topically altered pitches were on their way out. In the National League Grimes was the ace of the Dodgers' rotation, winning twenty-three games and leading them to the World Series against the Indians, who had charged past the wounded White Sox in the last weeks of September despite the loss of Chapman. In Game 5 of the Series Grimes surrendered a grand slam to Elmer Smith, the first in postseason history, and a home run to opposing pitcher Jim Bagby. Removed from the game, he saw his replacement, Clarence Mitchell, hit into an unassisted triple play. The Indians won the Series, behind three wins from their own spitballer, Stan Coveleski.

After that season the spitter and other such trick pitches were banned, as had been expected. Grimes was one of only seventeen major leaguers who were grandfathered in—permitted the continuing use of the spitter for the rest of their careers—so as not to deprive them of their livelihood. Grimes continued to pitch in the majors until he was old enough to be a grandfather, and in 1934 he had the honor of throwing the last spitball—legally, that is.

TO 1960

The summer of 1941 had been a glorious one, with Joe DiMaggio's fifty-six-game hitting streak, Ted Williams's .406 batting average, and a thrilling Yankee-Dodger World Series, the first of many to come. But then the raid on Pearl Harbor thrust the United States into the war that had already embroiled most of the world, and suddenly baseball was not very important anymore, neither to the players nor to the fans. Or so some politicians thought.

Judge Landis was ready to shut baseball down if President Roosevelt wished, but FDR, a fan himself, thought otherwise. He knew that the American war effort needed all able-bodied men to come to the aid of their country, including ballplayers, but America also needed recreation, perhaps now more than ever before. Baseball would serve to ease tension on the home front and help retain an air of normalcy even in those extraordinary times. "Here is another way of looking at it," the president wrote to the commissioner, "if 300 teams use 5,000 or 6,000 players, these players are a definite recreational asset to at least 20,000,000 of their fellow citizens—and that in my judgment is thoroughly worthwhile." Roosevelt even encouraged Landis to schedule more night games so that day-shift workers would also derive the benefits of baseball; however, the military's need for every bit of scrap metal delayed the planned installation of lights at, among other venues, Chicago's Wrigley Field.

As the nation mobilized to fight the Axis powers in World War II, baseball played its part, with war bond rallies, free admission to men in uniform, and war relief games (on one such occasion, between games of a benefit doubleheader on August 23, 1942, Babe Ruth squeezed into his old uniform and hit a homer off Walter Johnson). Even the St. Louis Cardinals' program for the 1943 World Series had a message for Berlin: "Victory is in the Cards—but not for you, Adolf!"

The first player drafted was Hugh "Losing Pitcher" Mulcahy, who entered the service in March 1941. The first to enlist was super slugger Hank Greenberg, whose military identification card is on display here. Bob Feller followed Greenberg into the service (the day after, in fact) and did not pitch in the majors again until September of 1945; the navy gunner's goggles shown here are his.

Twenty-six other future Hall of Famers contributed, too, including Ted Williams, Joe DiMaggio, Pee Wee Reese, Stan Musial, Yogi Berra, Luke Appling, Phil Rizzuto, and Warren Spahn. But they were hardly unique: in the spring of 1945, *The New York Times* reported that of the 5,800 professional baseball players in the country at the time of Pearl Harbor, 5,400 went into the service. More than fifty professional players lost their lives in the war, and many came home with injuries that effectively ended their careers.

FDR was right: baseball was important to Americans, and not only on the home front. The hand-hewn, taped-up bat used by American diplomats while detained in Germany at the start of the war is testament to that. And the strangely carved balata baseball, captured from hostile troops, is testament that baseball was Japan's game, too.

——★——

Only four men in baseball history had reached the level of three hundred career home runs when Hank Greenberg of Detroit knocked this ball out of the park in 1946. Greenberg went on to lead the American League that season with forty-four, his fourth homer title, the fourth time he had hit forty or more.

What this three hundredth home run ball doesn't tell us is that its date might have come four years earlier were it not for World War II. Greenberg was an awesome slugger, driving in a staggering 183 runs in 1937 and belting 58 homers the following season. When he was drafted into the military early in 1941, before World War II started, he was the top right-handed hitter in baseball, coming off a season in which he had once again led the American League in homers and RBIs. Greenberg was discharged on December 5 of that year and, having ful-

filled his military obligation, could have expected to resume playing ball in 1942, alongside Joe DiMaggio, Ted Williams, and other league notables.

Two days later, however, the Japanese attacked Pearl Harbor, and Hank immediately enlisted, the first ballplayer to do so. He served in the Far East well into 1945. His first day back in the bigs he hit a homer. Then he slugged a grand slam the last day of the season to give the Tigers their first pennant in five years.

——★——

Twenty-one represents the year Warren Spahn was born, his age when he first reached the big leagues with the Boston Braves of 1942, the number of major-league seasons he pitched, the precise number of games he won in his first full season and in each of seven seasons thereafter! You wouldn't want to play blackjack with this guy.

Two quotes define the majesty and mastery of Warren Spahn. One is his profoundly simple definition of the two jobs in baseball: "Hitting is timing. Pitching is upsetting timing." The other, unattributed, describes his remarkably easy, high-kicking motion: "If Martians landed in the middle of a game Spahn was pitching, they might have no idea in the world what he was doing, but they would know immediately he was the best in the world at doing it." Spahn won 363 games, the most by any left-hander in baseball history, before finally quitting the game after the 1965 season, at age forty-four. But, as Stan Musial said, "I don't think Spahn will ever get into the Hall of Fame. He'll never stop pitching."

Spahnie still felt that his arm was only twenty-one—hadn't he waited until his thirty-ninth year to throw his first no-hitter, then followed up with another the next year? So, rather than bow to Father Time, he resumed his pitching career two years later in the Mexican League, delaying his induction into the Hall until 1973.

——★——

If the sight of this uniform number doesn't provoke a knowing smile, you are as folklorically challenged as Eddie Gaedel was challenged vertically. The diminutive Eddie had only one occasion to wear this unique St. Louis Browns uniform—in the second game of a doubleheader with the Detroit Tigers on August 19, 1951—but it is safe to say that no event in baseball history tops it for notoriety or hilarity.

Between the games, Browns owner Bill Veeck

staged an elaborate fiftieth anniversary celebration for the American League, attended by Commissioner Happy Chandler. The celebration featured acrobats, antique cars, a band made up of Browns players, and, for the finale, an anniversary cake. Gaedel jumped out of the cake wearing this uniform, originally made for the son of former owner Bill DeWitt.

As the Browns came to bat in the first inning of the second game, the crowd roared and Tigers pitcher Bob Cain doubled over with laughter as Gaedel strutted to the plate as a pinch hitter for the leadoff batter. After Browns manager Zack Taylor provided assurances to the umpire that Gaedel was legally under contract and on the Browns roster, Cain was instructed to pitch to him. Cain walked him on four pitches—all, naturally, high. Little Eddie trotted to first base, where he was replaced by a pinch runner.

Although Chandler found the incident entertaining, American League president Will Harridge was not amused. He banned any further appearances by midgets.

"Fine," Veeck said. "Let's establish what a midget is in fact. Is it three-feet-six inches? Eddie's height? Is it four-feet-six? If it's five-feet-six, that's great. We can get rid of Rizzuto."

stocky strength gave him stamina: he was a complete-game pitcher. Eight times he completed more than twenty games in a season; he led the league in complete games six years in a row. And Roberts had superb control: only twice since 1922 has a pitcher led his league in both fewest walks per nine innings and most strikeouts. Both times it was Robin Roberts. As his fastball slowed later in his career, Roberts began giving up a lot of home runs, but not a lot of runs. Because he was always around the plate, good hitters could tee off on occasion. But because he was such an excellent control pitcher, there was hardly ever anyone on base. The Roberts model seems particularly apt for pitchers in today's homer-happy game.

—————★—————

A baseball archetype of days gone by: the excellent pitcher laboring year after year for a losing team. Today such a pitcher would reach free agency and his downtrodden team would not only be unable to afford him but would be delighted to see him go, in his "walk year," in exchange for a passel of young talent that might turn the team's fortunes.

In Robin Roberts's third season with the Phillies he won twenty games and his "Whiz Kids" went to the World Series. It had been thirty-five years since the Phils had been there, and it would be thirty more until they got there again (and that year they actually won the Series, which made them the last of the original sixteen franchises to do so).

Roberts was a kind of pitcher that every team seemed to have in the 1950s—a big, strong workhorse right-hander who threw a lot of innings. The Pirates had Bob Friend, the White Sox Virgil Trucks, the Cubs Bob Rush, the Tigers Frank Lary, the Yankees Bob Turley, the Indians Early Wynn, Bob Lemon, and Mike Garcia. Roberts was the best of them. After that 20–11 season in 1950, he won twenty games or more five years in a row, including a 28–7 mark in 1952. But the Phutile Phils stuck around the .500 mark. Meanwhile Roberts was *averaging* 319 innings pitched a year, a number that in today's world of relief specialists seems as absurd as the six-hundred-inning seasons hurled in the nineteenth century.

Roberts was a fastballer, and his ball was "heavy": it had a lot of downward movement. His

They were the "Go-Go Sox" before he arrived, but Luis Aparicio brought a new dimension not only to the nickname but to the game itself. The stolen base had been disappearing from baseball ever since Babe Ruth started banging out homers. Dom DiMaggio led the American League in steals in 1950 with fifteen, about two weeks' work for

Rickey Henderson in his prime; only four men in the whole league had double-digit totals. After that, the Chicago White Sox led the league in steals every year for the next eleven, led first by Minnie Minoso and Jim Rivera, then by Little Looie. Seven years in a row no one in the American League outstole him. Then he went to Baltimore and led the league as an Oriole two more years. Three years in a row he swiped more than fifty bases; no one had done that since Ty Cobb.

His aggressive base stealing culminated in a World Series appearance for the Chisox in 1959, their first since the dark days of 1919. His opposite number at shortstop in that Series was Maury Wills of the Dodgers, a speedy rookie who, with Aparicio, would make the stolen base the offensive hallmark of the pitching-dominated 1960s.

In 1984 Aparicio became the fourth Latin-born player elected to the Hall of Fame, following Roberto Clemente, Martin Dihigo, and Juan Marichal.

—★—

Bob Feller exploded onto the big-league scene when he was just seventeen years old. The farm boy from Van Meter, Iowa, had a blazing fastball that brought to mind the hard ones of Walter Johnson, Lefty Grove, and Amos Rusie. But some said he was even faster, the fastest pitcher of all time. In his first major league start he set down fifteen Browns on strikes. A month later he set the American League record by whiffing seventeen Athletics. Two years later he broke that record with eighteen. In his first sixty-two big-league innings he struck out seventy-six batters. Then he headed back to Iowa to get his high school diploma.

Feller's heat was made even more terrifying by his huge windup which, for a disconcerting fraction of a second, presented his back to the hitter. And there are dozens of stories of hitters being intimidated by Feller's smoke. Allegedly, Lefty Gomez lit a match at the plate one overcast afternoon when it was his turn to bat. The unamused umpire said, "I don't think that will help you see Feller any better." "No," Lefty replied. "I just want to be sure he can see me."

Feller won forty-one games in his first two full seasons, then started the 1940 campaign with a bang, no-hitting the White Sox on Opening Day. He threw two more no-hitters before his career was over, including the April 30, 1946, gem against the Yankees, from which the final ball is displayed here. Feller was at the absolute peak of his career when World War II began, yet he was the second big leaguer to enlist. He spent 1942 pitching for the Norfolk Military Training Station and other All-Star teams, but then requested transfer to a combat unit, where he earned five campaign ribbons and eight battle stars as an antiaircraft gunner, feeding the opposition a different kind of heat.

Feller returned to the Indians at the end of 1945, having missed almost four full years. He certainly would have been a three-hundred-game winner if the war hadn't intervened, and if he had maintained his 250-strikeouts-a-year average he might have passed Walter Johnson as the all-time whiff king. Like Johnson, Feller rarely had the opportunity to pitch for a championship team. Feller won "only" nineteen games in 1948, but his team caught fire to end the season tied with Boston and then topped the Red Sox in a one-game play-off to reach the Series.

Feller was masterful in Game 1, but the Braves' Johnny Sain was his equal. There was no score as the two teams began the last of the eighth. Feller walked the leadoff hitter. Pinch runner Phil Masi moved up to second on a sacrifice bunt. Feller spun and threw a strike to playing manager Lou

Boudreau at short (that's him on the Series program), and the whole world thought Masi had been picked off. Everyone but ump Bill Stewart, that is. A single by Tommy Holmes followed (only the second hit Feller would allow), and the Indians lost the opener. Feller also lost Game 5, but his team took the Series.

Not winning a World Series game was a disappointment for Feller, but it looms insignificant in a career studded with superlatives. "Rapid Robert" was a hero in baseball for a long time, but his greatest attribute may have been his sense of perspective. When duty called in December 1941, he knew who he was and what he had to do.

——★——

It is the greatest of baseball stories because it is greater than baseball itself: Jackie Robinson's combination of courage, tenacity, and conviction in the face of unparalleled pressures. He bore the twin burdens of hope and hatred with a dignity and strength that became legendary. His story ascends to the level of myth, like George Washington and the cherry tree or Paul Bunyan and his blue ox, but right now, in the afterglow of the fiftieth anniversary celebration of Jackie Robinson's integration of baseball, there is still time to appreciate the man as he was rather than as the revered figure the nation needs him to be. Best to recall him not as a martyr, not as a savior, not as a sociocultural icon, but as a great baseball player, one whose fiery competitive spirit finds its equal in Cooperstown only in the person of his fellow Georgian and spiritual opposite, Ty Cobb. His presence in the Hall of Fame adds to the stature of the institution and the game.

In 1947 Jackie Robinson was the first Rookie of the Year, at the advanced baseball age of twenty-eight, and now the award bears his name. In 1949 he won a batting title, was named the National League MVP, and he played in the second of his six World Series. But tucked beneath the mementos of that year are items that recall the political realities that made Robinson a standard-bearer for integration, before his major-league career and after it.

Ten years ago, during a research visit, I came upon a box that *Look* magazine had shipped to the Hall in 1954. Inside it were strips of photographic contact sheets, including those displayed here. The photos showed a very youthful Robinson and two other black players going through batting and base-running drills. The players were wearing uniforms that read "Royals." The sheets were dated October 7, 1945, a full two weeks before the announcement of Robinson's signing to play with the Montreal Royals, the Dodgers' Triple A farm team. I was perplexed. Over the next few weeks, with the help of historian Jules Tygiel and a visit to the Library of Congress to research the Branch Rickey papers, I was able to piece the story together.

Rickey had met with Robinson in the Dodger offices on Montague Street in August 1945, ostensibly to discuss his playing in a new Negro League for a team that Rickey had announced in May, the Brooklyn Brown Dodgers. But what Rickey really had in mind as his scouts fanned out across the nation to contact several black players was to find the men who would integrate his major-league Dodgers, thus fulfilling his lifelong conviction that segregation was morally wrong and giving his team an enduring competitive and economic edge.

Rickey knew the value of manipulating the press and public opinion and wanted to insure that his motives behind the signing were clearly depicted. So he asked writer Arthur Mann, a close friend (and later a Rickey employee) to write a long piece for *Look* titled "The Negro and Baseball:

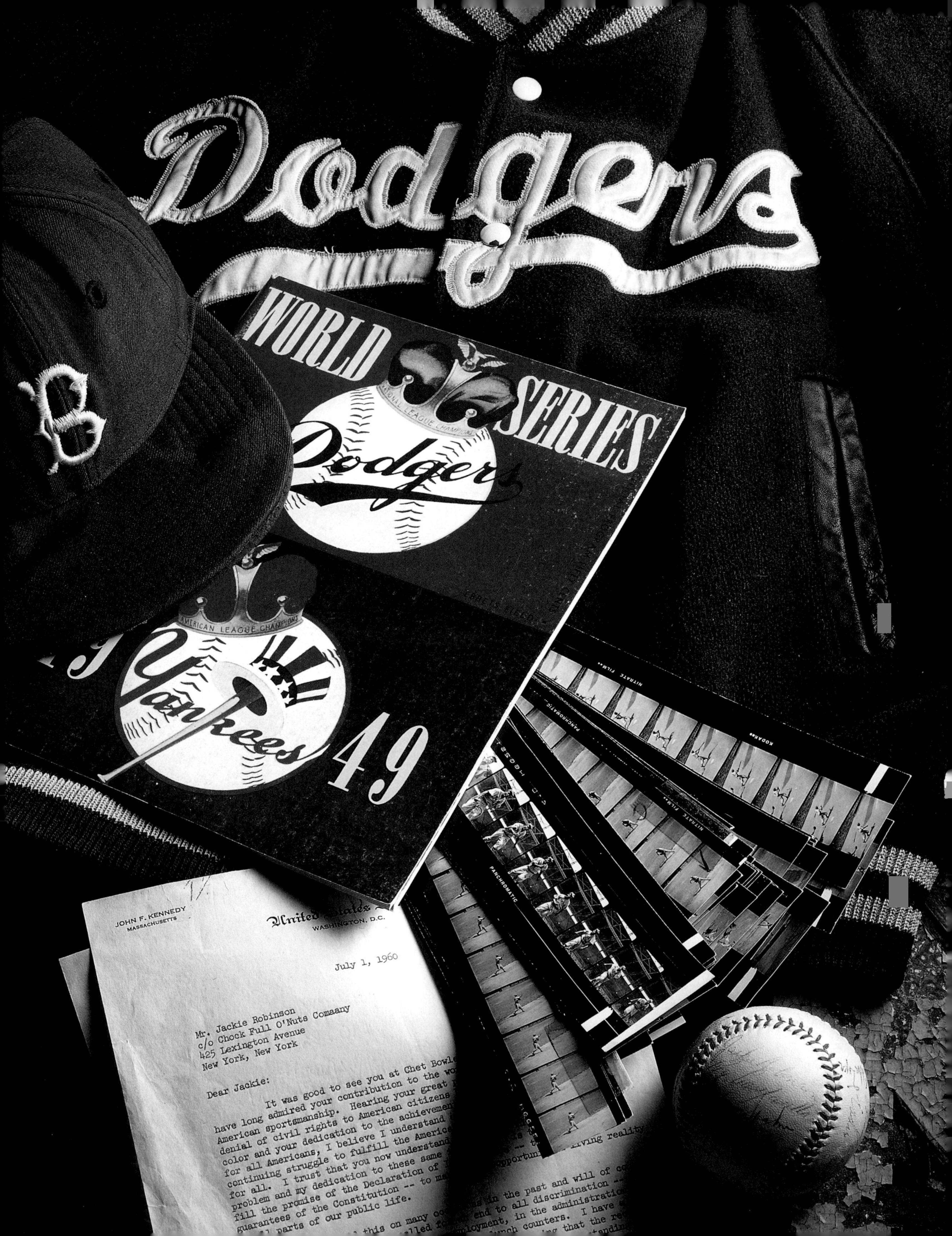

Dodgers
WORLD SERIES
NATIONAL LEAGUE CHAMPIONS
Dodgers
AMERICAN LEAGUE CHAMPIONS
Yankees
49
JOHN F. KENNEDY
MASSACHUSETTS
United States
WASHINGTON, D.C.
July 1, 1960
Mr. Jackie Robinson
c/o Chock Full O'Nuts Comaany
425 Lexington Avenue
New York, New York
Dear Jackie:
It was good to see you at Chet Bowle
have long admired your contribution to the wo
American sportsmanship. Hearing your great
denial of civil rights to American citizens
color and your dedication to the achievement
for all Americans, I believe I understand
continuing struggle to fulfill the America
for all. I trust that you now understand
problem and my dedication to these same
fill the promise of the Declaration of
guarantees of the Constitution -- to ma
parts of our public life.
NITRATE FILM
PANCHROMATIC
KODAK

The National Game Faces a Racial Challenge Long Ignored." The photographs were meant to accompany the article, which was to be held until the signings were to be announced, after the major-league meetings in December 1945, or even later. The "Royals" name that had thrown me a curve was not that of the Montreal Royals but the Kansas City Royals, a barnstorming team Robinson was playing for in California. *Look* photographer Maurice Terrell was stationed high in the empty grandstand at San Diego's Lane Stadium, snapping shots of Robinson and his fellow Royals, who were unaware of the photographer's presence.

The secrecy of Rickey's plan was near perfect. The manuscript, with his annotations in the margin, was revealed in the previously closed Rickey papers in Washington. Mann makes it clear that Rickey had never planned for one black man to deal with all the problems alone; he had meant to announce the simultaneous signing of several others. Don Newcombe and Sam Jethroe were supposed to have been Robinson's teammates at Montreal, and Roy Partlow, John Wright, and Roy Campanella were to have been assigned to another farm club.

But during the 1945 World Series Rickey wrote Mann and told him not to go through with publication of the article. "There is more involved in the situation than I had contemplated." What he meant was that it was becoming a divisive and public issue in New York City politics, and Rickey no longer had time to execute his master plan. In order to deter the Communist Party or Mayor Fiorello La Guardia from taking credit for pushing baseball to integrate, after all Rickey's years of work behind the scenes, he had to rush the signing of Robinson and Robinson alone. The grand plan—several players signed at once, the *Look* magazine scoop and accompanying photographs—dissolved. Rickey had Robinson, and that was all. Luckily for us, it proved more than enough.

After his retirement from baseball following the 1956 campaign, Robinson continued his advocacy of racial justice and integration, for which he had become a potent symbol. In the letter at the lower left, Senator John F. Kennedy sought his support in the 1960 presidential campaign. But Robinson backed Richard Nixon instead, which came as a disappointment to the liberal community but was consistent with who Jackie Robinson was and where he came from. Proud of his race, his community, his family, he asked nothing more of government than he asked of baseball: neither sympathy nor entitlement, but equal opportunity and a level playing field.

—★—

Some men's characters are summed up in their physical presence. As a young 6'1", 150-pound catcher, Cornelius Alexander McGillicuddy ("Slats" Mack to all but the census takers) presented so odd a specter that when he teamed with the equally bony pitcher Frank "Shadow" Gilmore in Washington in the 1880s, they were called "The Grasshopper Battery." Writer Wilfrid Sheed said that as a manager of the Philadelphia Athletics in his later years Mack, with his angular body and patrician bearing, looked "like a tree from the Garden of Eden."

We paint a mind's-eye picture of him as upright (in both the physical and moral senses of that word) as he sat in the dugout in a business suit and positioned his players with a wave of the scorecard. Yet the real Mr. Mack (it seems almost blasphemy to call him by his first name) was, like his old rival Clark Griffith, a very sly fox indeed. As a catcher (note his primitive face mask) his fine defensive skills were, shall we say, augmented by his ingenuity. In those days any caught foul tip was an out, so Connie liked to make a noise that resembled a ball hitting a bat on a swinging strike. He was also good at impeding a batter's swing with the brush of his glove, invariably offering apology for his clumsiness. When he became manager of the Pittsburgh Pirates in the 1890s, it is said he put the baseballs on ice the night before the game to deaden them.

Mack's earliest days as a player were with his hometown nine of East Brookfield, Massachusetts, a village of barely 1,000 but so in love with baseball that it raised $100 to bring Cap Anson's Chicago White Stockings to town one day in 1883. No wonder the silk shown here for the "Presentation of the Prize Bat" stayed with Connie Mack for more than seven decades. Mack joined the professional ranks the following season with Meriden, at the "stupendous" salary of $90 per month, then moved up to Hartford, and, at the season's end, his contract was purchased by the New York Mets of the American Association, a big league at the time. But he never played for the Mets, who sold him along with four other players to Washington for $3,500. He became a solid player with the Solons and enjoyed his best year with the bat with Buffalo in the lone year of the Players League, 1890. He concluded his eleven-year career as a player with the Pittsburgh Pirates, who also gave Mack his first managing post, but he left in 1896 in a dispute with a meddling owner.

He moved on to manage the Milwaukee entry in Ban Johnson's Western League, which in 1900 became the American League. When the American League challenged the National League by putting a team in Philadelphia, Mack got the chance to manage there. He also bought 25 percent of the club's stock. Connie, who had salted away some of his salary, retained the job of manager through 1950, a prodigious run of fifty-one years.

John McGraw, no fan of the new American League or Ban Johnson, its president, who had virtually banned him for his umpire baiting as manager of the 1901–1902 Orioles, said the Philadelphia operation was doomed to be a "white elephant"—a sure money-loser. The canny Mack wore the insult as a badge of pride and adopted a logo that survives to this day, mystifying the fans in Oakland. The A's topped the American League in 1904, but McGraw extended the feud by refusing to match his Giants against them in the World Series, inaugurated the year before between Boston and Pittsburgh. When the Giants defeated the A's in five games in the all-shutout Series of 1905, Mack vowed to gain revenge. His white elephants stomped McGraw's men handily in 1911 and 1913, by which time they were cavorting in the new concrete-and-steel palace that would one day be named for Mack but which had been christened Shibe Park after the A's majority owner, baseball equipment magnate Ben Shibe.

Mr. Mack was beloved by his players and known for his ability to build a pitching staff around young talent. But when his highly favored A's were toppled in the 1914 World Series by the "Miracle Braves" of Boston—he suspected that gamblers had reached some of his players, he later wrote to Red Smith—he dismantled his franchise. His team fell to last place in 1915 and stayed there for seven years. Mack felt his operation could be more financially successful with a first-half contender that settled into third or fourth place than with a pennant winner, which would certainly inspire the players to demand higher salaries. Gradually, he built another powerhouse, featuring such future Hall of Famers as Lefty Grove, Jimmie Foxx, and Al Simmons. The A's of 1929–1931 won three pennants and two World Series, right when Ruth and Gehrig were at their peaks. But the stock market crash and ensuing Depression brought the team to its knees, and once again Mack sold off his stars, this time from dire necessity. From 1934 through 1950 his team finished in the first division only once, but even though he was past the age of seventy, Mack didn't fear for his job; since 1937 he was the A's sole owner.

While the Atlanta Braves are the oldest continuous franchise in baseball, descending from the Boston Red Stockings of 1871, and the Chicago Cubs could trace their lineage back just as far if it weren't for the Great Fire of that year, the name "Athletics" is the oldest team nickname that has been in more or less constant use. The Athletics were formed as an amateur team in Philadelphia in 1860.

And that's where our geography lesson starts, baseball fans. This shirt is from the Philadelphia Athletics' last year, 1954. It epitomizes the greatest three years of upheaval in baseball franchises in the past ninety-plus years. In 1952 there were five cities with two (or, in the case of New York, three) major-league teams each, and all but the two St. Louis

teams were east of the Mississippi and no farther south than Washington, D.C. Three years later there were only two cities with two or more teams, New York and Chicago, which is where things remain today, except that we have major league baseball outposts stretching from the East Coast to the West and from Florida to Canada.

The Athletics, twice an American League dynasty, were forced to move to Kansas City in 1955 for economic reasons. Two years before, the Boston Braves had packed up their bags for Milwaukee. In

1954 the St. Louis Browns became the Baltimore Orioles. Despite expansion and player movement that have left us all a bit dizzy, no franchise has pulled up stakes since 1972.

During the fifty-year reign of tightfisted Connie Mack, the Philadelphia Athletics had been for the most part a horrific club. In the previous twenty years, they had finished last or next to it fourteen times and never got higher than the lofty perch of fourth. Prior to that stretch, in the late 1920s and early 1930s, they were one of the game's powerhouse franchises, winning three consecutive flags and two world championships. Mack had also built an A's dynasty from 1910 through 1914, when they took four pennants and three World Series.

But Connie Mack knew he made more money if he sold the stars he had developed and didn't spend much on the rest. Arnold Johnson extended from Mack's paradigm in the Athletics' years in Kansas City, turning them into a virtual farm club for the Yankees. At last Charlie Finley applied some unorthodox models to building his team, including spending on young, unproven talent such as Reggie Jackson, Catfish Hunter, Rick Monday, and Vida Blue, to make the Athletics champions again.

——★——

You hear it said, by fans, officials, and even folks at the Hall of Fame, that there ought to be a way to honor fame that's more fleeting than a ten-year career, the minimum required to merit consideration for a plaque. Such a "Rotunda of Records" might house the feats of Bobby Thomson and Don Larsen and Johnny Vander Meer and Mark Whiten—and Walt Dropo.

Here's the ball that the Detroit Tiger first baseman (surely a trivia answer) rapped for a double in Griffith Stadium in 1952 to tie Pinky Higgins (his partner in trivia) for most consecutive hits—an even dozen. But Higgins had walked once during his 1938 streak, so Dropo's is the "purer" record.

The other ball is a testament to one "hot" and one "cold" player during the 1946 World Series. The frigid batsman was Ted Williams, quite possibly the best hitter who ever lived, yet who managed just five singles and one lonely RBI during that Series. The other was Enos "Country" Slaughter, who

not only ripped the ball at a .320 clip but scored the Series' winning run on one of its most breathless plays.

In Game 1 of that Series, Slaughter had slugged a triple with two out and wanted to try to keep going on to score, but third-base coach Mike Gonzalez held him up, and Slaughter was stranded when the third out was made. Enos griped to manager Eddie Dyer about Gonzalez and was given the go-ahead to run on his own if he felt he could make it. He got his chance in Game 7. The Sox had just scored twice in the top of the eighth to tie the game when

Dom DiMaggio doubled in two runs, but he hurt his ankle on the play and was replaced in the outfield by Leon Culberston—nowhere near DiMaggio's equal as a thrower. In the bottom of that inning, Slaughter was on first with two out when Harry Walker lifted a liner into left center. Slaughter was off like a shot and refused to stop at third. Shortstop Johnny Pesky may have hesitated before he threw home or maybe not, but in any case Slaughter charged home with the winning run of the Series. Ted Williams would never play in a World Series again.

———★———

This is the batting helmet that Phil Rizzuto wore. But there was no such thing as a batting helmet in 1946 when Nelson Potter of the Browns beaned him with a high, hard one. And there was no such thing when Hughie Jennings and Frank Chance and Ducky Medwick and Don Zimmer and countless others were brutally injured, or when Ray Chapman was killed in 1920. Wally Moses had experimented with a rudimentary helmet for the A's back in the late 1930s, but no one seemed to like it. Then Branch Rickey had his Pirates wear helmets in the early 1950s; before long wearing one became common practice. Then it became the rule. Rizzuto suffered from dizzy spells for years after the beaning, and his offensive promise (he hit .307 and .284 in 1941 and 1942, the two seasons he played before he was hit) eroded. Until 1950, that is, when he rapped

the ball at a .324 clip and was named American League MVP.

For years Rizzuto was linked with Pee Wee Reese, his counterpart on the Dodgers, and Alvin Dark, his counterpart with the Giants; they were the "Willie, Mickey, and the Duke" of New York City shortstops. Reese was a fine defensive player, but a much more serious offensive threat than Rizzuto. Phil shone with his glove, his bunting, and his leadership. Dark was their equal at the bat but had limited range in the field. Reese was elected to the Hall of Fame in 1984; Rizzuto had to wait till ten years later. Dark remains on the outside looking in.

The issue of how important defense is to earning election to the Hall remains a conundrum. Defensive superstars such as Mark Belanger, Davey Concepcion, and Frank White will probably never see election. Bill Mazeroski, the Babe Ruth of defense, has never even come close. Let's see what happens when Ozzie Smith's number comes up in 2001.

In 1969, the centennial year of professional baseball, Major League Baseball conducted a poll among sportswriters as to who was the greatest living baseball player. The winner was Joe DiMaggio. Had it been conducted twenty-five years later, when baseball marked the 125th anniversary of the professional game, the answer might well have been the same.

Joe DiMaggio's stellar career stands squarely at the historical center of the longest tradition of excellence by any team ever—the Yankees' forty-four-year domination of baseball. It began with the arrival of Ruth in 1920 and Gehrig as a regular in 1925; DiMaggio arrived in 1936, missing Ruth by just two seasons and overlapping with Gehrig for three full seasons. In that 1938 campaign Joe D had taken center stage from the fading Gehrig. Painfully shy and self-conscious, DiMaggio was an introvert whose aversion to publicity just whetted the public's appetite for any tidbit about him. By 1938—the year when he used the glove and bat depicted here—the son of a San Francisco Bay fisherman had become a Wheaties champion, even winning the approval of invented radio personality "Jack Armstrong, All-American Boy." In 1941 his name was on everyone's lips as he hit in fifty-six straight games, and "Joltin' Joe" never fell from favor in all the years he played ball. In his final year as a Yankee, 1951, a new kid named Mantle joined him in the outfield. This is Joe's last uniform.

DiMaggio was consummate grace, with the style that comes with seeming effortlessness. Yankee announcer Mel Allen loved describing DiMaggio's "gliding" across center field to snag a hard-hit fly ball or "sailing" around second to advance the extra base on a single. "The Yankee Clipper"—what a perfect nickname.

Joe DiMaggio has always been our most mysterious and distant hero. Some have taken his shyness and reserved manner for aloofness or even hostility. But with the perverseness of celebrity in this country, Joe D and everything about him are of consuming interest to the public, who most want what they cannot have: his privacy and dignity. In his postplaying career, as spokesman for products and institutions and as a living icon of an America gone by, Joe DiMaggio has achieved—like Henry Aaron—that most difficult of feats: trading on his fame without becoming a prisoner to it. Though he has made far more money in the years since he hung up his spikes than he ever did as a player, he has done it his way.

Miracle of Coogan's Bluff" was the title of Red Smith's column for *The New York Herald Tribune* on October 3, 1951, the day after the New York Giants defeated the Brooklyn Dodgers, 5–4. And he wasn't exaggerating. The Giants had made up a thirteen-and-a-half-game deficit on August 12 by finishing the season with thirty-seven wins in their last forty-four contests, to wind up in a final-day dead heat for the pennant. The story is not only familiar, it is leg-

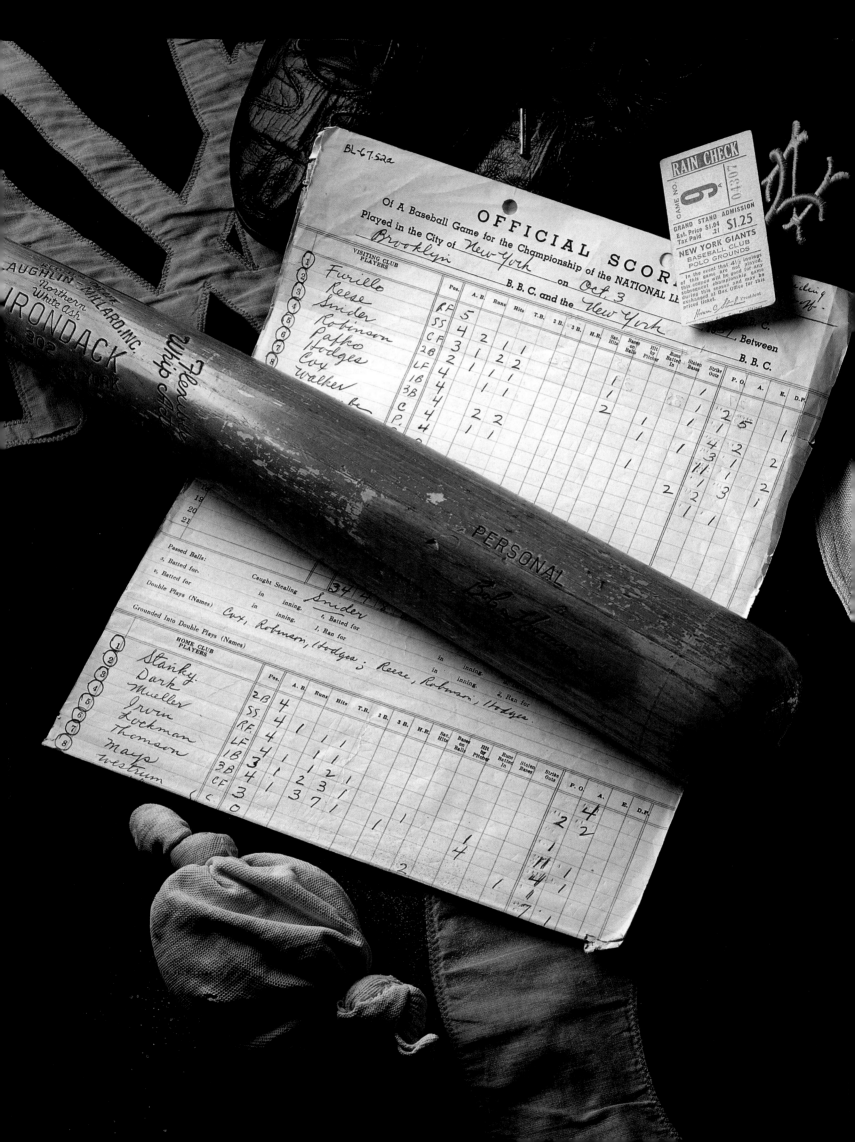

end: Giants win Game 1 of the best-of-three-play-off, defeating Ralph Branca, but the Dodgers take Game 2 behind Clem Labine and lead Game 3 comfortably, 4–1, going into the bottom of the ninth at the Polo Grounds. But the Giants score a run and put two runners on while using up one out; Bobby Thomson steps to the plate against Ralph Branca, who has just been brought in to replace the tiring Don Newcombe.

"Now it is done," Smith began his report. "Now the story ends. And there is no way to tell it. The art of fiction is dead. Reality has strangled invention. Only the utterly impossible, the inexpressibly fantastic, can ever be plausible again."

The 1950s belonged to New York's three teams, as every World Series showcased the Yankees, Dodgers (in Brooklyn and Los Angeles), or Giants—and five times presented a Subway Series. But heartbreak was the specialty of the Brooklyn Dodgers, who had appeared in the Series five times without a championship, including the excruciating loss in 1941, when Mickey Owen's missed third strike led to defeat; the Dodgers, who had also lost a play-off in 1946 after tying the Cardinals for the pennant (losing pitcher Branca); the Dodgers, who had lost to the Phillies on the final day of the 1950 season when a win would have forced another play-off. A World Series title in 1955 brought a measure of redemption, but not enough. Flatbush fans were meant to suffer, so the Dodgers lost to the Yanks the next year and left Brooklyn altogether the year after that. But for gnashing of teeth, for rending of garments, for abject misery, nothing could top the Brooklyn view of 1951.

What a rich, dense array of memorabilia this is, what an assortment of delights for Giants faithful, and what a rack of torture instruments for Dodgers fans. This is the official score sheet, with the H.R. column bearing an innocuous "1" alongside Thomson, the sixth batter in the order. This is the bat with which Bobby Thomson hit the humpbacked liner that eased into the left-field stands in the Polo Grounds and turned a whole season on its head. This is the rosin bag that Branca slammed into the dirt as he looked out to left field, displaying the number 13 on his back to the TV cameras behind home plate as he helplessly watched Thomson dance around the bases. These are the shoes in which "The Staten Island Scot" danced. This is the cap that flew from Thomson's head as he leapt onto home plate and was buried under a swarm of incredulous, adoring teammates. And this is the ticket to the game that half a million people should have in their collections if personal reports of attendance are to be believed (in fact it was one of 34,320 sold).

After the celebration in the clubhouse, Thomson did what he did after every home game: he headed for the subway, paid his fare, and took the Staten Island Ferry home. After their careers ended, Thomson and Branca, the two men united forever in history, became inseparable pals, at social, charitable, and sporting events. They even sold insurance together.

Like all great games, Game 3 of the National League Playoff of 1951 has been studied and second-guessed over and over. Why did manager Charlie Dressen keep an exhausted Don Newcombe in so long on this Wednesday afternoon, after the Dodger right-hander had thrown a shutout on Saturday and five and two-thirds innings of relief on Sunday? Why was first baseman Gil Hodges holding Alvin Dark on first with a three-run lead, which permitted Don Mueller to poke a single through the vacated hole? Why did Dressen bring in Branca? Hadn't Thomson already homered off him in the first game? One pitch, one swing—one goat, one hero—and the 156 games that have gone before, and the countless opportunities for victory along the way, are all forgotten in an instant. It's unreasonable, and it's cruel, but it's baseball.

There was one famous personage who missed the Thomson homer. Yogi Berra, there to check out the team his Yankees would be playing in the World Series, left with the Dodgers leading 4–1 in the top of the ninth. This is the man who would go on to coin the ultimate baseball tautology, "It ain't over till it's over."

—★—

Distressingly for one who saw his first major league game in Ebbets Field, it has come to the point that I must ask the question: did you know that the Los Angeles Dodgers once played in Brooklyn?

The Brooklyn Dodgers' only world championship, in 1955, is more distant from this book's year of publication than it is from the opening of Ebbets Field in 1913. The Dodgers have met with more success in their four decades in L.A. than in all their years in Brooklyn, where they were established as a major-league club in 1884. Yet the soul of today's Dodgers will always reside 3,000 miles away, in the borough whose heart they broke after the 1957 season. Has there ever been a team more beloved by its fans? The Brooklyn Dodgers—sometimes daffy, sometimes "supoib," always the pride of the city that was no longer a city. Think about it: we don't call New York's American League team the "Bronx Yankees" or its National League representative the "Queens Mets." Yet even to the end, some sixty years after what was once the third largest city in the land became only the second largest borough of New York, the Dodgers were still named for Brooklyn, a city that never ceased to be unique in the minds of its citizens and every opponent who dared come to Ebbets Field.

When Walter O'Malley moved the Dodgers to Los Angeles in 1958, a trust was broken with several million people. But in reality the nation had changed in the aftermath of World War II, and O'Malley was right to think that its national pastime would have to change with it. Despite the Dodgers' six pennants in the previous ten years and final-day contention in two others (1950 and 1951), attendance at Ebbets Field had declined 40 percent from its postwar peak and in all but one year of the 1950s it fell short of the prewar high of 1941. The franchise was dying. Sentiment aside, O'Malley was right. He tried to get the city of New York to build him a new stadium with adequate parking, but he was rebuffed. The game had to go where the people were, and they were leaving urban areas like Flatbush for the suburbs, they were deserting mass transportation for the pleasures of the automobile, and they were leaving the industrial north and midwest for California. The pity was that for Los Angeles to get a team, Brooklyn had to lose one. On Tuesday, September 24, 1957, a sad day marked by the ticket stub and baseball shown here, the Dodgers played their last game in Brooklyn. Only 6,702 fans showed up.

The team began play as the Trolley Dodgers, endured some years as the Brooklyn Bridegrooms (several players had wed in the off season), and next emerged as the Brooklyn Superbas (their manager was Ned Hanlon, and a celebrated acrobatic troupe of the day was "Hanlon's Superbas"). They were once again the Dodgers, however, when Ebbets Field was opened in the "Pigtown" section of Brooklyn in 1913, named for the garbage strewn there and porcine patrol that kept it manageable. Charles Hercules Ebbets, whose father had employed Alexander Cartwright as a teller in the Dime Savings Bank in the 1840s, was the majority shareholder in the team and the visionary behind the

park's construction, a detail guy who may well have specified the shade of red in the usher's uniform shown here. His son, Charles Hercules Ebbets, Jr., went from the initial share of stock shown here, granted him in 1905, to 10 percent of the team by the opening of Ebbets Field.

In the 1920s and 1930s they were called the "Daffiness Boys" and "Dem Bums," a collection of lovable losers and formidable players that included Dazzy Vance and Babe Herman and long-suffering managers Wilbert Robinson and Casey Stengel. But it was Branch Rickey's efforts in the 1940s that made the Dodgers America's team for all time: he brought together Jackie Robinson, Duke Snider, Roy Campanella, Gil Hodges, Don Newcombe, and Pee Wee Reese. The mere roll call of these names still stirs the souls of those who saw them play and inspires by example those denied the privilege.

—★—

Apparently the nickname came about because of the way he walloped Dodger pitching. "Here comes that man again," one forlorn Brooklynite was heard to say, and "that man" became "The Man": Stan "The Man" Musial. As a moniker it is surprisingly apt, both in its connotations of strength, stolidity, and indispensability, but also in its curious blandness. This is no "Splendid Splinter" or "Yankee Clipper" or "Sultan of Swat." Musial was definitely "The Man" when it came to batting feats; his stats are awesome, and in his day no one disputed that he was the best hitter in the senior circuit, as Ted Williams was in the junior. Yet he never seems to receive the same recognition as some of his peers, flashier perhaps in their style of play. This quiet composition of Musial treasures contains a Silver Slugger Award and an MVP plaque, one each of several he won, but it also contains such humble items as his spikes, stirrups, and locker-room stool.

"The Man" is one of only six players to have more than 400 homers *and* 3,000 hits. When he retired he was the major league leader in lifetime total bases, and he topped the National League in hits, games played, and runs scored. (Pete Rose went on to pass him in all three categories; interestingly, Musial's final hit was a line drive past a diving rookie second baseman—Pete Rose.) He had a curious peekaboo stance that uncoiled in a corkscrew swing that swatted line drives everywhere. He won seven batting titles. Five times he led the National League in runs. And he was surprisingly spry on the base paths, although base stealing wasn't considered necessary in his day: nine times he hit more than forty doubles, three times more than fifty, and five times he led the league in triples, twice hitting twenty. In 1948 he led the league with his .376 batting average, 230 hits, 46 doubles, 18 triples, 135 runs scored, 131 RBIs, an on-base average of .450, and a slugging average of .702. What did he not lead in? Home runs—his thirty-nine was just one behind the league leaders.

Musial was born in Donora, Pennsylvania, a steel town southeast of Pittsburgh (Ken Griffey and Ken Griffey, Jr., would also be born there). He began his career as a pitcher, but an arm injury had the Cardinals close to releasing him in 1941. Given a second chance to play outfield in Class C ball, he began to show the form that would make him "The Man." In eighty-seven games there he slugged twenty-six homers and was bumped up to AAA ball with Rochester late in the year. At the tail end of the season the Cards called him up; in a dozen games he hit .426. He wouldn't see the south side of .300 for eighteen years. After three seasons below the .300 mark, he made a sensational comeback at age forty-one to hit .330.

Musial won his first Most Valuable Player Award (called the Kenesaw Mountain Landis Memorial Award since 1944—why doesn't anyone ever call it that?) in 1943, his second in 1946, and his third in that memorable season of 1948. Then he finished second in MVP voting three years in a row. Consistency, thy name is Musial. One stat makes the point: when he retired after the 1963 season, he had exactly the same number of hits on the road as at home.

—★—

The year is 1949. Jackie Robinson wins the MVP in the National League, Ted Williams in the American. The Dodgers and the Yankees go to the World Series. George Kell of the Tigers and Ralph Kiner of the Pirates stay home; well, they're a big part of the year in baseball, too. These bats tell the story.

George Kell was the best third baseman in the American League in 1949, and he would remain so for years to come. He routinely led all American League third basemen in assists, fielding percentage, and chances. He was also a line-drive hitter with some extra-base power. He was no Ted Williams, but in 1949 Kell kept him from a third Triple Crown, winning the batting average title by less than two ten thousandths of a point. In the closest such race ever, the final numbers were .342911 for Kell, .342756 for Ted.

The other bat commemorates a man who had a short but extraordinarily explosive career. Ralph Kiner came to the woeful Pittsburgh Pirates in 1946. Playing in cavernous Forbes Field, the young slugger swatted twenty-three homers to lead the league. The next year Pirate management made some adjustments: they signed Hank Greenberg, who was ready to retire, for one final season, then moved in the left-field fence thirty feet, creating a bull-pen area.

The more homer-friendly space was dubbed "Greenberg Gardens," and Greenberg tagged twenty-five homers, but more important, he tutored Kiner in the art of the long ball. Ralph responded with fifty-one, the most of any National Leaguer since Hack Wilson's fifty-six in 1930. Though he dropped to forty the next year, in 1949 he reached his high-water mark of fifty-four. In fact, Kiner led the National League in homers every year from 1946 through 1952—a seven-year string unmatched even by Babe Ruth, who is the only man ever to hit home runs more frequently than Kiner. The silver-plated bat shown is from Kiner's 1948 campaign.

Both Kell and Kiner became broadcasters, Kell for the Tigers, Kiner for the brand-new Mets in 1962. Their bats crossed in 1949, and their fame linked at Cooperstown, where Kiner was inducted in 1975 and Kell eight years afterward.

—★—

Satchel Paige must have been born old. Either that, or what he saw early in his life blessed him with the wisdom of age and it shone in his eyes. He was forced by the color of his skin to watch organized baseball from the outside until he was at least forty-two years old (the oldest rookie ever). His homespun philosophy ("Avoid fried meats, which angry up the blood." "Don't look back, something may be gaining on you.") has therefore become a larger aspect of his legend than his pitching feats, recorded sparsely in dozens of years of Negro League and barnstorming play.

Satchel claimed to have pitched between 130 and 160 games a year for all that time (his custom was to start a game, pitch a couple of innings, then give way to a collaborator like Hilton Smith). He had great stories of his prowess and his range of pitches. "I got bloopers, loopers and droopers. I got a jump ball, a be ball, a screw ball, a wobbly ball, a whipsy-dipsy-do, a hurry-up ball, a nothin' ball and a bat dodger." His best, though, was the "be ball," named "'cause it 'be' right where I want it." One Paige story is that he walked the bases full in a World Series game just so he could end the contest by striking out Josh Gibson, a former teammate and the Negro Leagues' greatest slugger. His pinpoint control was the secret to his long-lived success and huge income, according to legend more than that of any white player except Ruth.

But happy as he was to be the king of black baseball, Paige was distressed when the Dodgers made Jackie Robinson the first of his race to reach the modern major leagues. "I'd been the guy who started all that big talk about letting us in the big time. I'd been the one the white boys wanted to barnstorm against." His first complete game in the majors, in 1948, was in front of 51,000 fans at Comiskey Park. In August of that year he threw his second complete game, this time for 78,000 appreciative hometown fans in Cleveland. He even got to pitch two thirds of an inning in the World Series that year.

Integration pioneer Bill Veeck (the story is told that the owners kept him from buying the Phillies in the 1940s because he planned to sign a lot of Negro Leaguers) brought Paige with him from Cleveland to the Browns in 1951, and he averaged more than forty appearances a season there for three years. (It's delightful to contemplate that juvenile Palmer Cox brownie adorning the sleeve of this superannuated Brown.) He returned in 1965, at age fifty-nine or so, to throw three scoreless innings for the Kansas City A's against the Red Sox; only one man, Carl Yastrzemski, got a hit off him.

———★———

E ven though he baffled everyone from sportswriters to congressmen with his stream-of-consciousness double-talk, Casey Stengel had both a keen baseball mind and, by the time he retired, more than fifty years of major league experience to back it up. His name must come up in any discussion of the greatest baseball manager (who else won nine pennants in eleven years?), greatest clown, greatest thinker, and, ultimately, greatest survivor. Asked how best to describe himself, an elderly Casey reflected a moment and said, "I'm a man that's been up and down."

His nickname was "K.C.," for the town where he grew up, but it quickly was transformed into "Casey," the ultimate baseball handle. Having tossed aside a career opportunity in left-handed dentistry, Stengel broke in with Brooklyn in 1912, when Christy Mathewson and Honus Wagner were still superstars. For one day he imagined he might ascend to that level, as he broke in with a four-for-four performance against Wagner's Pirates, topping off his day by crossing over to bat right-handed and drawing a walk. He became a huge favorite of the Brooklyn fans, even more so when he inaugurated Ebbets Field the following season with a game-winning home run in an exhibition contest against, of all teams, the Yankees, with whom he would at last reach the heights.

Stengel was an inconsistent player, so he wore out his welcome mat at Brooklyn, Pittsburgh, and Philadelphia before being traded to the Giants in July 1921. His manager at Brooklyn, "Bad Bill" Dahlen, had noticed that Casey hit right-handers a whole lot better than he did lefties. The idea

of platooning was already a staple of John McGraw's tactics, so when Casey was summoned to the Polo Grounds he knew his playing time would shrink, but he didn't care; he was rejuvenated by going from a tailender to a team on its way to the World Series. "Wake up, muscles," Stengel said to himself. "We're in New York now." Casey hit .368 in part-time duty in 1922 and .339 the next season. But he had his greatest moments as a player in the 1923 World Series, in which the Giants were seeking a third consecutive victory over the upstart Yankees and Babe Ruth.

In Game 1, the teams were tied at four when Stengel batted with two outs in the top of the ninth. He smashed a drive into deep left center and began to run full tilt. But a heel pad he wore to cushion an aching foot came loose in his shoe. Stengel thought his shoe was falling off, but he wouldn't stop running. Damon Runyon immortalized Casey's antic hobble in his column the next day. Runyon thought Stengel was old and wheezing; Casey was just trying to keep his shoe on. He reached home with an inside-the-park homer that won the game. Two days later he hit another homer, this one out of the park, the only run in the Giant victory and, in true Casey style, thumbed his nose at the booing Yankee fans as he rounded third.

After Casey's two final big-league seasons in Boston, team owner Judge Emil Fuchs bought a minor league team in Worcester and made him the playing manager there. It was the beginning of his second professional baseball career, the more important one. After six years of managing the Toledo Mudhens he was hired by Brooklyn as a coach in 1932 and was elevated to the manager's post in 1934. The club was terrible, Stengel couldn't make chicken salad out of chicken feathers, and he was canned, which proved the same story later on, after six years at the helm of the hapless Boston Braves.

Aging and seemingly on a treadmill to oblivion, he spent six more years bouncing around the minors, managing Milwaukee, Kansas City, and Oakland, where he spent some very happy and productive years taking a ragtag bunch of fading big-league stars and green kids to the Pacific Coast League title in 1948. Even though he was widely credited with a great performance as manager, when the Yankees signed him in 1949, there was something of a revolt by players and press, who remembered Casey as nothing more than a good-natured clown who had joked his way out of the majors. Casey was fifty-nine years old and had to prove himself. All he did was take a hobbled team of veterans, for whom only one outfielder was able to play one hundred games, and defeat the Boston Red Sox on the final day of the season to win the flag. It took just five games for the Yanks to dispatch the Dodgers in the World Series, and for the following four years, the Yankees repeated as Series champions. They finished second in 1954, then won another four pennants before falling to third in 1959.

Stengel won again in 1960, but his World Series managerial decisions were widely criticized when the Yanks were startled in a seven-game loss to the Pirates, and Casey was given his walking papers. His take on the situation: "I'll never make the mistake of being seventy again." In 1962 the expansion Mets suited up for play, and Casey provided the world with four more seasons of delightful quotes and perplexing strategy.

How much heartache exudes from this little pin! There was a time in baseball, and it wasn't so long ago, when there were no divisions, no League Championship Series, no "wild cards." If you wanted to be in the World Series and therefore have a chance to become that season's champion, your team had to be the best in your league, over the grueling march of 154 or 162 games. No second chance. No percentage points. No tiebreaking criteria. First, or back home.

More often than not, the pennant winner locked up the flag with a week or more to go in the season. But on rare occasions the final week saw two teams scrambling for the title, sometimes playing each other in tense do-or-die matches. Even more rare were three- or four-team battles. This World Series press pin was never used; like other franchises in the same situation, the Phillies were in the hunt in the final days of September and thus had to commission the pins for credentialing the visiting press, but the team just fell short at the finish.

Late in 1964 manager Gene Mauch seemed to have his Phils where he wanted them: six and a half games in front with a dozen games to go. Superstar-to-be Dick Allen and reliable Johnny Callison would finish with sixty homers between them. Chris Short and Jim Bunning were having fine years on the mound. Of their final twelve games, the Phils horrified not only their fans but all of baseball as they lost the first ten. As the slide deepened Mauch panicked, starting Bunning and Short three times each on just two days' rest. It didn't work. The gasping Phils won their next-to-last game and had a chance to tie for first if they could win their final effort and the Mets topped the Cardinals. The Phils won gloriously, 10–0, but the Mets didn't help.

(Gene Mauch never made it to the World Series in all his years of managing that followed. In fact, the fates tortured him once more in 1986, in the ALCS, in the ninth inning of Game 5: his Angels were one strike away from advancing to the World Series when Dave Henderson hit a monumental home run for the Red Sox.)

— ★ —

This beautifully composed image takes Willie Mays from his first contract with the New York Giants in 1951, when he made far less money for the season than utility infielders today make per game, to his glorious (although, in retrospect, amazingly few) seasons in the Polo Grounds; on through the fifteen years in San Francisco (shown here is his 1972 road jersey); and concluding with his sentimental return to New York in 1973, marked by final appearances in the All-Star Game (the pin depicted is his twenty-fourth, a record of enduring achievement), and an Amazin' World Series. In between he was the most exciting baseball player anyone has ever seen, and he left his footprints all over the record books. The bat you see is the one with which he collected his three thousandth hit; the ball is from his six hundredth home run; the flag that forms the backdrop carried the Giants' fame atop a distant stadium. And the glove, well, it made "The Catch," of which there is more to be said.

Mays had taken the Giants to the World Series back in 1951; they lost to the Yankees, who had a rookie of their own named Mantle. In 1952–1953 the "Say Hey Kid" gave his all for Uncle Sam, and the Giants went nowhere. But in 1954 he returned to patrol center field in the Polo Grounds, led the league in batting at .345, added 41 homers and 110 RBIs, and the Giants swept the mighty Cleveland Indians (111–43) in the World Series. The Giants moved to San Francisco for the 1958 season, where they are still looking to win their first world's title since that epic season, 1954.

With the new technologies available today, if you want to see a whole basketful of great defensive plays you can rent a video or pop in a CD-ROM. Which is why The Catch—the ball that Willie Mays snagged over his shoulder off Vic Wertz's bat in the first game of the 1954 World Series—has such historical significance. It was the first such play captured by the movie cameras. (If you're wondering, I don't believe Al Gionfriddo's catch in the 1947 World Series can be mentioned in the same breath as The Catch.)

There had been great catches before, of course. Mays himself said that the 1954 catch wasn't even his personal best (but what about that throw?). Since then we have been treated to Kenny Lofton and Jim Edmonds and Ken Griffey, Jr., and the 11 P.M. wrap-ups provide a numbing dose of improbable dives and leaps and snags. But in 1954, when Mays made The Catch, he created an eternal symbol of extraordinary athleticism and, recognizable only in retrospect, genius.

Mays was an utterly complete talent; his speed made him both an outfield legend and a base-running demon; his arm was outstanding—some say the best ever; and as a batter he had much more power than his smallish frame would indicate. Only he and Ralph Kiner ever hit more than fifty homers a season more than once in the National League. Willie's lifetime total of 660 is seventy-four more than the next guy. He's third in lifetime total bases, too, and in the top ten in hits and RBIs. But for all his great statistics, no one can describe to the fans of a future generation the thrill of seeing Willie Mays. Fortunately, graybeards like me will simply refer them to The Catch.

TO DATE

No bat ever caused a bigger brouhaha than this one. It happened on July 24, 1983, and took several days to sort out. George Brett of the Kansas City Royals was batting against flamethrowing Yankee reliever Goose Gossage in the top of the ninth with his team down by a run, two men out, and a Royal on base. Brett timed one of Goose's fastballs and ripped it into Yankee Stadium's right-field

stands. Royals lead, 5–4. But what's this? Yank manager Billy Martin wants Brett's bat; he's showing it to home-plate ump Tim McClelland. McClelland takes the bat, lays it down next to home plate, then raises his arm and signals "Out!" The rules say that no bat shall have pine tar more than eighteen inches from the handle, so as not to transfer a sticky substance to the batted ball. By comparing the tar to the seventeen-inch-wide plate, McClelland rules Brett has used an illegal bat and is therefore out. The game is over. Yanks win. But Brett, usually the most congenial of fellows, goes berserk. He charges toward McClelland at home ("I can still see his bulging eyes and red face," McClelland recalled much later), and it takes several men to restrain him.

How could this be? How could a hitter as great as George Brett be cheating? Actually, he wasn't. The Royals protested and league president Lee MacPhail upheld their protest, saying, "The umpire's ruling, while technically defensible, is not in accord with the intent or spirit of the rules and the rules do not provide that the hitter shall be called out for excessive use of pine tar." The game was to be replayed from that point on, later in the season.

But illegal bats have been a part of baseball for a while. Some bats have been shaved down one side to make for a flatter hitting surface. Others have had nails driven in to make them harder. Norm Cash won a batting title with a corked bat in 1961. (Cork reduces the weight of the bat barrel, thus permitting greater bat speed and harder hits.) Amos Otis admitted to playing the last fourteen years of his career with a bat full of cork. Even legitimate slugmeister Albert Belle was suspended for using a corked bat. So was Billy Hatcher. In 1975 Bill Buckner and Ted Simmons were caught with bats into which they had cut fine grooves to create greater distance. The most exciting discovery of a tampered bat probably happened in 1974 when Graig Nettles broke his bat and six Super Balls came flying out of it.

— ★ —

It's been called "The Curse of the Bambino"—the fact that the Boston Red Sox have never won a World Series since they performed the unforgivable sin of selling Babe Ruth. But as of eleven-thirty or so, Eastern time, on the night of October 25, 1986, it seemed to be ending. The Sox were two runs up and three outs away from winning the World Series against the Mets. Reliever Calvin Schiraldi retired the first two batters. The electronic message board congratulated the Red Sox on their impending World Series championship. The champagne bottles were being wheeled into the Red Sox locker room. But, in Roger Angell's palindromic encapsulation of the situation, the great victory was to be "Not so, Boston."

Singles by Gary Carter and Kevin Mitchell put men on first and second. Then the wearer of this cap, Ray Knight, blooped another single to center and a run came home. Bob Stanley's wild pitch to Mookie Wilson tied the game and allowed Knight to move up. Then Wilson topped a roller toward first, and Bill Buckner saw it squirt between his legs, waking up the echoes of Fred Merkle and Fred Snodgrass and, who knows, Fred Mertz. Knight came in to score the winning run from second, smacking his hands to his batting helmet as if to convey that his brain couldn't absorb the enormity of the moment.

And the Mets won the Series two days later, in Game 7. You can run the film in your mind and see this cap bouncing on Knight's head as he tore home, and you can stifle a moan or mouth a silent "Yesssss!"

— ★ —

"Lefty" used to be one of the most common baseball nicknames. It implied not just the arm the person threw with, but also an attitude, one somewhat at odds with conventional thinking. All that seemed to go away when Steve Carlton took over the nickname in the early 1970s. He made it his own. And rightfully (what did you expect me to say—leftfully?) so. Carlton was always aloof, answering only to himself. He refused to talk to the media for years. He maintained an unusual conditioning ritual, involving acts such as forcing his hand into a barrel of rice and using martial arts techniques and even a little Zen meditation. Three years into his career, he developed a hard slider, which became one of the nastiest pitches in the history of the game.

In 1968 he fanned nineteen Mets, the most strikeouts in the National League in eighty-five years, although he lost the game, 4–3. He won twenty-seven games for the last-place Phils in 1972, which is especially remarkable when you consider the Phils in total won only fifty-nine. These are his four Cy Young Awards (no pitcher has ever won more, al-

though Greg Maddux is trying). The award design itself looks more like a hood ornament than something that evokes the greatness of its namesake. Carlton spent the end of his career bouncing around among the Giants, White Sox, Indians, and Twins. But who was going to tell him he'd lost his stuff?

When he did retire, only Warren Spahn among fellow lefties had won more games; only Nolan Ryan had struck out more hitters. Despite Lefty's eccentric notions, and despite his shunning the press during his career, the Baseball Writers Association voted him into the Hall of Fame in 1994, the first year he was eligible.

— ★ —

After watching Mike Schmidt complete his first full season in a big-league uniform, in 1973, you would have given pretty good odds that he wouldn't last long enough to outhomer Dick Groat, let alone Mickey Mantle. (Schmitty's final total: 548.) His average of .196 that year was the worst of anyone in the bigs who played full-time. But as Schmidt tells the story, after that season he was playing winter ball and found a new, more relaxed swing. "That sucker went off my bat for a mile," he said. Mike brought the swing north with him and won the National League home run title that year and the next. And the next. He'd lead them all in long balls five more times before he retired. And he was a sensational fielder, too; only Brooks Robinson won more Gold Gloves at third. No less than Pete Rose called Schmidt the greatest player he had ever seen. The 1981 season, split in two by a players' strike, could have been Schmidt's best ever. His final stats led the abbreviated campaign in runs, homers, RBIs, walks, on-base average, and slugging percentage.

— ★ —

In 1955, just his second full season, Al Kaline won the batting title with a .340 average (he also belted 27 homers and knocked in 102 runs). He had never played an inning of minor league baseball, and he wasn't yet twenty-one years old. The kid played on and on, through twenty-two seasons, until he became a Detroit institution. Though his career never again reached those lofty heights, he became known and loved for his consistency—averages over .290, homers in the twenty to twenty-five range, and a Gold Glove year in, year out. Kaline's team was hardly ever a contender. In 1961 the Tigers won 101 games, but the Yankees won 109. The Tigers got tough in 1968 and took the American League flag by a dozen games. But Kaline had had his arm broken by a pitch in May, and by the time he returned, his right-field job had been taken over by Jim Northrup. Manager Mayo Smith wanted Kaline in the World Series, so he moved right fielder Mickey Stanley to shortstop and Northrup to center. Kaline hit .379 in the World Series, with two homers and some superb defense, and the Tigers topped the Cards in seven games.

The years began to wear on Kaline, and he became a designated hitter in 1974. Tiger fans groused about losing their right fielder, but his range had diminished and he had become prone to injury. As a DH, Kaline registered 558 at-bats that season, the most he had had since 1961. And on September 24 that year he used this bat to hit a double off Dave McNally for his three thousandth hit. When he was elected to the Hall of Fame in 1980, he was one of that incredibly rare breed who had gone from high school to the Hall wearing just one uniform. Kaline was always a Tiger.

roken blossoms. In the days after Mickey Mantle's death on August 13, 1995, his fans left these flowers, this poem, and other modest, heartfelt tributes beneath his plaque in the Hall of Fame Gallery. The Mick was sixty-three when he succumbed to liver cancer—too soon, but not truly an athlete dying young; he had outlived Babe Ruth and Jackie Robinson by ten years. We mourned as much for ourselves, for a vital part inside of us that died, as we did for him.

We remember where we were and, more important, who we were when "The Commerce Comet" picked up a random bat (the Loren Babe model shown here), strode to the plate at Griffith Stadium one afternoon in 1953, and parked a Chuck Stobbs pitch 565 feet away. We remember his astonishing blend of power, speed, and grace; his dash into left-center field to snare a Gil Hodges line drive and keep Don Larsen's perfect game alive. We remember his chase of the Babe's record in 1961, when he kept pace with Roger Maris until a September injury forced him to the sideline. We remember his baseball cards, and his Maypo commercial, and that silly movie he made. We remember the Copacabana scrape, and the drinking and carousing, and the bad business deals he got into.

We remember the pain he endured, from the bone inflammation that almost cost him his leg as a teenager to the torn-up knee in his rookie year to the wrecked shoulder and the wounds that the yards of tape could never heal, especially his belief that he, like his father, would die young. "If I'd have known I was going to live this long," he would say, half jokingly, "I would've taken better care of myself." Yes, we will remember him.

"As a ballplayer," President Clinton said after the announcement of his death, "Mickey inspired generations of fans with his power and grit. As a man, he faced up to his responsibilities and alerted generations to come to the dangers of alcohol abuse. He will be remembered for excellence on the baseball field and the honor and redemption he brought to the end of his life." Maybe in some larger way his passing even served to redeem baseball itself. The ticket stub shown here was for the last game the Yankees played during Mantle's lifetime; within hours

of its end, Mickey would meet his. The game took place a year to the day after baseball shut down in 1994, the season without an end.

Heroes provide role models through their achievements and their ability to overcome adversity. Their greatness enlarges us all. The greatest achievement of Mickey Mantle's life was not his home runs or MVP trophies or World Series heroics; it was the dignity he brought to his death when he said to America's youth, "Don't be like me." As Lou Gehrig's death did so much for the funding, treatment and, one day, cure of ALS, Mickey Mantle has done more than anyone for the cause of organ donation.

His exploits are on display in the record books, and his likeness is on a plaque at the Hall of Fame; his legacy, not so easily captured, is everywhere.

— ★ —

Some teams seem never to be able to find a third baseman; others move their spares to first or right. Some teams can never locate a decent leadoff hitter; others have them scattered throughout the lineup. And every team always needs another left-handed pitcher. But there are also traditions of excellence in one position that last with one team for decades, with the predecessor handing off to the successor as cleanly as a quarterback to a runner. From 1936 through 1966 it was either Joe DiMaggio or Mickey Mantle in center for the Yankees. Luke Appling was at short for the White Sox from 1932 through 1949 (although out for a couple of war years), then Chico Carrasquel handled the position admirably for six seasons before Luis Aparicio moved in and played Hall of Fame style there for seven more.

This jersey was worn by the centerpiece in a three-person string of great left fielders for the Boston Red Sox. Ted Williams had handled the position for the Red Sox (with time out to serve his country) from 1939 through 1960; Jim Rice took over in 1975 and, with some time interspersed at DH, played with his back to the Green Monster until 1988, with a final season as a full-time DH.

In between Rice and Williams stands Carl Yastrzemski. That first year the phenom was slumping, and having to follow in the footsteps of one of the greatest hitters of all time wasn't making things any easier. The Sox tracked down Williams, fishing in New Brunswick, and he came to Boston to put

Yaz's mind at ease. Then Carl proceeded to put together a Hall of Fame career of his own, including three batting titles and a Triple Crown in that heart-stopping season of 1967, when the Sox battled three teams down to the last day to take the flag and Yaz was driving in the big runs every single night. But while Williams strove to be the greatest hitter who ever lived, and he might well have been, Yaz never thought he was very good at all. He went about his job with a fierceness, a tension that might have made him the great player he was—or he just might have been great without all the worry.

— ★ —

Only Santa Claus owns a whole month as completely as Reginald Martinez Jackson owns October. Although he was a fine outfielder for four teams (he could run and throw well enough in his early years to play center field, which few fans re-

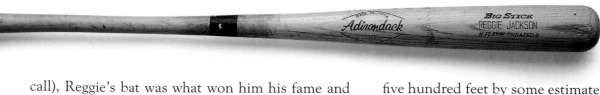

call), Reggie's bat was what won him his fame and his name: "Mr. October." The label was applied derisively by teammate Thurman Munson, but Reggie lived up to it, and, as Dizzy Dean used to say, "It ain't bragging if you can do it."

Yankee Stadium, Game 6 of the 1977 World Series, Yankees leading the Dodgers three games to two, Dodgers leading 3–2 in the fourth, when Reggie stepped to the plate against Burt Hooton with Munson on first. The first pitch was deposited into the right-field bleachers and the Yanks had recaptured the lead. The next inning, one on and two out

and, on the first pitch from Elias Sosa, Jackson repeated the feat. Another long two-run homer. The Yankee fans were in absolute heaven. Now the score was 7–3. Then, once more for legend's sake. In the last of the eighth, Charlie Hough threw a knuckle curve to Jackson that didn't do either, and this ball went even farther, five hundred feet by some estimates, to dead center. Three home runs on three swings to win the World Series! Jackson smote a total of five homers in that Series, setting the all-time record.

That wasn't the only superstar Series for Reggie. In twenty-seven Series games he hit ten homers, knocked in twenty-four runs, and batted .357. He homered six times in League Championship Series play, and on that fateful afternoon in 1978 when the Red Sox had a last gasp at winning the division title in a one-game playoff, his home run provided the margin of victory.

———★———

When Ted Williams first saw Johnny Bench, he autographed a ball for the youngster. "To Johnny Bench," it read. "A future Hall of Famer, for sure."

Ted's keen eye wasn't limited to the strike zone. Bench is that most highly prized phenomenon in baseball: a superb defensive, power-hitting catcher. And he didn't grow slowly into stardom. His first full season with the Cincinnati Reds, at just twenty years old, he batted .276, belted fifteen homers, and set a record for games caught by a rookie—154. Not surprisingly, he was named Rookie of the Year. Bench developed a special catching style, using a hinged-pocket catcher's mitt, which let him snag pitches with just one hand. It prevented the rash of broken fingers and torn nails that typically plagued most other backstops, and it kept Bench's bat healthy and in the lineup. In fact, he set records for durability: in his first thirteen seasons he caught more than one hundred games every year. In 1970 he swatted 45 homers and knocked in 148 runs to lead the National League, batting .293 at the same time.

Although a solid glove man and astute handler of pitchers, his defensive signature was the cannon attached to his right shoulder. His arm was magnificent, perhaps the best any catcher ever had. He didn't throw out many potential base stealers, though; few of them even bothered to try. Moved to third and first late in his career, Bench knew

when it was time to quit. He refused a million-dollar contract (big news then) because he couldn't play up to his previous benchmark. It wasn't enough for him that nobody else could, either.

———★———

This may be the ugliest of the jerseys Gaylord Perry wore in his travels with eight different teams in twenty-two years in the big leagues, but he did win a Cy Young Award while wearing it, thus becoming the only man to win one in each league. He finished with 314 victories and was elected to the Hall of Fame in 1991.

So why did he bounce around so much? Well, Gaylord Perry was somewhat . . . elusive . . . slippery . . . evasive. The title of his autobiography, *Me and the Spitter*, gives a clue. He threw a spitball, all right, but it was the *possibility* that he might throw one that he really used to his advantage. He was in a constant fidget on the mound, touching every part of his face, belt, belly, shoulders, and arms before every pitch; no one could tell when he was loading one up.

———★———

As a Brooklyn Dodger, Gil Hodges was the quietest man on a quiet team. He drove in plenty of runs and hit his share of homers and was, like Joe Adcock and Ted Kluszewski, the prototypical 1950s big slugging first baseman. Not as huge as his peers, he was nonetheless usually considered the strongest, with hands so big some said he didn't really need a first baseman's mitt. Gil was a smoothie around first base, graceful and agile, one of the best ever. He had come to Ebbets Field as a catcher, but Leo Durocher gave that job to Roy Campanella in 1948 and asked Hodges to try first base. That move sent Jackie Robinson to his more natural position, second base, and solidified the Dodger infield for the glory years of 1949–1956.

Gil spent his last two years as a part-timer on Casey Stengel's expansion Mets of 1962 and 1963, splitting first-base duties with "Marvelous Marv" Throneberry. Perhaps his grim experience of going 0 for 21 in the 1952 World Series prepared him for life with losing teams, for after he retired as a player he went on to manage the expansion Washington

Senators for five years. Then the Mets acquired him in a "trade" ($100,000 and a pitcher) and in 1968 made him their manager.

Previous Met helmsmen had mastered the art of comedy: Casey Stengel (who said to Tracy Stallard of his 1963 team, "After this season they're gonna tear this place [the Polo Grounds] down; the way you're going the right-field stands will be gone already"), and Wes Westrum (after a close game he said, "That was a real cliff dweller"). But Hodges, not exactly a jolly sort, was brought in to win. He instilled discipline and inspired performance. His 1968 team improved by a dozen games. The next year brought two equally implausible events: man walking on the moon and the Mets winning the World Series. The Shea Stadium version of Mission Control was named Gil Hodges.

———★———

These balls prompt some old schoolboy musings. You know the Philosophy 101 stumper, "If a tree falls in the forest, and no one is there to hear it, does it make a sound?" Here's the answer, in baseball terms. In 1972, when Roberto Clemente knocked in run number 1,273 of his career with this ball, the Pirates maintained that he had tied Pie Traynor for the all-time Pirate record. He hadn't. Honus Wagner had 1,732 RBIs, 1,475 of them with Pittsburgh. But many runs old Hans drove in were not "official" because league authorities didn't deem them worth counting until 1920, and Honus drove in his last run in 1917. So was this ball rendered meaningless? Not at all. Remove the number, and you still have an artifact of a man who would not leave many more behind him. On December 31 of that year Roberto Clemente lost his life in a plane crash while bringing aid to the earthquake victims of Managua, Nicaragua.

The other ball memorializes the three thousandth strikeout by Ferguson Jenkins, a quiet man who only once in nineteen seasons led his league in K's. He surely wasn't as fast as Rob Dibble or Steve Dalkowski or even such notables as Sandy Koufax and Bob Gibson—yet he had more strikeouts. Does that make him a strikeout pitcher? This gets to what a pitcher's job is, precisely—to conquer batters with the decisiveness of a strikeout or to prevent runs and win games? And it gets directly to what earns a man a plaque in the Baseball Hall of Fame: durability, longevity, hard work, and consistency—all qualities worth prizing over the sizzle of sudden, peacock success. Jenkins had one of the more quiet Hall of Fame careers, quietly great. There's much to be admired in that.

———★———

The man who wore this Pirates number 21 uniform is still referred to in Pittsburgh simply as "The Great One." Roberto Clemente was more than a supremely talented baseball player; he played the game with a passion and brilliance that heightened the intensity of both teams. Roger Angell described him "playing a kind of baseball that none of us had really seen before—throwing and running and hitting at something close to the level of absolute perfection, playing to win but also playing the game almost as if it were a form of punishment for everyone else on

the field." Never really appreciated on the national scene, Clemente smoldered while fans recognized Aaron and Robinson and Mays. Until, that is, the 1971 World Series, in which he made his own seven-game statement of personal excellence. Not only did he bat almost a hundred points higher than anyone else on either team, collecting a dozen hits, but no one exceeded his doubles and homers. Perhaps more important, he stunned Baltimore base runners into submission with one sensational throw. "I play this way all the time," he told reporters. But Clemente's passions extended beyond the playing field. A true humanitarian who did his good deeds with no thought of self-promotion, he gave or generated hundreds of thousands of dollars in charity for many people, especially the children of his homeland of Puerto Rico.

In 1972 Clemente's Pirates fell to the Cincinnati Reds on a wild pitch in the final inning of the National League Championship Series, so they didn't return to the World Series. Clemente, at age thirty-eight, had just finished his eighteenth season, posting a batting average of .300 or better for the twelfth time in the last thirteen years. He was actively accumulating donations of money, food, and medical supplies for the victims of an earthquake in Nicaragua when he heard that some of the donations were being pirated by unscrupulous people. So he boarded a tired old plane full of supplies headed for Nicaragua on New Year's Eve, 1972. It crashed shortly after takeoff, killing all on board. The ticket stub is from September 30 of that year, Clemente's last regular-season game, in which he belted a double off the Mets' Jon Matlack for hit number 3,000 and, as it turned out, his final hit.

—★—

The Orioles discovered Brooks Robinson playing second base in a church league in Little Rock, Arkansas, and signed him after he finished high school in 1955. "He couldn't run, couldn't throw, and—when he first came up at eighteen, nineteen years old—he couldn't hit," Yankee shortstop Tony Kubek recalled. Even in later years, after he was universally acclaimed as the greatest third baseman in the game, teammate Jim Palmer described him as "the worst athlete I ever saw—from the waist down."

Ah, but from the waist up, that was another matter. Fast reflexes, fast hands, quick release on the throw—Brooksie had it all. He led the Orioles to the World Series in 1966, when they swept the Dodgers, and in 1969, when they were shocked by four straight losses to the Mets after an opening-game victory. But in 1970 the Orioles returned to their winning ways against the Cincinnati Reds, and Robinson put on a veritable fielding clinic. That year had seen him win his eleventh straight Gold Glove (he would win it five more consecutive times), so it was hardly a surprise when, in Game 1, Robby made an outstanding play. With the score tied, the Reds' Lee May walloped what looked to be a sure double over third, but Robinson fielded the ball deep in foul territory behind the bag and threw him out.

But the show was only beginning. The next day he made two diving catches to steal sure hits from Bobby Tolan and May again (the latter he turned into a double play). In the first inning of Game 3, with two men on and nobody out he snagged a tough high chopper from Tony Perez and converted it into a twin killing. The next inning he charged a swinging bunt off the bat of Tommy Helms, grabbed it bare-handed, and threw Helms out. In the sixth, another dive to his left took a base hit away from Johnny Bench. In the final game Bench smashed a line drive to Robinson's right.

(b) The Club's right to renew this contract, as provided in subparagraph (a) of this paragraph 10, and the promise of the Player not to play otherwise than with the Club have been taken into consideration in determining the amount payable under paragraph 2 hereof.
11. This contract is subject to federal or state legislation, regulations, executive or other official orders or other governmental action, now or hereafter in effect respecting military, naval, air or other governmental service, which may directly or indirectly affect the Player, Club or the League and subject also to the right of the Commissioner to suspend the operation of this contract during any national emergency.
Commissioner
12. The term "Commissioner" wherever used in this contract shall be deemed to mean the Commissioner designated under the Major League Agreement, or in the case of a vacancy in the office of Commissioner, the Executive Council or such other body or person or persons as shall be designated in the Major League Agreement to exercise the powers and duties of the Commissioner during such vacancy.
Supplemental Agreements
The Club and the Player covenant that this contract fully sets forth all understandings and agreements between them, and agree that no other understandings or agreements, whether heretofore or hereafter made, shall be valid, recognizable, or of any effect whatsoever, unless expressly set forth in a new or supplemental contract executed by the Player and the Club (acting by its president, or such other officer as shall have been thereunto duly authorized by the president or Board of Directors, as evidenced by a certificate filed of record with the League President and Commissioner) and complying with the Major and Major-Minor League Rules.
Special Covenants
PLAYER TO RECEIVE $3000.00 CASH WHEN CONTRACT IS APPROVED BY PRESIDENT OF AMERICAN LEAGUE
Approval
This contract or any supplement hereto shall not be valid or effective unles
League President.
Signed in duplicate this 1 day of June
Brooks C. Robinson Jr. (Player)
By
106 Denison St.
(Home address of Player)
Social Security No. 432 66 0691
JUN 3 1955 195
Approved William Harridge
President, American League of Professional Baseball Clubs
Brooks C. Robinson Sr. Father
BOYHOOD PHOTOS OF THE STARS
BROOKS ROBINSON

Another diving catch into foul territory. The Reds had seen potential rallies snuffed and extra-base hits disappear into Robinson's glove over and over again. He had dived, he had charged, he had gone to his left, to his right, deep into the hole, and behind the bag. They were utterly demoralized. Appropriately, the final out of the Series was recorded when Pat Corrales made the familiar mistake of hitting the ball to Brooks. Oh, and Brooks hit a little, too—a pair of home runs, a .429 batting average, and a team-leading six RBIs.

From little acorns mighty O's doth grow. Brooks had to have his father countersign his contract because he was still a minor, but he became a major leaguer three months later. Despite two subsequent dips back down into the minors, Brooks went on to a fabulously long and productive career in Baltimore, where he remains one of the most popular men in town.

—★—

The difference between sustained excellence and a great moment is further illustrated in these two bats. The black one was used by Willie McGee to swat two homers in Game 3 of the 1982 World Series and single-handedly win the game for St. Louis. A classic moment, and an early one in a fine career. But the other belonged to Billy Williams, who, like his longtime Cub teammate Ferguson Jenkins, was a superb player for a long time who *never* played in a World Series. Williams won just one batting title and never won a home run crown or MVP. For a long time, people like Billy Williams weren't rated very highly. We wanted supernovas—Mark Fidrych, Joe Charboneau—players who were impossibly good for a short while.

Interestingly, baseball (and sports in general) had previously rewarded the opposite. The legendary nineteenth-century racehorse Eclipse (who gave his name to the Louisville baseball club of the American Association) was undefeated in his career, even though he had lost several races. His record was untarnished because in his day a horse had to take two out of three heats to win a match, and you could beat Eclipse once but you couldn't beat him twice in the same day. Recently, sports fans seem to have turned back the clock, prizing the time-honored qualities. Cal Ripken's glorious effort in breaking Lou Gehrig's "unbreakable" consecutive-games streak was the biggest sports story of 1995. Nolan Ryan's unparalleled longevity has assured him of Hall election. Billy Williams and Fergie Jenkins have company.

—★—

This weighted bag is an unwieldy thing to steal, and it would seem to offer little profit: it does take four of these to make a run, which is the stuff that wins are made of. At least that's the theory behind discouraging larcenous thoughts by the lead-footed.

Caution flew out the window, however, when the thief's name was Lou Brock. Not much chance of his being caught in the act. This Willie Sutton of the base paths stole 118 bases in 1974 to demolish the mark of 104 set by Maury Wills twelve years earlier (this base is the one that gave Brock the record). Lou went on to top Ty Cobb and Billy Hamilton for career steals as well, although he has since been surpassed in both areas by Rickey Henderson.

CHAPTER FIVE

Special Historical Exhibits

BLACK BASEBALL

He was so unruffled by the possibility of pitching before a large crowd at age nineteen that he was nicknamed "Cool Papa." But the speed that would make James Bell famous was not in his left arm but in his feet. Some of the stories are apocryphal (he was called out for being hit by his own line drive as he slid into second, he could turn off the light switch and be in bed before the room got dark), others more reliable (in a barnstorming game against white major leaguers Bell, at age forty-two, scored from first base on a sacrifice bunt). But there

is no doubt he was the speediest base runner in Negro League history, and maybe the fastest in any league, anytime (his zip around the bases in twelve seconds is 1.3 seconds faster than anyone else has done it).

Even his shades are ineffably cool. But he didn't wear them to evade the glare of publicity; society took care of that, sentencing him and his other talented counterparts to exhibit their skills in the shadows of the major leagues. While Tris Speaker and Kiki Cuyler were eating big steaks and staying in plush hotels, Bell's barnstorming teammates often had to sleep on the team bus because African-Americans were not allowed in local hotels.

According to some reports Bell once stole 175 bases in a two-hundred-game season and compiled a .480 batting average in another year. When baseball slowly opened its doors to these superb talents, Bell was offered a contract with the St. Louis Browns. He was forty-eight years old. He declined, saying it was time for the younger men. In fact, he deliberately lost the 1946 Negro League batting title to Monte Irvin because he knew it would improve Irvin's chances of making it to the white majors. And when he was elected to the Hall of Fame in 1974, he said it was not the biggest thrill of his life. That had come, he said, "when they opened the doors to black ballplayers." For years before his death in 1991, Cool Papa, frail but proud, was a fixture at the annual induction ceremonies.

———★———

For white America, electric floodlights were not powerful enough to bring black ball out of the shadows. And when Jackie Robinson broke the color line, he left many Negro League stars behind, too old to perform at peak level before a new audience. Satchel Paige became the glorious exception, when in 1948 he became the majors' oldest "rookie" at age forty-two. But boys like me grew up in the 1950s and '60s loving baseball and not knowing a blessed thing about Rube Foster or Judy Johnson or Martin Dihigo or Oscar Charleston; it was left to the Hall of Fame to right a historic wrong and, beginning in 1971 with Paige, include the men who had been excluded from the playing fields in their prime. Inspired by Ted Williams's advocacy of the Negro Leaguers in his own induction speech in 1966, and informed by the dedicated research of such writers as John Holway and Robert Peterson, the Hall of Fame has given us the great gift of Josh Gibson, Cool Papa Bell, Pop Lloyd, and more.

For black America, there had never been any question about the greatness of these men; all the same, a young generation of African-Americans could take pride in seeing their legendary heroes honored in Cooperstown. The Museum has an educational mission, and in this area it serves a particularly notable purpose.

Although the Negro Leagues survived into the 1960s, the last players of note they produced were in the early fifties: Willie Mays, Ernie Banks, and Hank Aaron. This collage only hints at the rich character of that shadow-ball time: on the one hand, the prejudice, the privation, the struggle for recognition; on the other, the innovation, the tenacity, the adaptability required for survival.

The ageless Satchel Paige, he of the flawless control and the surprising be ball, was one of the few established stars in the Negro Leagues to make the bridge to Major League Baseball (others were Monte Irvin, Larry Doby, Roy Campanella, and Sam Jethroe; Jackie Robinson played only one season with the Kansas City Monarchs). Here is Satchel's ghosted autobiography. "The Pitchin' Man" played for many teams in his long day at the park, and he always was "the attraction."

The bat belonged to Buck Leonard, the man known as "The Black Lou Gehrig," in counterpart to his teammate Josh Gibson, "The Black Babe Ruth." Leonard was a smooth-swinging and slick-fielding first baseman for twenty-seven years, mostly with the Homestead Grays. The glove, cap, and shades belonged to Cool Papa Bell, the epitome of equanimity and the sultan of speed.

The black leagues not only had excellent players; they had visionaries like Rube Foster, the portly pitcher who founded the first Negro League in 1920. They had inventive executives: in 1930 Kansas City Monarchs owner J. L. Wilkinson worked out a way to transport lights to his team's games. A truck carried the portable lighting system, and the truck's engine generated the power. "What the talkies are to movies," he said, "lights will be to baseball." He was right.

Baseball's integration was a wonderful event for white America, but for black America it was a mixed blessing. Access to the broader range of national experience was gained, but some vital things were lost, too: entrepreneurial opportunity, pride of ownership, and a culturally binding institution. The extent of that loss has become painfully clear in recent years. More than half a century after Jackie Robinson, young African-Americans are growing up wanting to be like Michael Jordan, not like Ken Griffey, Jr. Baseball has another big job ahead.

Sol White wasn't just a sure-handed, line-drive-hitting infielder in black baseball of the nineteenth century; he was one of its founding fathers and its historian. White and Philadelphia sportswriter Walter Schlichter founded the Philadelphia Giants in 1902, and they were the most powerful black club of their time. According to the records, they played 680 games from 1902 through 1906 and won 507 of them. In 1903 they played the Cuban X-Giants in the first-ever Colored Championship of the World. A young pitcher named Rube Foster won four games for the Cuban X-Giants to upset White's team. The next year Foster came over to pitch on White's side, and they won. Although there was no formal league structure, in 1905 the Philadelphia Giants won 134 games and lost just 21. They challenged what they thought was the second-best black team to a World Series; the opponents never showed. After going 108–31 in 1906 they issued a challenge to play the winner of the white World Series to see who was truly best. No one answered then, either.

This incredibly rare 1907 book is a work of both

history and advocacy; in it White cautions black players that their skills are more valuable than showboating or clowning. He looks forward to the day when black and white players will be able to play together: "An honest effort of his great ability will open the avenue in the near future wherein [the colored player] may walk hand in hand with the opposite race in the greatest of all American games—baseball." Born just three years after the Civil War, White lived to see his dream come true. He died in 1955.

— ★ —

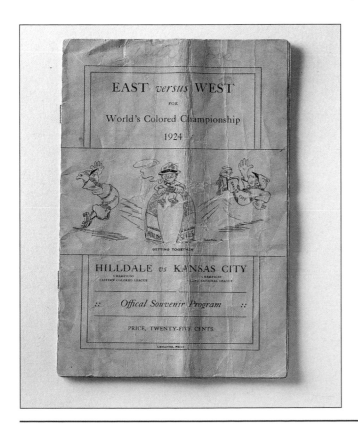

By 1920 the best black players were not barnstormers but men who played in a real league, with regular schedules, rules, and umpires. Former pitcher and highly successful manager Rube Foster was the founding father of the Negro National League. Using his own money and superb organizational abilities, he made sure the league was strong. He was the sole boss, yet because he continued managing, other teams thought Foster's men got the better of the umpires' decisions. And why not? Foster wrote the umps' checks.

This is the program from the first interleague World's Colored Championship, in 1924. Foster's counterpart and founder of the Eastern Colored League was Ed "Chief" Bolden, a retiring and dapper little man who worked for the post office. His quiet style was the opposite of Foster's bulk and bluster. Bolden ran the Hilldale team when they were just semipros and built them into professionals, before joining with other owners to create the new league in 1923. But Bolden had a nervous breakdown in 1927, and, without his keen organizational skills, the league collapsed. Six years later he recovered and founded the Philadelphia Stars, who became members of the Negro National League.

Hilldale's opponents in this Series were the Kansas City Monarchs, who became a perennial powerhouse with stars like Bullet Joe Rogan, Newt Allen, Chet Brewer, and, of course, Cool Papa Bell and Satchel Paige. But that's getting ahead of ourselves. The star of this Series for the victorious Monarchs was an old-timer, José Mendez, who in postseason exhibitions in Cuba in 1911 had defeated Christy Mathewson. Mendez's brilliance in a one-hitter against the Cincinnati Reds three years earlier, followed by his handcuffing of Ty Cobb in a series the following season, had prompted John McGraw to say he would pay $50,000 for him if only he were white.

But Mendez was not, so he was available to star in the 1924 Negro League World Series.

UMPIRES

This display is like a Roz Chast cartoon in *The New Yorker*, captioned simply "Umpire's Eyeglasses." The man who wore these, Frank Umont, would see the humor behind the admission of human frailty, but he wouldn't take any lip about it.

After all, he had been a professional football player before becoming an umpire. While his career in Giants blue lasted only three years, his time in umpire's blue ran to twenty years, from 1954 through 1973.

Bill Klem, the Babe Ruth of umpiring (his first sixteen years in the majors he umpired home plate for every game; no one disputed that he was the best), always felt that eyesight was far less important than insight. He was often quoted as saying, "I never missed one." What actually happened is that John McGraw ordered the Polo Grounds architect to climb the new scoreboard and double-check whether a fly ball that Klem had called foul had actually been fair. The dent showed the ball had been foul by three inches. When the architect reported that to Klem, the ump replied, "I never missed one of those in my life." The misquote made him sound stubborn and arrogant, so in later years Klem added a phrase to the "I never missed one" quote: "in my heart." But that line makes "Old Catfish" (he hated that name) seem more cuddly than he was. Nearer to the truth of the man—and the profession—is this one:

After a close play at the plate that would decide the game, players from both teams gathered around Klem, who had yet to make the call. "Well, what is he?" one player shouted. "Safe or out?"

"He ain't nothing till I call it," Klem replied.

——★——

This looks like an ancient tribal fetish, but it was the whisk broom of Jocko Conlan, one of the feistiest umpires of all time. Jocko used it not only to keep things tidy around home plate but also to control the situation when nerves were becoming frayed. As a judicial symbol of authority, the whisk broom conveys all the authority of a gavel. For a quarter of a century, this broom in

Conlan's hands kept order. But as a player, Jocko was no fan of umps. In the minors he was suspended for verbal abuse. He was on the bench as a White Sox sub one day in 1935 when umpire Red Ormsby was felled by the hot weather. By agreement of the teams, Conlan moved into the ump's spot. The next season he hung up his bat and picked up the broom. As an ump Conlan had the most trouble with managers who shared his fiery attitude, like Leo Durocher, with whom he got into a celebrated shin-kicking contest in 1961. As usual, the law won. Jocko was wearing shin pads and toe plates.

—★—

Whoa! What's going on here? This ball-strike indicator was actually used by a major league umpire in 1887. In its formative years baseball experimented with the rules, trying to find the ultimate combinations that would allow for excitement both offensively and defensively. The distance from home to the pitcher's mound was moved from forty-five feet to fifty feet in 1881 and then to the current sixty feet six inches in 1894. In 1884 overhand pitching was made legal. Until 1887 a player could request a "high ball" or "low ball" to hit—in effect, there were two separate strike zones. In some seasons it took nine balls to get a walk, in others six or seven. In 1887 the number of called balls that sent a batter to first base was five, and, uniquely in that year, the umpire's call was "Four strikes—you're out!" In 1888 the number of strikes was restored to three; the next season four balls became the standard for a walk, and that combination hasn't changed since.

In another development unique to 1887, the scoring rules were changed to count walks as hits. Among the temporary results (altered by major-league baseball edict in 1968) was a .492 batting average for Tip O'Neill of the St. Louis Browns, along with fifteen other .400-plus seasons! (When the walks were recomputed as neither outs nor hits, only O'Neill (.435) and Pete Browning (.402) stayed above the .400 line.

—★—

For more than half a century *The Saturday Evening Post* was the magazine of Middle America, and for most of that time Norman Rockwell was creating covers that became targets for stuffy art critics and milestones of American social history. Not surprisingly, baseball, "America's Game," was the subject of many a *Post* cover and story. Rockwell's art first graced a *Post* cover on May 20, 1916, and its subject was, in equal parts, boyhood and baseball. But this was not his first published baseball illustration—credit for that must go to the cover and internal plates for Ralph Henry Barbour's novel *The Lucky Seventh*, published one year earlier. When *The Post* shut its doors in 1969, Rockwell had delivered 317 covers and baseball remained as close to his heart as it did to the heart of America. During his lifetime, Rockwell's work was considered "illustration," not art, a false distinction if ever there was one. But the American people were ahead of the critics, and not for the first time nor the last; now he is reckoned as a master of his craft and of his era, an utter original.

Among his most memorable baseball pieces was an oil painting entitled (pick one; they've all been in common use) *Game Called Because of Rain, The Three Umpires,* or *Tough Call.* It was published as a *Post* cover on April 23, 1949. Wonderful as the finished art is, this preliminary study in monochrome is more interesting for what it reveals to the student of Rockwell's method.

The three umpires (that's all there were for most games in the late 1940s) are detecting a few raindrops falling from the sky on an Ebbets Field afternoon. On the far right, Pirate manager Billy Meyer is huddled over, feigning that he is being drenched and that the game should be called. His Brooklyn counterpart, coach Clyde Sukeforth, doffs his cap and points to the clearing sky that only he can see. The umpires—from left to right, Larry Goetz, Beans Reardon, and Lou Jorda—are judiciously assessing the elements and the prospects. The rationale for this complicated tableau can't be detected from the sketch, but the final illustration tells the tale. On the scoreboard, Meyer's woeful Bucs are (amazingly) leading the vaunted Dodgers, 1–0, in the last of the sixth. A rain-out would mean a Pirate victory, quite a rarity against the Dodgers of the time. This sketch also has something the final doesn't; the AVOID FIVE O'CLOCK SHADOW: USE GEM BLADES sign in right field was changed to an SCM sign.

MINOR LEAGUES

In the entire history of Major League Baseball from 1871 through 1997, only once in 167,135 games did two men throw no-hit ball against each other for nine innings or more. On May 2, 1917, righthander Fred Toney of the Reds and lefthander Hippo Vaughn of the Cubs went through nine innings of their no-hit duel, broken up in the tenth as Cincinnati's Larry Kopf hit a clean single and came home on a Jim Thorpe roller to the mound. I used to be able to call this game a double no-hitter, until a recent scoring rule change deemed a no-hitter to be a complete game in which no hits were allowed, thus wiping not only Hippo Vaughn but also Harvey Haddix from the honor roll. Oh, well, they've still got no-hitters in my book.

And so does Scott Bakkum, who pitched hitless ball for Winter Haven in the Florida State League on August 23, 1992. The Boston Red Sox prospect allowed a run to Clearwater on a cou-

ple of walks, a sacrifice, and a squeeze play, so he lost the game to Phillies farmhand Andy Carter, who had the perspicacity to throw a shutout as well as a no-hitter. Like Toney and Vaughn, the right-handed Bakkum and the left-handed Carter are linked in baseball history forevermore, and nothing can break that bond.

——★——

The term "minor league" connotes inferiority and subordination to a greater league. Yet in the 1990s, as Major League Baseball was coming

apart at the seams, minor league parks were the place to be. Promoting community, innovation, value, and fun, as they have always had to do to

compete with the big boys, the minors are a living museum of what baseball once was and may yet become again.

The minors also used to be a hothouse of entrepreneurial wizardry, from racial integration and night ball to theme nights and aluminum bats. In the days before Branch Rickey dreamed up the farm system, in which a parent club bore the player-development costs in exchange for the right to a player's future services, minor league teams were independently operated. They scouted and signed and nurtured the talent, and they profited not only by keeping the turnstiles spinning but also by selling their best players to the big leagues. That idea has been revived recently in such examples as Miles Wolff's Northern League, where fans flock with as much enthusiasm and loyalty as they once did to the leagues whose names are festooned on these season passes.

———★———

The radar gun and tuning fork, the stopwatch, the index card, and what you can't see, the heart and mind and instinct: the tools of the trade for that most underappreciated of baseball figures, the scout. Scouts are on the prowl for tomorrow's legendary star, and the best ones have created their own legends. Joe Cambria became a scout after a minimal playing career and several years of owning minor league teams. He signed Mickey Vernon, Early Wynn, and legions of Cuban players for the Washington Senators. Paul Krichell discovered Lou Gehrig and Whitey Ford. Howie Haak kept the Pirates supplied with Latin stars. Tony Lucadello signed Fergie Jenkins, Mike Marshall, and Mike Schmidt. In the Negro Leagues their counterparts were retired players Oscar Charleston and Buck O'Neil.

Scouts used to work for only one team, seeing hundreds of high school, college, and American Legion games every year, sleeping in their cars, and eating blue plate specials in greasy spoons, beating the bushes to flush out one prize catch. Nowadays the work is much more corporate; there are scouting bureaus and combines that generate information not for one team, but several. The card here shows the report written by then scout Tommy Lasorda on a college pitcher, Tom Seaver. Seaver was originally signed by the Braves, but the commissioner voided the contract because Seaver's college team had already started its season. Three teams—the Braves, Phillies, and Mets—put their names in a hat, and the Mets won. Note that Lasorda comments not only on Seaver's mechanics and speed ("Real good command of point of release") but his attitude ("Boy has plenty of desire to pitch and wants to beat you"). Don't you think Tommy gnashed his teeth every time Seaver took the mound against his Dodgers?

The All-American Girls Professional Baseball League began as a softball league and changed the size of the ball nearly every year, as these balls (from newest to oldest, left to right) show. On the far right is a regulation softball (12″ circumference). By 1954 the league had reduced the size to a Major League Baseball standard 9¼″ (far left). Overhand pitching wasn't allowed till the sixth year of the league's existence. The difference between traditional softball and what the league played was in base running. Chicago Cubs owner Philip K. Wrigley wanted the excitement of taking leads and stealing, which isn't allowed in softball. It was this decision that made the women's game so exciting and such a crowd pleaser. Hits were few and far between, but double steals were commonplace. Sophie Kurys was the Maury Wills of the AAGPBL. She was named Player of the Year in 1946, when she swiped 201 bases in 203 tries! The writers dubbed her "Tina Cobb."

★

One of the reasons for the league's success was that its managers were often former major-league stars who really enjoyed making the game more baseball-like. Hall of Famer Max Carcy, for one, sensational base stealer for the Pirates in the teens and twenties, taught the women the art of base running. At the helm for other teams in the league were former big-leaguers Carson Bigbee, Dave Bancroft, Bill Wambsganss, and, of course, Jimmie Foxx, whose lack of interest in the whole venture was parodied by Tom Hanks in the movie *A League of Their Own.*

Wrigley, like most Americans at the time, felt that sports was a manly thing to do, and so women who were athletic had the onus of proving how feminine they were. There were strictly enforced height and weight limits, and the girls of the AAGPBL got charm-school lessons and lipstick instruction.

To evaluate ballplaying talent we have the statistical record and the memories of those who played in the league. Dottie Kamenshek of the Rockford Peaches was labeled (by a perhaps overheated press agent) "the greatest defensive first baseman—man or woman—of all time," and she hit .292 over a ten-year career. Connie Wisniewski, Grand Rapid Chicks pitcher, was dubbed "Christine Mathewson" and "The Iron Woman" for all the innings she threw. Doris Sams and Jean Faut were the only women named Player of the Year twice in the league's twelve-year (1943–1954) history. And the Weaver sisters posted stupendous batting marks in the league's final years, including a .429 mark by Joanne in 1954.

The Women in Baseball exhibit is now one of Cooperstown's most popular. And Major League Baseball tells us that more than 40 percent of all fans attending its ball games are women. Historians trace this trend to the introduction of radio in the 1930s or to Rosie the Riveter and the introduction of women into the workplace during World War II; sociologists attribute women's interest in baseball to the theory of the leisure class. It would probably be wrong to attribute the whole transformation to the eye-catching uniforms of the AAGPBL.

The away uniform in orange for the Rockford Peaches belonged to Dottie Ferguson Key, who had been a champion speed skater and hockey player in her hometown of Winnipeg. She was a second baseman and center fielder on the Peaches' champions of 1946, 1948, and 1949. Signed in 1945, she stayed with the league till its bitter end in 1954, when the bus-less Peaches had to drive their own cars to their games. The green cap is from the Kalamazoo Lassies, winners of the last AAGPBL game—the 1954 championship. The home uniform of the Peaches was worn by Dolores Dries.

—★—

As wartime manpower shortages threatened to close Major League Baseball down for the duration, Cubs owner Phil Wrigley launched the All American Girls Ball League, a softball circuit that, he thought, might fill the impending void in big-league stadiums. As it became clear that men's baseball would endure, because President Roosevelt thought it was necessary to help maintain home-front morale, Wrigley's original impulse seemed extreme. The minors, however, were losing teams and whole leagues by the handful, and soon the idea transformed into placing women's baseball teams in small cities in the Midwest that had lost their National Association teams. That newer idea became, in 1943, the All-American Girls Professional Baseball League, although only underhand pitching was allowed until late 1946, when sidearm came in, followed by overhand in 1948. A larger-than-regulation-size baseball continued to be used until the league's final year, 1954. The base paths started at sixty-five feet long and were later adjusted to sixty-eight feet and seventy-two feet before reaching their final specification of seventy-five feet in 1953.

The All American Girls Professional Baseball League fielded fourteen teams in its twelve years of existence. The Springfield Sallies and Chicago Colleens, whose pennants are shown here, each lasted just one season—1948. The league expanded from midsize towns into major cities like Milwaukee, Minneapolis, and Chicago, but the league's champions and its stars came mostly from the smaller cities like Rockford, Kalamazoo, and Muskegon. The "1st Ever Womens' Baseball World Series" took place in 1943 and was won by the Racine Belles of Racine, Wisconsin (that's *Ray-seen* to you, bub; this ain't no French playwright). And the league had its stars: outfield rifle "Rockford

Rosie" Gacioch, who threw out thirty-one runners trying to take the extra base one year; hitters like Joanne Weaver and her older sister Betty Weaver Foss, and pitchers Jean Faut, who threw a perfect game in 1951, Connie Wisniewski, who won sixty-five games in two seasons, and Joanne Winter, who pitched the Racine Belles to the championship in 1946 by going 33–10 with a 1.19 ERA and then pitched a fourteen-inning shutout to win the final game of the Shaughnessy Series, the league championship. This is the ball that recorded the final out and the pin that was awarded to each of the victorious Belles.

BASEBALL ABROAD AND TOURS

The wearing of this jacket helped us win World War II. When the United States planned a baseball tour of Japan in 1934, the last player added to the roster was third-string catcher Moe Berg. There were good reasons, and they had nothing to do with his bat or glove. (Although Moe was an excellent catcher, hitting wasn't his thing. He was the inspiration for Mike Gonzalez's immortally terse scouting report: "Good field, no hit.") Moe was supremely intelligent, a summa cum laude Princeton graduate, and certainly the best-read player in baseball history. He was master of a dozen languages, in none of which, it was observed, could he hit. Moe gave a welcoming speech in perfect Japanese and even addressed the Japanese legislature. He didn't have much to do on the field; Babe Ruth took care of that, hitting thirteen home runs in the six-

teen-game tour. If there was a chance of rain, Babe played right field carrying an umbrella; first baseman Lou Gehrig wore galoshes. But Moe was still busy; suddenly, photography became his new hobby. He spent much of his time on the hotel roof taking pictures of Tokyo, with emphasis on industrial and military installations. General Jimmy Doolittle is said to have used the snapshots eight years later in the first bombing runs over Japan.

——★——

In 1913 American entrepreneurs worked up their nerve for a world tour despite previous results that could at best be termed indifferent. The moment seemed propitious, for baseball had been on display as an experiment at the 1912 Olympic Games in Stockholm. The World Tourists consisted of Chicago White Sox and New York Giants,

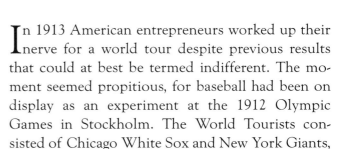

and their exploits were recorded by Ring Lardner, a Chicago reporter whose national fame was still a few years off. The man who wore this jacket, "Wahoo Sam" Crawford, never played for Chicago, but when invited along leapt at the chance.

—★—

This brilliant jacket was worn by Harry Wolter, former Yankee outfielder and a coach of the 1936 United States Olympic team managed by Les Mann, another former big leaguer. But isn't baseball a newly adopted sport at the Summer Olympics? Wasn't 1992 the first year of official competition? Yes, but baseball has been an experiment at Olympic sites since St. Louis in 1904 and a demonstration sport at such odd intervals as 1912, 1936, 1952, 1956, 1984, and 1988.

What made the 1936 games special was that the United States played an intrasquad night game at Berlin Stadium before the largest crowd ever to watch a baseball game anywhere—an estimated 110,000. Les McNeese broke up a 5–5 tie with a seventh-inning home run, and the United States defeated itself (nominally, the "World Champions" beat the "Olympics"). The huge German throng never got the hang of this baseball thing; what they loved most was the umpire. Apparently, his broad "safe" sign resembled the Nazi salute enough to delight the crowd.

It has been a sobering and splendid experience for the United States to lose in the Olympics to Japan, Cuba, and Taiwan. The quality of play in the Olympics is not yet the equivalent of a World Series, but when professionals are permitted to play, as they have been in basketball and hockey, baseball will truly be the world sport that Albert Spalding and Harry Wright envisioned more than a century ago.

—★—

They set out from Chicago on October 20, 1888, and didn't return to the United States until April 6, 1889. It was Albert Goodwill Spalding's world tour, an attempt to spread the baseball gospel (and his sporting-goods empire) to the four corners of the known universe. Previously, Spalding, Al Reach, and the Wright brothers had organized a midseason English tour in 1874 that pulled the Boston Red Stockings and Philadelphia Athletics out of league play for nearly two months. Cricket teams from Britain had toured the United States as early as 1859, and Harry Wright and Al Spalding wanted to return the favor. But when they got there, the Brits didn't want to see baseball, they wanted cricket. The baseball players complied, and their unorthodox style of slugging won bemused praise.

The 1888 tour was comprised of the Chicago White Stockings, led by Cap Anson, who had also been part of the English tour fourteen years earlier, and an all-star group selected from other teams in both leagues (the All-Americas). After departing by rail from Chicago, the barnstormers played games in St. Paul and Minneapolis, then meandered through the West with stops to play in Cedar Rapids, Des Moines, Omaha, Hastings, Denver, Colorado Springs, and Salt Lake City. They reached California in early November, buttressed by such stragglers as John Ward and Cannonball Crane, who had been detained in St. Louis to complete the Giants' victory in the World Series.

The All-American Tourists, shown in this oversize, singularly splendid lithograph, played games in San Francisco and Los Angeles before setting sail (and steam) for the Sandwich Islands, known today as Hawaii. The main isle of Oahu had been the home for nearly forty years of none other than Alexander Cartwright, an original member of the Knickerbocker Base Ball Club of New York and known to Spalding and Ward as a pioneer of baseball. Hawaii was the first stop for Spald-

ing's Tourists, but they arrived in port late, on a Sunday, when ballplaying was out of the question. More important, they had to make up for days lost at sea, so, after a day's festivities, the players didn't even stay the night. Spalding never did get to meet Cartwright.

The tour continued to New Zealand, Australia, and onward to Ceylon and Egypt. It proceeded to the mainland of Europe, with scenic stops to play ball at the Borghese Gardens in Rome (they tried for the Coliseum and were rebuffed) and next to the Eiffel Tower in Paris. They finished up in the British Isles, where the Queen's subjects admired the way the Americans fielded but disapproved of the pitching (too difficult) and the batting (too weak and, unlike cricket, too soon over).

The returning heroes were honored at a banquet at Delmonico's restaurant in New York on April 8, 1889, where former National League president Abraham G. Mills declared that baseball was purely an American invention, and the audience responded by pounding the tables and shouting, "No rounders! No rounders!" Mark Twain, unwittingly assuming that the Tourists had played in Hawaii, reminisced about his own four months in the Sandwich Islands in 1866. He pointed up the incongruity of that sylvan setting and baseball, "the very symbol, the outward and visible expression of the drive and push and rush and struggle of the raging, tearing, booming nineteenth century."

The beautiful silk memento of the White Stockings' subsequent return to Chicago is tattered now, but it is not only an evocative capstone to the tour but a harbinger of baseball in the century to come. It was handed down from attendees at the banquet, Mr. and Mrs. W. H. Gray, to Judge Kenesaw Mountain Landis. The ball may be history's most traveled, having been in play across several continents.

In the years to come, Spalding ballyhooed the importance of his two tours, but in truth both were artistic, financial, and ideological flops. The game took off in places visited not by ambas-

sadors of baseball but by our military and our missionaries—Japan, Cuba, the Caribbean basin, Mexico. A 1913–1914 tour (populated by Nixey Callahan's Chicago White Sox and John McGraw's New York Giants) made a stop in Japan, and later had a grand return celebration in March 1914, as the program from the Biltmore Hotel and the Reception Committee badge attest. That tour also zigzagged across the American West before heading across the ocean. Sixty-seven people were in the traveling party, including players' wives and a recording scribe, Ring Lardner.

But the most important baseball tour took place in 1934 and is represented here by the official jacket and two balls (one of which, richly embellished with player autographs, was turned into a cigarette lighter in baseball's tradition of wacky collectibles). This tour was the second by major leaguers to Japan in the decade (another group had traveled there in 1931, including Hall of Famers Lou Gehrig, Lefty Grove, Al Simmons, and Frankie Frisch, as well as baseball's unofficial ambassador to Japan, Lefty O'Doul). But the 1934 visit is the one given credit for finally turning the Japanese into huge baseball fans. Part of the reason was the cast: Babe Ruth, Jimmie Foxx, Charlie Gehringer, Lefty Gomez, and Rabbit Maranville, as well as Gehrig, Frisch, Simmons, O'Doul, and the spy Moe Berg. The Japanese lost every one of the eighteen games played, by wide margins, except one: Eiji Sawamura was the losing pitcher in a 1–0 thriller in which he struck out Gehringer, Ruth, Gehrig, and Foxx in succession. Two years later, Japan formed its own professional league.

Pedagogical demonstrations did not make baseball flourish in Colombo or Cairo, but competitive play turned the trick in Osaka and Tokyo.

—★—

E ast is East, and West is West," wrote Kipling, "and never the twain shall meet." Yet isn't it fascinating that baseball is the national game of the United States and of Japan, and is regarded by each country as the embodiment of its unique culture? We seem very different, Americans and Japanese, so how can baseball/*beesubooru* perfectly mirror both? Is the game so different in each locale, or are the two peoples perhaps not so different after all?

The game had been played in Japan since 1873, when instructor Horace Wilson taught it to his Japanese students. Visiting University of Washington students played Japanese teams in 1908 and lost four of ten games; the Reach All-Americans also came to Japan that year. Professional tours followed, with major-league baseball aggregations playing in Japan in 1913, 1920, 1922 (including Casey Stengel), 1928 (led by Ty Cobb), 1931, and 1934. In 1927 and 1932 the Philadelphia Royal Giants of the Negro Leagues toured, and they greatly impressed the Japanese with their competitive spirit (many of the white All-Stars took the exhibitions less seriously than the Japanese felt they should). By 1936 Japan had its first professional baseball league. After a cessation of tours because of growing hostility between the nations, culminating in the Second World War, a U.S. team (Lefty O'Doul's San Francisco Seals) returned to Japan in 1949. After that, November was typically marked by the appearance of a U.S. major league team, including the Dodgers, Yankees, or Giants.

These artifacts show some of the splashier mementos of the tours and the Japanese game, in-

cluding an ornately bound scrapbook of a Cincinnati Reds visit, a graphic luggage tag, and an eye-brow-raising ball-bat-glove ashtray given to sportswriter Fred Lieb in 1931.

The 1934 tour was memorable for the massive display of affection for Babe Ruth. In retrospect, however, when we think of that tour, we think of catcher-soldier-spy Moe Berg, whose visiting card at the upper left does not hint of his various occupations and preoccupations.

The glove and shoes are of more recent vintage and relate not to U.S. players touring Japan but to the glories of Japanese baseball itself. The golden slippers were awarded to Yutaka Fukumoto, he of the fleet feet, who led Japanese baseball in steals thirteen straight years. When he received these mementos of his one thousandth stolen base, no ballplayer on earth had ever stolen more. The glove belongs to that fascinating hero of Japan, Sadaharu Oh, who hit more home runs than any other man, a staggering 868 in nearly 3,000 fewer at-bats than Henry Aaron. Oh's autobiography tells how he applied the Asiatic martial arts of kendo and aikido to slugging a baseball.

Kipling could not have imagined this.

CHAPTER SIX

The Changing Game

BATS

This handmade bat from 1852 looks more like something you'd use to chase the neighbor's kids out of your garden. But the baseball bugs of that era didn't have access to Spalding Sporting Goods catalogs. So they carved bats out of whatever they could find—wagon tongues (the long piece of wood jutting out from the wagon to which the horses' reins were attached), ax handles, cordwood. Before the Civil War, the style of bat favored for bat-and-ball games like town ball, rounders, and shinny (the ball game of New York City in the 1830s) was shorter (eighteen to twenty-four inches) and slimmer, so that it could be swung with one hand; in town ball such a bat was called a "dellil." The fascination of this artifact lies not merely in its antiquity and primitive strength, but in its having been shaped with care to perform a particular function no longer practiced.

———— ★ ————

He was the original "Louisville Slugger," and the bat was named after him. This bat, alas, is not the authentic relic but rather an exact replica—not really museum quality, but interesting as a takeoff point for a story, one that goes like this:

One day in 1884 Pete Browning of the Louisville Eclipse broke a favorite bat while Bud Hillerich, whose dad owned a woodworking shop, was sitting in the stands. Bud offered to make the hitter a new bat, and Pete joined him at the factory to make sure it suited him. The next day Browning rapped out three hits, and soon other ballplayers sought out Hillerich. The Hillerich company turned out a model first called the "Falls City Slugger," after Louisville's popular nickname of the day; by 1894 it had become known as the "Louisville Slugger."

There is no doubt that Browning was a sensational batsman. He broke in with the Eclipse (the only ball club named after a racehorse) in the first year of the American Association. The league was known as the "beer and whisky league" because its parks permitted booze to be sold in the stands. Ol' Pietro was a charter member in all respects. He won three batting titles and even topped the .400 mark once. His lifetime average of .341 is the highest of any eligible player not in the Hall of Fame. But Pete was strictly a hitter; glovemanship held no allure for him. Once during dinner Pete complained to the waitress that there was a fly in his soup. "Don't worry," a teammate commented. "You'll never catch it."

He also suffered from mastoiditis, a debilitating infection that rendered him partially deaf, rather clumsy, and susceptible to the relief that comes from malt and spirituous drink. "The Old Gladiator" (called that as much for his battles with fly balls as with pitchers) once said, "I can't hit the ball until I hit the bottle." The problems with the infection, exacerbated by the alcohol, finally resulted in his being committed to a mental asylum, where he spent the final years of his short life.

— ★ —

In the latter part of the nineteenth century, hitters were less interested in bat speed than they were in making contact. Errors were common and home runs were not, so keeping the ball in play was the key to scoring runs and winning games. Accordingly, a thick, scarcely tapered bat with a huge sweet spot assured hitters that even if they were fooled a little by a drop or an outshoot, they could still hit the ball hard.

This bat, called the "mushroom" because of its handle (it was cheaper and easier not to cut off that bulb of wood sticking off the end), was a favorite. Batters of that time didn't deliver the long, smooth swings we are so familiar with today. They chopped at the ball, often adjusting their grip on the bat as the ball approached (sliding the top hand down for a fat pitch, so they could drive it; leaving the hands spread apart to squib a tough pitch through the infield). Casey Stengel baffled his 1960s Mets when he hollered, "Gimme some butcher boys out there! Butcher boy! Butcher boy!" What he meant (Casey had been around a long time) was to swat at the ball like a butcher chopping a piece of meat and let your legs get you a base hit.

The "Spalding" on this bat was Albert, great player turned sports merchant turned team owner turned sporting-goods millionaire. Of the National Association's key players from 1871 to 1875, Spalding was not the only player to create a sporting-goods empire; so did George Wright (who combined with Henry A. Ditson to manufacture the official ball of the Union Association rebels of 1884) and Al Reach (who manufactured the official ball of the American Association, 1882–1891). By the 1880s there was at least one company making balls and bats in every big city, including such long-gone names as Louis Mahn (official supplier of balls to the Players League of 1890), the Victor Company (which made the official ball of the Federal League—do you detect a pattern here?), Ben Shibe, Draper & Maynard, and Goldsmith. New York had at least a half-dozen "baseball emporia," giant stores to supply individuals, teams, or whole leagues, including E. I. Horsman's Base Ball and Croquet Emporium, Andrew Peck (later Peck & Snyder), and A. B. Swift and Company. In another All-American move, Spalding bought out the rest in 1892, including Reach, Wright & Ditson, and Peck & Snyder, to form a new company, valued at $4,000,000.

— ★ —

This flat bat is a replica of a model advocated by Harry Wright and actually legalized for major league play in 1885. Wright, originally a cricketer, felt that this bat would help players place the ball more accurately when they hit it. In practice, however, batters found that a decent fastball would turn the bat in their hands, producing nothing more than a weak dribbler to the box. Though the flat-bat option remained on the books until 1893, by the end of its debut year it was as out of fashion as the bustle is today. In cricket, putting the ball precisely where you want it is a large part of that highly strategic game. Baseball would later have its "Hit 'em where they ain't" man, Willie Keeler. But the "scientific art" of pushing and poking and slicing the ball remained a vestige of the British sport. Just trying to wallop the heck out of it was the American thing to do.

— ★ —

For the first half of our century, this bat looked even weirder to the modern eye than the mushroom bat, but when Heinie Groh swung his "bottle

bat" he was really pointing the way to the future. The bottle bat had a slimmed-down handle offset by the bludgeonlike hitting end. Note the tape on the handle, which must have cracked dozens of times on inside fastballs. Groh was a smallish man, and his hands had trouble wielding the war clubs of the day, so he devised this model. He hit over .300 four times with it. Of course, he still used the swat-and-chop swing. Today's bat handles are thinner than ever (count how many broken bats you see in a game), and most players generate bat speed with no thought of fighting off an inside pitch for a defensive swing and a bloop hit.

BALLS

And it wasn't only the bats that were going through changes. Look at the differences in this display—in size, stitching, even color. The early balls, handmade and machine made, had the "lemon-peel" construction of four leather panels around a ball made of string and India rubber strips. Other stitching variations were common into the professional era, before the "figure eight" style of today (a two-panel configuration perhaps invented by Ellis Drake in the late 1860s) became standard in the mid-1870s. The regulation or uniform ball—one that behaved in a predictable way—was largely an invention of Ben Shibe, who created machines to wind the yarn and cut the holes in the leather to make the stitches (still done by hand) to exacting specifications. Spalding managed to lock up the big-league ball business by paying the National League a dollar for each one of his balls its teams used. Then he used that imprimatur to trumpet the quality of his balls to everyone else in the country. (This is a perfect example of why people desirous of selling their products continue to seek the license of Major League Baseball.) Notice how flat the stitches are in the nineteenth-century baseballs. No wonder the early curve ball was simply a pitch that sailed laterally; without good, high stitches, it's mighty tough to get a ball to drop, too.

There is an interesting story-behind-the-story here. While the gold ball at the top, second from the left, has been placed in the exhibit as an example of the early, oversized baseball of the 1850s, it is more important than that, being the ball used (yes, one ball for the whole game) on July 20, 1858, at the Fashion Race Course Ground on Long Island for the game between the best players in New York and the best players in Brooklyn. The right fielder for the victorious New York squad (score, 22–18) was Harry Wright of the Knickerbockers, and the catcher was fellow Knick Charlie DeBost, who was struck by the ball in midgame yet, according to accounts of the day, played the rest of the way with "indomitable pluck and spirit." It was DeBost's family who donated the ball to the National Baseball Hall of Fame.

———★———

The very first time I went to the Baseball Hall of Fame, some twenty-five years ago, this was my favorite exhibit. The fact that German bisque baseball-player dolls of a somewhat later period were wedged inside the case diminished its curatorial standing somewhat, but its charm not a whit. I knew that the great Centennial Exhibition in Philadelphia in 1876 was designed to celebrate American ingenuity and productivity, and for the life of me I couldn't figure out how a case of baseballs qualified for display alongside huge dynamos and time-saving household implements. But then it struck me—it was the dazzling variety, the cornucopia of insignificant differences, that provided a model for stoking the fire of American consumerism. Where barely twenty years before, baseballs were either handmade or commodity items, perhaps distinguishable by their liveliness, here was a supermarket in a single case: Ben Shibe was not yet famous for his concrete-and-steel baseball palace; at the Centennial Exhibition he was merely a sporting-goods dealer, though one with a fertile imagination. There was the Professional Dead Ball; the Practice Ball; the Treble Ball (did it last three times as long or go three times as far?); the Amateur Dead Ball; the Philadelphia Regulation Ball; the Practice, the Mutual, the Champion, the Centennial; there was the Atlantic and, surely somewhere in Ben Shibe's offerings, the Pacific; and there was one that still makes an appearance in big-league parks with artificial surfaces—the Bounding Rock.

———★———

The Federal League lasted just two seasons, but it put a scare into the established National and American leagues. The ball was pretty lively; Federal League batters hit twice as many home runs in 1914 as their counterparts in the American League, for example. (Fed operators were smart enough to know fans like to see scoring.) The company that made the official ball was Victor, but the league it backed would soon be the Vanquished. After the 1915 season, the Feds succumbed to the strain of war and to the blandishments of the older leagues, which offered cash settlements and, in some cases, club franchises. A couple of owners were permitted to buy teams in the National and American leagues, but some Federal cities—Indianapolis, Newark, Buffalo—never saw major league ball come their way again.

William A. Hulbert was the most important man in the early history of Major League Baseball. He isn't one of the purported inventors of the game, like Cartwright, or a ceaseless proselytizer like Chadwick, or an innovator like Harry Wright. But Hulbert was the man who asserted the control of capital over labor in the emerging business of baseball, who created the National League through an act of will (and piracy), and who stuck by his principles even when it appeared his league would fail in only its second year, 1877.

But until 1995 Hulbert had no plaque in the Hall. It seems that in 1937, voters, wishing to honor the founding of the National League and its model, looked in the record books, saw that Morgan Bulkeley was the league's first president, and so inducted him as an appropriate symbol of the time and the venture—which, oddly, he was. No one wanted to be president, and Hulbert disqualified himself from consideration when the eight team owners met on February 2, 1876. Bulkeley, president of the Hartford club, drew the proverbial short straw.

Hulbert ran the league in 1876, as Bulkeley remained a figurehead, and he ended the charade the following season by openly taking the reins. He transformed the chaotic, gambling-run, drunken course of the player-owned National Association into the businesslike, organized, owner-run National League, though his success was not immediate. If he had to break a few rules to do it, well, so what? Hulbert, when he had been owner of the Chicago team in the National Association in 1875, lost his star shortstop, Davey Force, to the Philadelphia Athletics because of contract irregularities. Upset that "the West" (meaning Chicago) was faring so poorly against "the Eastern establishment," he first raided the other clubs for players. Then, in consort with Al Spalding—the star pitcher for the Boston Red Stockings who in mid-1875 had been secretly bound to Chicago along with Ross Barnes, Cal McVey, and Deacon White—Hulbert cooked up the new league to prevent the National Association's eastern wing from voiding his contracts with his raided players. (He also took Cap Anson from the Athletics in revenge for the loss of Davey Force.)

Hulbert was not merely venal and self-interested, however. He instituted innovations such as a balanced schedule, paid umpires, and the reserve clause (to which only five players per team could aspire). Then, in 1877, in an act of principle that precursed Landis, he expelled the teams from New York and Philadelphia because they declined to play out their schedules, leaving him with only a six-team league and a precarious future. Even this was compromised further by four members of the Louisville club who sold games to gamblers. Hulbert's response was to expel them for life. He died in 1882, after the seventh year of his league, but his legacy remains.

———★———

These are some of the oldest items in the Hall's collection, and I love them beyond all reason. They come from a time when baseball was new, when real people came to a fork in the road and, as Yogi Berra has suggested, took it. Somehow we arrived at a game of three strikes to the out, three outs to the inning, nine men to the side; somehow we turned away from flat bats, a batter-selected strike zone, and a one-bounce out. These artifacts make us think differently about Abner Doubleday and Alexander Cartwright; they breathe life into Harry Wright and Jim Creighton, and they summon up, if just for a moment, such long-ago stars as Joe Start, Johnny Holder, and John "Death to Flying Things" Chapman.

Every year of baseball prior to the onset of the Civil War saw experiments in attitudes, styles of play, and rules. Names of teams long gone—Gotham, Eagle, Enterprise, Baltic, Flyaway, Wide Awake, Mutual, Empire, and hundreds more—today provoke curiosity or whimsy, but for one who loves the period, they are magical incantations, like "Open Sesame."

Why does the baseball fan of today know so little about the game's golden age? Because its history has been left to academicians who have interpreted the game rather than reveled in it. By viewing the period through such prisms as class and culture, urban modernization, and labor-management strife, they have reduced the grand old game to simply another socioeconomic microcosm of America at large. What did it feel like to be there, then, to scheme with Cartwright at the Elysian Fields or wave in futility at a Creighton riser? I want to experience the thrill felt by the men who held these artifacts when baseball was new.

The Doubleday Ball is a small, handmade product of the sort used to play town ball in northeastern localities in the 1830s and 1840s. Soft enough to permit "soaking," the ball was lemon-peel-stitched, just like the larger baseballs that Daniel Lucius "Doc" Adams made for the Knickerbockers in the 1840s. It was not until the next decade that entrepreneurs like E. I. Horsman came along to manufacture baseballs for purchase at his sporting-goods emporium. As the demand for baseball equipment boomed, better-financed competitors like Peck & Snyder entered the business and Horsman expanded to the manufacture of toys and board games, ultimately inventing the teddy bear.

Entwining the historic baseballs and booklets is a belt worn by a player for the Eagle Base Ball Club, a little-noted entity that points to a baseball history older than that defined by Cartwright. The Eagles were established as a baseball club in 1852, thus becoming the third to play under Knickerbocker rules after the Gothams (known as the Washingtons in 1850–1851) and the Knicks themselves. But the Eagles had been a formally organized ballplaying club since 1840. They played a rounderslike game of ball, on a field in the shape of a true diamond, with two oblique and two obtuse angles. The Eagle game was probably similar to the one played by the Olympic Club of Philadelphia, founded in 1833. The mysterious New York Ball Club, which had played various games of ball, including cricket, since 1832, was the Knickerbockers' first opponent, in the match game of June 19, 1846, and then seemingly vanished. But the New York Ball Club players simply migrated to the Knickerbockers and Gothams. An interesting account of early baseball in New York is offered by Charles Commerford, Gotham shortstop in the mid-1850s. Residing in his retirement years in Waterbury, Connecticut, he wrote in 1905 that the first baseball game he saw in the 1840s was played by the New York Club,

> which club had its grounds on a field bounded by 23rd and 24th streets and 5th and 6th avenues [i.e., Madison Square]. There was a roadside resort nearby and a trotting track in the locality. I remember very well that the constitution and by-laws of the old Gotham club, of which I became a

member in 1849, stated that the Gotham Club was the successor of the old New York City Club. When I was a boy and played ball, I remember, too, that the proper thing to do under the rules of play of the game of those days was to "soak the runners" between the bases to put him out of play—a regular rule of rounders, the latter game being then in vogue in Phila. and New England. Afterwards, when I joined the Gothams, we played under the Knickerbocker's rule of 1845, which put base runners out as now.

The constitution of the Knickerbocker Base Ball Club shown here is a venerable document. Although the club was not formally organized until September 23, 1845, for play at the Elysian Fields of Hoboken, its members had nonetheless been playing ball in Manhattan's Madison Square (near Twenty-seventh Street) and Murray Hill (near Thirty-fourth) since about 1842. The Knicks were not the first baseball team in New York or Brooklyn, nor the second, but their pioneer status is deserved. Not merited are the claims made for the solitary genius of Alexander Cartwright. Look instead perhaps to Lewis F. Wadsworth, the man who may actually have brought the diagram of a baseball diamond to the Elysian Fields and who without doubt created the nine-inning game, and to "Doc" Adams, who invented the position of shortstop, handmade the Knickerbocker baseballs and turned their bats, fixed the distance between bases and between pitcher and batter, championed the elimination of the one-bound catch, and more.

The Base Ball Player's Pocket Companion is the first baseball book, and its first edition of 1858 survives in only three known copies. In addition to detailing the Knickerbocker rules, the little book also provides the rules for the Massachusetts variant, at that time still a serious rival to the New York Game. The game with no foul territory, eleven to the side, and one out to the inning codified an amalgamation of many town-ball variants and inflamed New England for twenty years before yielding to the "more manly" New York Game. Furious local rivalries sprang up, culminating in the infamous Silver Ball Matches, annual championship games of the early 1860s that bred bad blood for generations to come. By giving way to the New York Game by the end of the Civil War, the Massachusetts Game represents baseball's "road not taken," but it was a wonderful game to play and to watch. Today Cooperstown's Leatherstocking Base Ball Club specializes in re-creating town-ball matches, played in authentic costume and by these published rules of 1858.

And then there are the glowing golden trophy balls of 1858 and 1860, displayed along with the humble ball from 1857, for many years the earliest in the Hall's collection that can be traced to a specific game (recently an 1854 ball has come into the collection). The Enterprise of Brooklyn (no, their captain was not named Kirk) defeated Young America, also of Brooklyn, by a score of 19–15. Both were junior teams, composed of fifteen- to eighteen-year-olds honing their skills and showing off for the big clubs of Brooklyn—the Atlantics, Excelsiors, and Eckfords. The Enterprise produced a string of talent, principally for the Atlantics, including such storied names as Bob Ferguson, the game's first switch-hitter and the player-president of the first professional league; John Chapman, who won the nickname "Death to Flying Things" for his famous over-the-shoulder bare-handed grabs of fly balls; and "Old Reliable" Joe Start, who caught everything that came his way at first base and played at the highest level (including the major leagues, when those were created) from 1860 to 1886, a career as long as those of Cap Anson and Nolan Ryan. Young America was the team on which Jim Creighton, baseball's first great pitcher, made his debut before starring with the Niagara, the Star, and the Excelsior until his death in 1862, at the age of twenty-one. The burnished ball from

1860 commemorates an Excelsior victory over the Olympics of Philadelphia, the club that had organized in 1833 to play another game of ball but by this time had adopted the New York Game.

Finally, and fascinatingly, we have the gold trophy ball from the Fashion Race Course Game of July 20, 1858, the All-Star affair that pitted the best of New York against the best of its rival municipality, Brooklyn (the two cities did not merge until 1898) and was termed "the Yankee Olympian games." This game on Long Island drew the biggest crowd up to that time and marked the first time admission was charged. Lewis Wadsworth, having moved from the Knicks to the Gothams, played first base for New York. Converted cricketer Harry Wright of the Knickerbockers played right field and batted ninth. New York won the game, 22–18, and the Knickerbockers took the ball back to their clubhouse. But the game's only home run was hit by Brooklyn's Johnny Holder, second baseman of the Excelsiors, who thus won a $100 mid-game(!) bet he made with a spectator, when that meant real money.

GLOVES AND MASKS

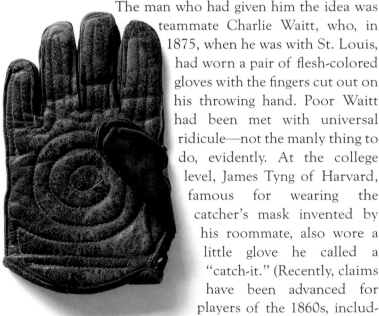

Who wore the first baseball glove? Albert Spalding, later famous for manufacturing gloves for the millions, told the story of how in 1877 he had felt personally mortified when he wore a modestly padded glove while playing first base. The man who had given him the idea was teammate Charlie Waitt, who, in 1875, when he was with St. Louis, had worn a pair of flesh-colored gloves with the fingers cut out on his throwing hand. Poor Waitt had been met with universal ridicule—not the manly thing to do, evidently. At the college level, James Tyng of Harvard, famous for wearing the catcher's mask invented by his roommate, also wore a little glove he called a "catch-it." (Recently, claims have been advanced for players of the 1860s, including Dave Birdsall and Doug Allison; an even earlier claimant is sure to come forth.) This glove, resembling a brakeman's glove, was an infielder's model of the late 1880s, the sort popularized by Philadelphia shortstop Art Irwin. No pocket, no webbing, no real construction except for a bit of padding at the palm—no wonder that shortstops of the era muffed one chance out of ten.

———★———

That's not a glove; it's a ham. This sort of catcher's glove was invented in the late 1870s by Frank Decker while in college at Princeton (he played major-league ball briefly in 1879). The mitt, from the 1890s, was designed to protect the hand more than to facilitate fielding, and from a safety standpoint this was a considerable advance upon the tiny, fingerless padded gloves worn by Buck Ewing and Silver Flint only a decade earlier. In earlier times catchers wore neither gloves nor masks nor chest protectors, and they took a fearful beating. (Later termed the "tools of ignorance," these devices seemed pretty smart at the time.) Broken bones, black eyes, split skin—these were the catcher's trademarks. Even the greatest of catchers seldom caught more than half his team's games; the physical strain was just too much.

The early rules, extending into 1884 in the major leagues, permitted a catcher to retire a batter on a foul bound (one bounce); this positioned him fifty

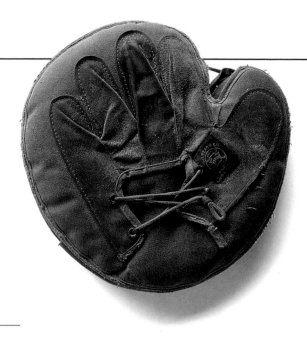

feet behind the batter unless a man was on base, at which point he had to move on up so he could throw out a potential base stealer. Also in that year, all restrictions on pitching deliveries were finally lifted (an underhand bowling motion had been mandatory until 1872, at which time an underhand whip motion was permitted; from then on there was an inevitable creep upward to sidearm, three quarters, and finally overhand). By 1890 a fastballer like Amos Rusie could turn a catcher's hand into a piece of raw meat. The battery of those days was more like assault and battery.

—★—

Now, this is a catcher's mitt with a pocket that no fist pounding made. This glistening hunk of leather belonged to Mickey Cochrane, and it caught the heavy fastballs of Lefty Grove and George Earnshaw. Unlike earlier models, this glove was not only for protection, it was flexible enough to make one-handed tags at the plate, as Cochrane often did. This 1930s glove evolved into the hinged-pad model of the 1950s and, twenty years later, into the contemporary model that, by way of Johnny Bench's one-handed style of catching, looks and feels much like a first baseman's glove.

Mickey was a tough guy, as most backstops were—his nickname, referring to his less-than-sunny personality, was "Black Mike." Once he gave pitcher Rube Walberg a swift kick in the trousers right on the mound to try to engage the hurler's attention. He was excellent at handling pitchers: both Schoolboy Rowe and Lefty Grove had sixteen-game

winning streaks with Cochrane behind the plate. He could hit with extra-base power, and his .320 lifetime batting average is best among all catchers. And he was a team leader, becoming a playing manager at age thirty-one. In 1934, his first year in that job, his Detroit Tigers won 101 games and the pennant; the next year they won the World Series. A beaning from Bump Hadley ended Cochrane's playing career in 1937.

—★—

The first player to wear a catcher's mask in the major leagues is said to have been Deacon White of the Boston Red Stockings, sometime in 1877. But he didn't invent it, nor did James Tyng, the Harvard man who wore it in an exhibition game between his college nine and the famous Reds in 1876 (Harvard won, 7–6, but that's another story). Tyng's college roommate was fellow baseball player Fred Thayer, who one year earlier had modified a fencing mask to preserve the fair features of friend Tyng.

Incredibly, the Hall possesses *three* Thayer masks: an original Thayer model worn by Tyng in 1876 and donated by the family of George Wright; another Thayer/Tyng model made for a player named Louis Trauschke, catcher of the Foster Base Ball Club of Lawrence, Massachusetts; and the 1878 patent model for the version produced commercially by

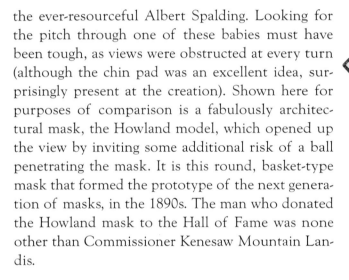

the ever-resourceful Albert Spalding. Looking for the pitch through one of these babies must have been tough, as views were obstructed at every turn (although the chin pad was an excellent idea, surprisingly present at the creation). Shown here for purposes of comparison is a fabulously architectural mask, the Howland model, which opened up the view by inviting some additional risk of a ball penetrating the mask. It is this round, basket-type mask that formed the prototype of the next generation of masks, in the 1890s. The man who donated the Howland mask to the Hall of Fame was none other than Commissioner Kenesaw Mountain Landis.

ORIGINAL MODEL of
THAYER BASEBALL MASK
Patented February 12, 1878, by
Frederick W. Thayer, Waverly, Mass.

PRESENTED BY THE CITIZENS OF
THE GEORGE "JUNIOR REPUBLIC"
"Smallest Republic in the World"
FREEVILLE, N. Y.

———————— ★ ————————

The first modern fielder's glove was designed by Bill Doak, and it changed the purpose of the glove from protection to better defense. Previously, players had labored for years to try and form a pocket in their gloves. Some guys even cut a hole in the middle of the mitt to give the ball a place to land. The usual method of catching a ball was to snag it the way you'd grab a ball with your bare hand, fingers closing down on the thumb and ball. The Doak model, introduced in the early

1920s, came with a pocket already in place and with webbing, rather than strings, between the thumb and forefingers. The difference it made was substantial; now the glove was a defensive tool. Fielding averages improved greatly. One historian said that even though Doak wasn't much of a pitcher, he caused more batters to be retired than anyone else in the history of baseball. Doak earned royalties on his invention for thirty-five years.

CAPS

This is a grouping of baseball caps spanning about sixty years, but all are of the same basic construction: a crown composed of six or eight panels, with airholes in each, and a board-covered bill of greater or lesser protrusion, with a sweatband of leather or (in the case of the Seattle Pilots monstrosity of 1969) cloth. As in the evolution of species, the greatest variety of styles was found at the dawn of baseball. The Knickerbockers' cap was not a cap at all but a straw boater, beginning in 1849 or so. The 1850s and 1860s saw floppy nautical caps, puffed-up baker's-style caps, and the Excelsior cap of 1860, a high-crowned prototype of the cap worn most frequently ever since. The 1870s produced the all-around-brimmed porkpie and no-brimmed fez style, as well as the cakebox style known as the Chicago cap, most recently worn by the Pirates of the 1970s and 1980s. (Several National League clubs also donned cakebox caps for the 1976 centennial season.) Brims have been short and crowns low (Boston-style, about 1910) and brims have been long, with crowns high (Brooklyn-style, same period).

When Casey Stengel was traded from the Dodgers to the Pirates in 1918, he went from a high-crowned to a low-crowned model. Nonetheless, upon his return to Ebbets Field, the resourceful Casey found room under his cap for a sparrow so that when the inevitable booing greeted him, he could doff his cap and send a message to his former fans.

———★———

The red-and-blue logo of 1922 has mellowed to a designer's vision in lavender and rose. But this is a rugged-looking cap worn by a rugged guy. It looks as though Frank "Pancho" Snyder was given to gnawing on the bill in tense situations. Snyder had a rather mundane career until John McGraw obtained him for the Giants in 1919. Pancho proceeded to hit .320, .343, and .302 as the number one catcher for the Giant teams that won consecutive pennants from 1921 through 1924. He caught pitchers such as Art Nehf, Rosy Ryan, "Shufflin' Phil" Douglas, Pol Perritt, and Slim Sallee—names so good they sound as if they came from the movie *Bull Durham*.

In the nineteenth century, the Boston National League club was one of the dominant teams of its era, winning eight flags. But at the turn of the century, as the new Boston Pilgrims (Red Sox) became the great attraction in Beantown, they went downhill. And stayed there. Since 1900, with the excep-

tion of the "miracle year" of 1914, the Boston Braves finished within ten games of first only *three* times through 1946. Eight times they were more than fifty games out. Ouch. In 1935 they finished with a record of 38 wins and 115 losses, despite the efforts of Babe Ruth; it was a winning percentage lower than that of the 1962 New York Mets.

In 1937 the Braves even changed their name—to the Boston Bees. They played a bit better and upped (yes) their attendance to 5,000 per game. This is the brilliantly pristine uniform of that year's stingers, worn by a thirty-three-year-old rookie pitcher named Jim Turner. "Milkman Jim" was a delightful surprise to the long-suffering Boston National League fans. He won twenty games that first year and led the league in ERA, complete games, and shutouts. He put together a thirty-one-inning scoreless streak. After a few years in Boston, Turner

went to Cincinnati, where he compiled a 14–7 record in the Reds' pennant-winning season of 1940. He then pitched in relief as a Yankee till he was forty-two (and, unknown to him because the stat was not yet being counted, led the league in saves that year). Turner was the archetype of the savvy hurler with fine control. "He knows all there is about pitching," manager Joe McCarthy said. Casey Stengel hired him as the Yankee pitching coach in 1949; he did two tours of duty there, ending in 1973. The old rookie who started with one of the worst teams in history wound up with ten World Series rings.

———★———

No, this isn't an All-American Girls League miniskirt. This is the earliest authentic uniform known to exist, from the Baraboo, Wisconsin, club of 1866. The belt and bib are of identical construction with a fireman's uniform of the day, which fits, for two reasons: (a) the fire hall was often the center of the community in many small towns (and large ones, too—even New York City's fire department was all-volunteer until the close of the Civil War), and (b) the companies that supplied uni-

forms to firemen were the same who later grew into sporting-goods emporia, and it was easy to cut a baseball pattern if it was identical to their stock-in-trade. Printing or embroidering a club's insignia on a detachable bib front made it easier for the supplier to stock generic shirts in inventory. The long sleeves were detachable, too, so that the basic model could be short-sleeved. Players wore long pants, banded at the ankle as a bicyclist would do today; knickers didn't become popular until promotional genius Harry Wright picked up on the idea for his Cincinnati nine, the better to display their well-formed calves.

—★—

This shirt has a sad tale. It was worn by Fred Snodgrass of the New York Giants in the 1912 World Series. Snodgrass was a center fielder with exceptional speed. He wasn't a superb hitter; his defense kept him in the game. But he made one bad play at a critical moment in a hugely important game, and like poor Fred Merkle and Bill Buckner and Lonnie Smith, the ballpark blunderer of 1991, and Tony Fernandez, whose error made the difference in 1997, he will forever wear the horns of the goat. Snodgrass's goof came in the last of the tenth inning of the eighth game of the 1912 Series (the second game had been called because of darkness

tied at 6–6). His Giants were up by one run at the time. But Clyde Engle, the first Boston batter, lofted a fly ball his way. Snodgrass dropped it. The story goes that his mother, sitting in a Los Angeles theater watching the Teletype reports of the game, fainted on the spot. On the very next play Harry Hooper lined a shot into deep center on which Snodgrass made an unbelievable catch, outrunning the ball. No one remembers that. Engle ultimately scored the tying run, and the Giants wound up on the short end. Snodgrass's error could have been overcome, but it wasn't. If the Giants had held on, he would be remembered for the catch he made, not the one he didn't. Instead, when he died in 1974, after a distinguished postplaying career and nearly sixty-two years after that dropped fly ball, the obituary headlines read, SNODGRASS DEAD AT 86; MUFFED 1912 SERIES. (See Chapter 12.)

—★—

This is the 1906 version of the warm-up jacket. Because of its odd combination of carnival jauntiness and morning-coat formality, such a jacket would be worn for pregame parades and festivities, photo opportunities, and the morning's wagon ride to the ballpark from the hotel. John Joseph "Red" Murray wore this jacket in his first big-league season, 1906. It was appropriate that young Red start out with the Cardinals, who had begun their existence as a National League franchise as the Maroons, to distinguish them from their opposing-league rivals, the Browns. Over time the Maroons became known as the Reds, echoing the city's Red Stockings franchise of the 1870s. Because of the confusion with Cincinnati's Reds and Boston's Red Stockings, the St. Louis Nationals became the Cardinals.

Murray moved on to the Giants and was a speedy right fielder on McGraw's pennant winners of 1911 through 1913. His most famous moment came in Pittsburgh's Forbes Field on August 16, 1909. The Giants were holding on to a 2–1 lead, but the skies were threatening as a dark and nasty storm blew in. Lightning flashed as the first Pirate hitter tripled. He scored the tying run a few minutes later, and the Pirates had runners on second and first with two out. Dots Miller smashed a ball deep into right center, which Murray and center fielder Cy Seymour went speeding after. It looked like a possible home run, or at least a triple. But at the last instant Murray reached out his bare right hand and snatched the ball, just as a lightning bolt lit up the sky. It was as though a thousand flashbulbs illuminated Murray's stellar catch. The rains came; the game ended in a tie. For years afterward the Giants loved to reenact the catch. In a train car with the lights out, Murray would pose as though he had just grabbed the ball and someone would light a match.

—★—

When the Pittsburgh Pirates and the Boston Pilgrims played a postseason "World's Championship Series" in 1903, most folks thought it signaled the end of the nasty battle between the National and American leagues. But it was an agreement between the two clubs; there was no league involvement. And there was no arrangement in place for 1904. John McGraw's Giants easily won the National League title that year, and it took a crucial wild pitch by New York's usually reliable Jack Chesbro to enable the Bostons to repeat in the American League. But McGraw wanted no part of

this World Series stuff. In his typical manner he announced that his players were the champs because they played in the "real" league and that playing those other guys would only "tarnish" their glorious season. His defiance hearkened back to his days in the American League with Baltimore, when he and league president Ban Johnson were always at odds over McGraw's umpire baiting. When Johnson suspended him in 1902, McGraw packed up some of his best players and headed for the Giants.

Things had settled down enough in 1905 for the leagues to sanction a postseason Series. And what a Series it was—for fans of great pitching. Every game of the five played was a shutout. Christy Mathewson threw three himself, in the space of six days. Now McGraw saw the advantage in playing the Series. And he proudly decked out his men in this World Champions uniform for the home opener of the 1906 season, in which the Giants circled the field in automobiles, bands played, and movie cameras whirred. Miraculously, the film survives.

And so does this uniform, worn that day by George Browne, McGraw's speedy leadoff hitter and right fielder. He's the fellow with the hat-hair in the lower right of the 1904 *Sporting Life* cover.

—★—

—★—

The changing face of baseball. Once upon a time there were only sixteen major league ball clubs, and they played in just ten cities, with only two leagues that, except for All-Star Games, never, ever played against each other until October. In the first half of the 1950s, the weaker sisters in three of the two-team cities pulled up stakes (Boston Braves to Milwaukee, St. Louis Browns to Baltimore, Philadelphia Athletics to Kansas City). In 1958 the Dodgers and Giants headed to sunny California. But in the 1960s (as with everything else, it seems), baseball exploded. In 1961 the Washington Senators moved to Minnesota, where they changed their name to the Twins. An expansion club, culled from the expendable players on the eight American League rosters, replaced the Washington Senators in D.C. and, like a hermit crab, took not only their home but also their identity. The American League joined the California gold rush with the expansion Los Angeles Angels, owned by singing cowboy Gene Autry, who was declared the twenty-sixth Angel.

In 1962 the National League expanded, too, into Houston and New York, giving us the Colt .45s (unlike the Chicago Colts of the 1890s, who were named for the youth of Cap Anson's players, the Houston nine became the only Major League Baseball team ever named for a weapon). And the expansion of 1962 also gave us the incomparable Metropolitan Baseball Club of New York, whose named recalled to life the Mets who had played in the first World Series, back in 1884, but whose play more closely resembled the Cleveland Spiders of 1899, who won 20 games that year while losing 134.

In 1969 the American League added Kansas City to replace the Athletics, who had also moved to California, and Seattle, whose management had been more hastily stitched together than their memorably grandiose uniform and cap. That year baseball became a truly international sport with the National League expansion into Montreal, and San Diego became the fourth National League expansion team (and the fifth team in California). The Seattle experiment lasted only a single season: by 1970 the Pilots were the Milwaukee Brewers, another name with a long and proud tradition. In 1972 the new Senators uprooted, becoming the Texas Rangers.

In 1977 the Toronto Blue Jays and Seattle Mariners entered the American League. The National League expanded again in 1993 to Florida and Colorado, balancing the leagues at fourteen teams apiece. But fans in cities like Charlotte, Phoenix, St. Petersburg/Tampa, and northern Virginia were still clamoring for new teams, and in the 1998 season the Tampa Bay Devil Rays and the Arizona Diamondbacks took the field.

Interestingly, when baseball expanded in the 1960s, it was quite okay for the new clubs to play in old parks, some of them woefully tired old minor league parks like Wrigley Field in Los Angeles or Parc Jarry in Montreal. Now the influence and power of baseball money has all but dictated that a city have a new park ready before a town can get an expansion team, which puts a new spin on the line from the film *Field of Dreams*: "You had better build it, or they won't come."

CHAPTER SEVEN

Ballparks and Fans

This Chicago trolley sign still provides a thrill: BASE BALL TODAY. Doesn't just reading the words on this page give an instant lift to your spirits? Today baseball and television help to define each other, but once upon a time the vital combination was baseball and transport. Media conglomerates buy baseball teams because of the synergy between the two: baseball provides cheap programming and draws traffic; the media does the promotion. In the same way, many teams in the early years of professional baseball were owned by trolley lines and short-line railroads—the "traction" companies that created enduring fortunes nationally and pretty profits locally. For example, a traction magnate would build a combination amusement-baseball-driving park at the end of his trolley line. Baseball, the horse races, and the carnival atmosphere provided the programming—a reason for people to use the trolley (particularly on weekends, when commuter traffic was down). The trolley lines promoted the game. Over time, the proximity of the ballpark and the trolleys led other businesses and residences to move there. The first major-league ballpark in Brooklyn was located at the intersection of five different trolley lines, so the fans headed for the game had to be careful where they walked. They became known as the "Trolley Dodgers," which, shortened to "Dodgers," became the home team's nickname. The name Los Angeles Dodgers is as interesting for its compacted history as the NBA's Los Angeles Lakers, who came to L.A. from Minnesota, the land of 10,000 lakes or, most amusingly, the Utah Jazz, formerly of New Orleans.

The magical number nine. Nine men on a side, nine innings to a game. This nine is especially charged with history. It comes from the manual

scoreboard at old Forbes Field, where in the ninth inning of the final game of the 1960 World Series it was the score for both teams when Bill Mazeroski (number nine himself) homered to upset the powerful Yankees. The hand-operated scoreboard that listed the score by inning for every game in both leagues was a small but rich pleasure for fans. You could catch every game going on at the same time. "What's that? The Dodgers scored three in the third? Haven't the Sox been up in the last of the sixth for a long time?" They even showed the numbers of the current pitchers, and the scorecard filled in the details. "Look! Buhl's been knocked out! Nottebart's in." As a kid I thought that if I couldn't be a big-league player, maybe I could be a scoreboard operator—that way I'd get to see all the games.

But, like many other things, that occupational window was closed as impractical when the "new wave" of monolithic, industrial-strength, multipurpose stadia began to appear in the 1970s. Fenway Park and Wrigley Field, two of the three oldest active parks, retained a human hold on the numbers. And when the "retro parks" such as Camden Yards and Jacobs Field came along, they brought back that delightful anachronism.

—★—

The cornerstone to Shibe Park, home to a million memories for fans of Philadelphia baseball. Except for home plate, which was moved to the new Veterans Stadium in 1971, this bleak reminder is all that is left of baseball's first palace for the fans.

Shibe Park began the boom in concrete-and-steel stadiums that came up like mushrooms in the decade that followed. It was named for Ben Shibe, owner of the A's and proprietor of a baseball-manufacturing company that produced more varieties of baseballs than the corner candy store had phosphates. An amalgamation of architectural fantasies and stolid middle-class virtue, Shibe Park had domes and turrets and arches and gingerbread icing, yet the dominant feature was its sea of red brick, red brick everywhere. It is hard to realize today how bold a statement its *permanence* made about the future of baseball in 1908, just five years since the American and National leagues had declared peace.

The A's had moved here from their previous home, Columbia Park, ripping up the sod and taking it with them as much for luck as frugality. In

years to come Shibe Park would be known as Connie Mack Stadium and, from 1938 on, would host the Phils as well as the A's. The Athletics left Philadelphia for Kansas City in 1955, and the Phils stayed on alone, until 1970. As this is written the team is agitating for a new baseball-only stadium to replace Veterans Stadium, the soulless multisport facility that replaced Shibe Park. I have a great idea for a design. . . .

These bits of paper are the kind of history few average fans would ever get to touch—season passes. Reserved for the working press and the famous or well heeled, they opened the door to any game the bearer wanted. Sometimes the passes were rendered in silver, with designs by famous artists, but for any baseball fan, even as cardboard they were more precious than gold. "Miss M. A. Vermilye" received hers in a handsome leather pouch. The typist in the Cleveland ticket office obviously didn't relish the challenge of spelling "Wambsganss," so he or she edited it to "Bill Wamby." Senator Hugh Scott was welcome at any Phillies game in 1965. The "Frank Adams" on the 1944 Yankee Stadium pass signed his celebrated "Conning Tower" columns "F.P.A." It was he who coined the eight-line verse "Tinker-to-Evers-to-Chance" in 1908. Ren Mulford was a hardboiled journalist who railed against both bad play and crooked dealings in Cincinnati and New York.

—★—

What's that dangling from the silk ribbon? A spittoon? A hard hat? No, it's a beanpot, commemorating the home of the bean and the cod, its Irish heritage, and its baseball team's most rabid rooters. Mike "'Nuf Ced" McGreevey, the boisterous bartender whose word was the ultimate authority on all issues, headed the Rooters (soon to add "Royal" to their name). The electroplate beanpot also celebrates the Boston team's unofficial nickname, "the Beaneaters." (Formerly they had been the Red Stockings.) The Rooters celebrated themselves with this "official" pin in 1897, a pennant-winning year for the hometown boys. Boston had a great team, with such future Hall of Famers as Hugh Duffy, Kid Nichols, Jimmy Collins, and Billy Hamilton. But they had to wrestle all season long before they finally nipped the equally great Baltimore Orioles, winner of the previous three flags, and their five future Famers John McGraw, Willie Keeler, Hughie Jennings, Joe Kelley, and manager Ned Hanlon. There was only one league in 1897, the National, so the first-place and second-place finishers squared off in a postseason contest for the Temple Cup. When the Boston team trained down to Baltimore after losing two of the three opening games in Boston, the Rooters accompanied them.

The Rooters rooted, but the Orioles prevailed. But that would be the last time the Rooters failed to sway the outcome of a Boston team in postseason play. In 1901, with neurotic logic, Beaneaters' owner Arthur Soden boosted his ticket prices in seeming disdain for the competition, a new American League team. The Royal Rooters switched allegiance. The Red Sox won all five World Series in which they next appeared—in 1903, 1912, 1915, 1916, and 1918—and the Rooters had a direct effect on the outcomes of at least two of them. You can look it up (in Chapter 10).

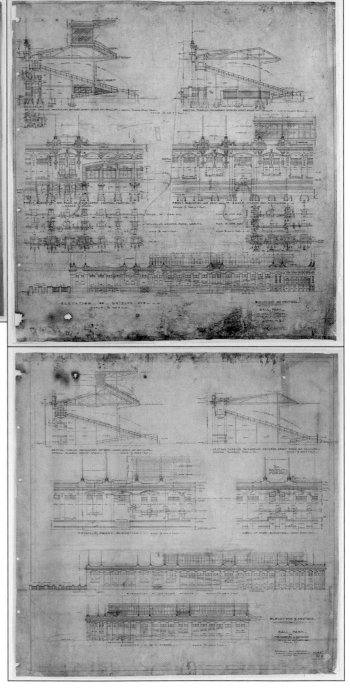

—★—

In 1906 the Chicago White Sox stunned the baseball world twice: by winning the American League pennant, even though they had the worst team batting average and slugging average in the league, and then by topping the powerful North Side Cubs, who had won 116 games that season—still the record—in the World Series. The Sox were quickly dubbed "The Hitless Wonders." Not surprisingly, the keys to their success were excellent defense and pitching, and "Big Ed" Walsh, of the scintillating spitter, was the pitching star. With the negotiation of a truce between the warring leagues, baseball was soaring in popularity. Forward-thinking owners in Pittsburgh and Philadelphia put up brand-new concrete-and-steel ballparks to hold many more fans than the old wooden contraptions. Sox owner Charlie Comiskey, who started out as a slick-fielding first baseman and then became a tough manager, felt that the time was propitious to abandon old South Side Park and build commodious new digs for his team.

The result was Comiskey Park, originally named White Sox Park, although some called it "Comiskey's Baseball Palace of the World." These original elevations and sections, discovered only upon the demolition of Comiskey Park in 1990, give some idea of the splendor of the detail. Like

Michelangelo executing a commission from Lorenzo de' Medici, architect Zachary Taylor Davis designed not for the city, not for the corporation, but a "Ball Park for Mr. Charles A. Comiskey."

Note that the ticket office is outfitted with a "tin roof with gargoyles" and the architect's hand extended even to the "turn stile" (spelled as two words, it reveals its simple meaning: a fence that turned). Even more impressive were the park's inside dimensions: 363 feet down the foul lines, 420 to dead (and we mean dead) center. During the design process, Davis and Comiskey consulted with Ed Walsh. Walsh, naturally, felt that cheap home runs were bad for the game, and Comiskey welcomed a player's perspective on what would provide the best brand of ball and help the team to win. They don't call it home field advantage for nothing.

———★———

This commemorative kerchief has been folded for many years, which diminishes its value in the collectibles hobby but enhances its charm for the baseball romantic. The signs of wear, even the hint of decay, are marks of character and testament to its worth. Keep your pristine Topps Mickey Mantle card from 1952; I'll take the one with banged-up corners and creases, the one that shows the touch of humanity.

The silk has been imprinted with remarkably crisp close-ups of five of the 1912 world champion Red Sox stars, subsequently star-crossed; a team photo; and a shot of the brand-new Fenway Park, today a creased memento itself.

On the far left is Smoky Joe Wood, easily the best pitcher in the American League that year. He spun an amazing 34–5 record and seemed poised for a superb career. Baseball fate took it away, as he ruined his arm after a slip on wet grass, though he stitched together an alternative baseball career as an outfielder by joining his Boston roommate Tris Speaker on Cleveland's world champions of 1920. Speaker and Wood would later be smeared, along with Ty Cobb, in a game-selling accusation by Red Sox teammate Dutch Leonard. Manager and first baseman Jake Stahl went from hero to unemployed in mid-1913 in a dispute with the club owner and

never managed again. Catcher Bill Carrigan took over for him and led the club to World Series victories in 1915 and 1916, then retired at the top, remembering what had happened to Stahl. Charlie Wagner (called "Heinie" in oblique reference to that shortstop named Wagner over in the other league) was thirty-two years old and past his peak even in 1912; that year turned out be his last good one.

———★———

Tickets are like bookmarks in the memory, stones in the river of time. The fans who held these stubs in their hands saw thrilling defensive plays, long homers, hustling doubles, and hidden-ball plays. They saw 0 for 4 days by .300 hitters, moments of glory by subs, surprise moves by managers. But what distinguishes all of these memories is that they are fixed in time in a way that an autographed bat or a genuine Cal Ripken statuette are not.

Some of these tickets were for Opening Day, when all teams are equal even if their prospects are not. A ticket might mark the birth of not only a new season but also a new ballpark, like Dodger Stadium and Comiskey Park, whose Opening Day tickets are shown here. A ticket might announce the birth of a new team, like the Baltimore Orioles of 1954, or hint

at the demise of another, like this rain check from the St. Louis Browns. A ticket can celebrate a century of baseball, the centennial of a team, a demicentennial of personal service, a return tour by faded heroes. It marks time.

Unlike World Series time, when everyone fortunate enough to get a ticket keeps it, regular-season tickets are throwaway items, which is why early ones are so highly prized. In fact, it's a good rule of thumb for building an interesting baseball collection of your own—keep what others would discard. You can't outsmart posterity, but this is the path to a collection of merit.

—★—

This beauty emerged from an envelope enclosed within a scrapbook in the Hall's basement, where it had reposed for decades. About fifteen years ago, while researching a picture history of nineteenth-century baseball for the Society for American Baseball Research, I came upon this earliest known season pass, admitting Mr. A. C. Johnson to the Jefferson Street Grounds of the Philadelphia Athletics. (A fine image of this ballpark, some eight years earlier, can be found in Chapter 11.) In the years since, an earlier season pass has turned up, but such discoveries detract not a bit from my pleasant memories of the hunt.

CHAPTER EIGHT

Special
Achievements

Tom Browning of the Cincinnati Reds was, at the end of the day, an ordinary pitcher—with a gift for the extraordinary. In 1985, his first full year in the big leagues, he was 9–9 in August, then ran out a remarkable string of eleven straight wins to finish 20–9 and narrowly miss Rookie of the Year honors. The next couple of years positioned him as a bulldog lefty who "threw strikes," "kept you in the ball game," and "gave you innings." In other words, exactly the kind of pitcher most major-league general managers wish they had more of, but no candidate for the Hall of Fame. But in 1988, at least, Browning had a Hall of Fame–caliber year. After splitting four decisions through the first two months of the season, he took a no-hitter into the ninth against the Padres before settling for a one-hitter. Including that win, he went 16–2 over the next few months, including a once-in-a-lifetime performance on September 16, when not a single Dodger reached first against him. It was then the fourteenth perfect game in baseball history. Fur-

thermore, over a span of three starts in which the perfecto was the centerpiece, he retired forty batters in a row, one short of the major-league record.

On July 4 of the following year Browning came within three outs of tossing his second perfect game, retiring twenty-four straight before Philadelphia's Dickie Thon opened the ninth with a double. He went back to being the reliable but prosaic pitcher he had been before, allowing more hits than innings pitched, until a string of major injuries shattered his career. But Tom Browning was no mere Joe Hardy— he tasted fame at the highest level, but he also delivered the everyday performance that entitles one to be termed a professional.

——★——

What is there to say about Babe Ruth that hasn't been said a thousand times over? That he was the greatest player ever? Sure, Ted Williams comes close in lots of batting categories and even tops the Babe in some. Henry Aaron hit more home runs and was undoubtedly a better outfielder. Willie Mays could throw with Ruth, and so could Roberto Clemente. The Babe was no threat to Rickey Henderson on the base paths. His lifetime batting average doesn't approach Ty Cobb's. And he couldn't have played shortstop like Honus Wagner. But none of these players, splendid as they were in their specialties and even in all-around ability, ever was called the best left-handed pitcher in his league. Case closed.

That he was the most popular player ever? The Babe signed thousands of items during his all-too-short lifetime, so it can't be said that his autograph is scarce. But it remains one of the most highly sought among collectors today; he could never have signed enough to meet demand. Things Ruth used or wore, or photographs and art that portrayed him, are precious beyond the dollars they fetch at auction. (In 1997 pitcher David Wells started a game at Yankee Stadium wearing one of Ruth's old caps, for which he had paid $35,000.) Only fifty years after his death, the Babe has attained an epic scale beyond that of such ancient worthies as Anson, Waddell, and Kelly, all honored in their day and mourned upon their deaths. Long ago I used to regale my eldest son, a baseball fan from the age of four, with tales of Ruthian exploits, such routine wonderments as "one year Ruth hit more home runs than any entire team in baseball besides his own." And I told him, in hushed tones, "In a World Series game, Ruth was getting a razzing from the opposing bench, so he simply pointed to center field, took a strike, pointed again, and took another—and then walloped a home run to the deepest portion of the park." When my son was six, I told him another story, evidently one more plausible. His response: "You mean Babe Ruth was a real person?"

Only Lincoln is loved more among American heroes, and only Paul Bunyan cut a mythic swath through the land like Ruth. As John Kieran wrote in 1927:

> He's the Bogey Man of the pitching clan and he clubs 'em soon and late;
> He has manned his guns and hit home runs from here to the Golden Gate;
> With vim and verve he has walloped the curve from Texas to Duluth,
> Which is no small task, and I beg to ask: Was there ever a guy like Ruth?

No, there was not. And the treasures on display here offer testimony.

—★—

In the mid-1920s Babe Ruth and Lou Gehrig were the stars of a western barnstorming tour that pitted the "Bustin' Babes" against the "Larrupin' Lous." In the collage you see the Babe's stylishly black but hellishly hot flannel jersey, with his signature sewn in at the collar. There is also a photo from that tour, when the Babe and Lou Gehrig were still the best of friends, before their celebrated feud. The story goes that Lou's wife, Eleanor, asked the Babe's new wife, Claire, why the daughter from her previous marriage was dressed more nicely than the Babe's daughter from his first marriage. As a result Babe and Lou did not speak for many years, until they reconciled at Yankee Stadium on July 4, 1939, when Gehrig said his memorable good-bye to baseball. More telling about Ruth's impact on the whistle-stop towns of his barnstorming days is the placard pasted into his scrapbook showing how the sleepy burg of Anaheim just about closed down to see Ruth play (and Walter Johnson was a pretty fair attraction in his own right).

Also shown here are a blackened, taped ball that Ruth is said to have used in his Baltimore bad-boy days, back at the St. Mary's home for orphans and incorrigibles (he was grouped with the latter, not the former). It was from St. Mary's that he rose meteorically in 1914 from an initial contract

with the minor-league Baltimore Orioles all the way up to the Boston Red Sox. Babe pitched splendidly from 1915 through 1919, his last year as a member of the Sox and his last as even a part-time pitcher (he started four games over the next fifteen years as a Yankee, and won them all). As a pitcher he could only benefit the club one day out of four. As a hitter in 1919, all he did was hit twenty-nine home runs, topping a record that had stood since 1884 and which had been tainted anyway (Ned

Williamson of the Chicago White Stockings had hit twenty-seven homers, but twenty-five of these came at home, where the distance to right field was less than two hundred feet).

The next year, his first with the Yankees, he shattered his 1919 mark by walloping fifty-four; the next season he outdid himself again, with fifty-nine. This feat, more than doubling his own record of only two years before, stimulated his admirers (President Warren G. Harding among them) to commission a "King of Swat" crown for Ruth, which he obligingly wore for photographers—the Babe never met a camera he didn't like. The silver cigar box was given to Babe by his teammates at the end of the 1932 season; Gehrig wasn't speaking to him, but he did consent to having his signature engraved.

The bat is the one with which he hit his 714th and final home run, wearing the uniform of the Boston Braves. The details are, like so much else, the stuff of legend. Almost forty and hopelessly out of shape, Ruth was released by the Yankees after the 1934 season because he wanted to manage the team and owner Jacob Ruppert wasn't inclined to fire Joe McCarthy to accommodate him. Ruth

hooked on with the Braves, but he was finished—hitting under .200, immobile at his new position of first base, and rapidly recognizing that he had been brought to Boston neither to play nor to be groomed for managing but as a gate attraction. In one final display of greatness and fury, like Samson, on May 25, 1935, he smote three epic home runs in Pittsburgh, the last one clearing the roof in Forbes Field for the first time in that park's history. It proved to be the Babe's final home run, as he quit a few days later. Although he coached for the Dodgers in 1938, he was never offered a job as a manager.

His wife, Claire, once said that he spent the rest of his life—only thirteen more years—waiting for the phone call that never came. In 1946 he was diagnosed with cancer. He rallied for a year or so, but the end was nigh. On June 13, 1948, at a celebration of the twenty-fifth anniversary of Yankee Stadium, Ruth sat before his locker, the one shown here, and put on this jersey, this cap, these shoes. As W. C. Heinz wrote, "He walked out into the cauldron of sound he must have known better than any other man." It was the last time; two months later he was gone. He had been, in the end, real enough.

This is a ball from a no-hitter that is no longer a no-hitter but retains this unchallengeable attribute: it is the greatest game ever pitched.

Harvey Haddix had a bit of a head cold the night of May 26, 1959, when he was scheduled to start against the Braves in Milwaukee's County Stadium, and the night was chilly and damp. It would have been a good night to take a rest. The pennant-defending Braves lineup featured potent sluggers Hank Aaron, Joe Adcock, and Eddie Mathews. But Harvey was a gamer. He set the Braves up and down in order, inning after inning. At the end of nine frames, he had retired twenty-seven consecutive batters. But his Pirate teammates had yet to break through and score against Lew Burdette. Three Pirate hits in the third produced no runs when Roman Mejias (playing in Roberto Clemente's slot for the evening) was thrown out heading for third on a hit to right. So Haddix kept on going. Through the tenth. And eleventh. And the twelfth, with not a single Brave reaching base by any means. The Pirates had a dozen hits, but still no runs.

To open the unlucky thirteenth, Pirate third baseman Don Hoak handled a routine grounder off the bat of Felix Mantilla, but he threw the ball wild. A sacrifice bunt by Mathews and an intentional walk to Aaron, who was batting exactly .442 at the time, brought up Adcock. Twice earlier Haddix had fanned him. Not this time. Adcock belted an appar-

ent home run into the night fog and over the center-field fence. Haddix had lost the game.

Aaron, however, thought the ball had fallen short and headed to the dugout, sure the winning run had scored. Adcock kept on going around second, which meant he was out for passing Aaron on the base paths. Fans and reporters left the game thinking the Braves had won 3–0. Only the next day did the league rule that Aaron was out, Adcock was to be credited with a double, and Haddix would be credited with a 1–0 loss in a perfect game. (The credit has become confused in recent years as the definition of a no-hitter has changed; Haddix and Ernie Shore have been "decertified" because neither threw a complete-game no-hitter of nine innings or more. Moreover Haddix allowed a hit in the thirteenth inning and Shore entered his game with a runner already on first base. This situation—perfect or imperfect—may well change again.)

A pretty remarkable award here—don't you love the three runners left forever in limbo while the fielder readies the tag? Recent research has verified that through the 1997 season there have been just 618 triple plays in major league history (since 1876). Cleveland shortstop Neal Ball was the first major leaguer to accomplish the feat unassisted in this century, when, on July 19, 1909, with this diminutive glove, he snagged a liner off the bat of Boston's Amby McConnell and retired Heinie Wagner and Jake Stahl on the base paths. Rochester first baseman Harry O'Hagen had been the first to turn the trick in professional baseball in this century against Jersey City of the International League

in 1902, a year in which he also spent significant time with three major league clubs.

But in a weird play that still provokes argument among baseball historians, Providence Grays outfielder Paul Hines may have collected an unassisted triple play on May 8, 1878, against Boston. And his effort was the most astonishing of all because he was an *outfielder*. As runners took off from second and third, Hines raced in from left field and snagged a liner into short left. Then he ran to third and stepped on the base. Because both runners had passed third, according to contemporary accounts, the tag of the base was all that was needed to retire them both (the man originally on third was out for

leaving too soon, the man originally on second would have had to retouch third on his way back). Hines then threw the ball to the second baseman, who tagged second base to be sure of the out. According to today's rules, Hines would be credited with a double play and an assist for the third out. But under the rules of 1878, the throw to second was unnecessary, placing Hines in the record books above all others.

The unassisted triple killing is so delightfully rare because it involves some heady defensive play along with some base-running blunders. It's more a flash of fate than of skill. The most famous of all, of course, took place in the 1920 World Series, when Cleveland second sacker Bill Wambsganss did in three Brooklynites in a flash. Among the eleven major leaguers who achieved the feat are two first basemen, Johnny Neun and George Burns, one outfielder (Hines), and eight middle infielders. None of these players (Ball, Wambsganss, Ernie Padgett, Glenn Wright, Jimmy Cooney, Ron Hansen, Mickey Morandini, John Valentin) were (or are) anywhere near Hall of Fame status, but their incredible moments live forever.

One of the most recent to accomplish the feat, Mickey Morandini of the Phillies, did it against the Pirates in 1992 and donated this uniform to the Hall. His sense of history was

lacking, however, when he made the play: Morandini didn't even keep the ball; he tossed it onto the mound. The next inning some Phil hitter fouled it into the stands. No one knows where it is today.

Who holds the record for hitting into the most triple plays, lifetime? None other than genuine Hall of Famer Brooks Robinson, with four. Much-traveled Joe Pignatano gets a special mention here. He ended his major-league career by rapping into a triple play in his last at-bat.

———★———

Three left-handed sluggers, one record. Before 1955 the record for consecutive games with a homer was six, by Ken Williams and Lou Gehrig. Pittsburgh Pirate Dale Long shattered that mark by cracking taters in eight straight games in May 1956. Long became an international celebrity overnight (proof—he made an appearance on *The Ed Sullivan Show*). Two weeks later Long fouled back-to-back pitches off his foot, tried to play through the injury, and proceeded to go 1 for 50. The next year he was traded to the Cubs. Twenty-one years after Long's feat, Yankee Don Mattingly matched the effort and exceeded it in some ways by hitting ten homers during eight games. That was also the year in which he hit six grand slams to set the major league mark. Blossoming superstar Ken Griffey, Jr., equaled this feat in 1993.

But perhaps the most amazing consecutive-game streak for home runs took place in 1968, the so-called Year of the Pitcher because hitters were an endangered species. Fighting the good fight for his kind was Frank Howard, the 6'7", 255-pound, right-handed slugger of the Washington Senators. Among the forty-four homers he belted that year were ten he hit in just six games in May.

———— ★ ————

The National League was still pretty green in 1880, its fifth season of existence. Reduced from eight to six teams in 1877, it had bounced back to eight, dropping Indianapolis and Milwaukee and adding Cleveland and such small-population franchises as Troy, Buffalo, and Syracuse, in 1879. In 1880 Worcester replaced Syracuse. This "baseball sketchbook" by H. H. Pollard, recounting "The Ups and Downs of the Worcester Base Ball Club, 1880," is a gem of cartoon art in fading purple ink. Each panel depicts the outcome of a Worcester game during its inaugural year in the National League, with colorful language and highly uncomplimentary depictions of opposing players (Cap Anson and his White Stockings were a favorite target) and cities (pigs running in the streets of "Porkopolis," or Cincinnati). Worcester finished that season twenty-six and a half games behind Anson's men, but the team made its mark for sure.

This scorecard tells the story of June 12, 1880, when Lee Richmond of the Worcester Brown Stockings threw the first perfect game, against the Cleveland Blues. Look closely at the fifth inning. See that "9–3"? Yep, Richmond's masterpiece stayed intact because right fielder Lon Knight threw out Bill Phillips at first base. Only five days later John Ward of Providence matched Richmond's perfect game. The feat didn't occur again till the estimable Cy Young performed it in the American League against Philadelphia in 1904. Four years

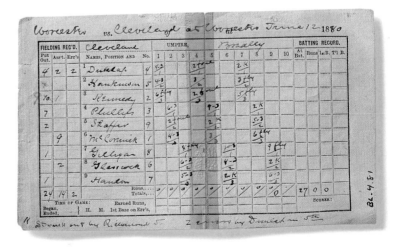

later Addie Joss of Cleveland also held the opposition runner-less for nine innings. The story is told that after Joss's gem someone ran into his son's schoolroom to shout, "Your dad just pitched a perfect game." The teacher wasn't thrilled. "So what?" he said. "So did I." The teacher was Lee Richmond.

———— ★ ————

Long before Babe Ruth, Mark McGwire, and Cecil Fielder, baseball had sluggers—that unique breed of musclemen who hit the ball a long way and, in so doing, created new levels of excitement and thrills for the fans. One of the first was Roger Connor of the Troy Haymakers and New York Giants in the 1880s and 1890s. Roger was no speed demon, but he belted a lot of triples because his long clouts couldn't leave the immense spaces of the old ballparks. In his career he hit 233 triples against only 138 home runs, the latter figure being unsurpassed until Babe Ruth in 1921!

No less than today, organizations saw the self-promotional value in giving awards for accomplishments large and small. Here *The New York Evening World* did its bit to promote itself as *the* sporting paper in the city. This gold watch fob was given to Connor for popping a ball over the distant center-field fence at the new Polo Grounds at Coogan's Bluff, on July 10, 1889. Landlord Coogan promptly

offered $100 to the next player who belted one over the fence. Connor had previously won such a prize for walloping the first ball out of the original Polo Grounds at Fifth Avenue and 110th Street, on September 11, 1886. There was no player more popular than "The Mighty Clouter" during his decade in New York.

Graphically, it's an exceedingly boring computer-printed ticket for a Reds-Padres game at Cincinnati in 1985. The magic comes from the notes penned on it: "Pete's hit 4192 . . . 93 . . . 8:01 time." The person who paid $3.75 for this ticket saw Pete Rose break the all-time hit record set by Ty Cobb, the long-thought-unreachable magic number

of 4,191. Perhaps. In independent researches, Pete Palmer and Paul MacFarlane uncovered the fact that in 1910, during the furious battle for the batting title (and the Chalmers auto that came with it), Ty Cobb had been credited with an extra 2 for 3 game in the records. So his actual (though not official) total was 4,189. Trust me that the story is more complicated than that, with other erroneous entries, but the correct—and now official—hit total is indeed 4,189. Rose had actually broken Cobb's mark the game before, in Wrigley Field. But the greatness of Cobb, and the greatness of Rose, consist of so much more than numbers.

Rose's stature as a player flowed, like Cobb's, from an incredible will to win. One of the most indelible memories of Rose is his headfirst dive home into catcher Ray Fosse to win the 1970 All-Star Game (and nearly ruin Fosse's career). Pete came to the park to beat you, nothing was clearer, and thus he was one of the game's most beloved players at home and one of the most despised on the road. He won three batting titles and led the league in hits seven times. Rose had ten two-hundred-plus-hit seasons; Cobb didn't do that.

The awful scandal and expulsion of 1989 tarnished even Pete's greatest accomplishments. So for years he has been perhaps the greatest player not in the Baseball Hall of Fame, forming a sad tandem with Joe Jackson.

You might well ask what a pitcher's bat is doing in the Hall of Fame. (No, it's not in the section for archaic equipment.) This is the bat of Rick Wise, a pitcher who finished just seven games over .500 (188–181) for an eighteen-year career but who had about as good a single day as anyone has ever had. His team, the Phillies, weren't known for scoring many runs. One day Rick was heard to say, "To win a game around here, you have to pitch a shutout and hit a homer!" Well, Rick went himself one better on June 23, 1971, when he not only hit *two* homers (one a two-run shot) but also pitched a no-hitter against the Reds. After the 1972 season Wise was dealt, even up, for the Cardinals' Steve Carlton, and most folks thought that was a fair trade, that's how good Rick Wise was (though he proved to be no match for Lefty and his four Cy Young Awards).

Braves hurler Jim "Abba Dabba" Tobin was another hurler who was a tough out. On May 13, 1942, Tobin slugged three home runs in consecutive at-bats against the Cubs. Two years later Tobin prefigured Wise when he homered and threw a no-hitter in the same game.

—★—

Baseball is the sport you play every day, which makes it (like life) a thing of peaks and valleys, ups and downs, hot and cold streaks. Which is what makes the man who wore this uniform so special. Henry Aaron didn't seem to blow hot and cold; although he had peaks, he never seemed to have a valley. His was a career of quiet, day-in, day-out excellence. And that is the only way to set the records he did: the lifetime best in home runs, runs batted in, extra-base hits, and total bases.

First in the record books because of his accomplishments as well as the alphabetical singularity of his name, Aaron also is last in a historical category that few recall: when he hit his record-breaking home run number 715, he was the last remaining major leaguer to have played in the Negro Leagues. First, last, and linked to generations of baseball players past and future, Henry Aaron is one for the ages. The most underappreciated superstar in any sport, Aaron nonetheless is the gold standard by which all players are judged. For all-around play—hitting, running, throwing, catching—he was the best.

He never hurried. Aaron said, "The thing I had on my side was patience. When you wait all your life for respect and equality and a seat in the front of the bus, it's nothing to wait a little while for the slider inside." Aaron's first professional baseball job was with the Indianapolis Clowns in 1952, as the Negro Leagues were winding down. Aaron was an awfully skinny second baseman on a team that was more about clowning than about baseball, but the Braves spotted the talent and bought him for $7,500. In his first full year with the Milwaukee organization, Aaron and two other players became the first blacks to play in the Southern Atlantic (Sally) League. The ring pictured here is from that season, when Aaron led the league in runs, hits, doubles, RBIs, and batting average.

Aaron got his chance at the majors when Bobby Thomson (of shot-heard-'round-the-world fame) broke his leg in spring training in 1954. The Braves and the Dodgers traveled north together, playing every day in towns along the way, and Aaron hung out with Jackie Robinson, Don Newcombe, Joe Black, and Roy Campanella. He learned about baseball and about dealing with racism in the majors. But nothing could have prepared him for what he faced as he moved toward breaking

Babe Ruth's lifetime homer mark. There were death threats, incredibly ugly verbal abuse, and a stream of letters from racist fans furious that a black man could make the Babe move over for him. The U.S. post office gave him an award for receiving the most mail—930,000 pieces—of any non-politician. He handled it all with the same quiet dignity he had demonstrated his whole career. "I don't want people to forget Babe Ruth," he said. "I just want them to remember Henry Aaron."

Here are the bat and ball he used to tie the 714 record, struck off Jack Billingham in Cincinnati on Opening Day in 1974, and the shoes he wore to break it, off the Dodgers' Al Downing back home in Atlanta. And there's fan stuff, too, from the road to 715. The title of Henry Aaron's autobiography, however, was not *I Hit a Homer*. It was *I Had a Hammer* (from his nickname, "Hammerin' Hank"), and in it he told of how he rang its blows not just for civil rights in baseball but for human rights everywhere.

—★—

The assault on Babe Ruth's 1927 record of sixty home runs had seen some close calls. Hack Wilson slugged fifty-six in 1930. Jimmie Foxx and Hank Greenberg had each reached fifty-eight before Ruth's record was a dozen seasons old. The mark of fifty would be reached just three more times before 1961. But that year the American League expanded, thrusting twenty pitchers into the league who wouldn't have made a major league staff the year before. Two Yankee sluggers made their move. Both Roger Maris and Mickey Mantle got hot in July, and the world cheered. For Mantle. The Golden Boy of the Yankees, the spiritual successor to Ruth and the direct descendant in center field of Joe DiMaggio was the one most fans wanted to break the record. The Yankees even considered changing their batting order, switching Maris to fourth and Mantle to third, to guarantee that Mickey would see plenty of pitches. (Maris did not receive a single intentional walk all year.) By July 25 Maris had hit forty, Mantle thirty-eight. In mid-September an abscessed hip knocked Mantle out of the running; he finished the season with fifty-four. Maris set his sights on the Babe.

Because the 1961 season had been expanded to 162 games, Commissioner Ford Frick—a former ghostwriter for Ruth—declared that Maris would have to break the record in 154 games for it to "count." Otherwise it would receive an asterisk in the books and in the minds of all Americans, figuratively if not literally. The pressure was unbearable. Not only was Maris daring to knock the legendary Ruth off a legendary pinnacle, Maris had none of the fan or media support that Mantle did. He began to lose his hair, in clumps. He had fifty-eight home runs when game 154 began. In the third inning he socked a line drive homer for fifty-nine. Six innings to go for Maris to catch the Bambino. In his next at-bat he hooked a drive ten feet foul, but he couldn't straighten it out with his remaining swings.

Maris had sixty home runs when the season's last game began at Yankee Stadium. Against Red Sox pitcher Tracy Stallard he finally did it—a single crack of the bat, a ball sailing into the lower-right-field stands, and the titanic record of Ruth had fallen. This is that ball, and this is that bat. The ball was snatched up by Yankee fan Sal Durante, thereby making himself the most famous fan since Brooklyn's Hilda Chester.

"It would have been a helluva lot more fun if I had never hit those sixty-one home runs. All it brought me was headaches," Maris said later. Maris won his second consecutive MVP title that year. But when he fell to thirty-three homers the following year, one publication called him "Flop of the

Year." The magic of baseball numbers is a funny thing. "Sixty" still sounds more like the pinnacle than "sixty-one" does. When a crop of today's young sluggers was asked about breaking the single-season homer mark, most of them referred to Ruth's record, not Maris's. The numbers we grew up memorizing are legends; the rest are just stats.

Something momentous for baseball fans changed when Maris hit sixty-one, just as something changed in 1974 when Aaron topped Ruth's lifetime homer mark. Yet for those who remembered the Babe, rather than feeling suddenly old and passé when "their" records fell, nothing much changed at all. And that's baseball, the way we like it.

— ★ —

No, this bat and helmet did not belong to the same player. They belonged to players who played for the same team seventy years apart. But their names will be linked forever because of what each accomplished in just one day. The bat is "Sunny Jim" Bottomley's. On September 16, 1924, Jim rapped out six straight hits against the Brooklyn Robins, managed by their namesake, Wilbert Robinson. But even more important, Bottomley also knocked home an even dozen runs, breaking the record Robinson himself had held for thirty-two years. Bottomley had the advantage of batting behind Rogers Hornsby, who was having a pretty fair season (he ended up with a .424 average). In the fourth inning, with his team down 5–1, Robinson walked Hornsby to get to Bottomley, who slugged a grand slam for his seventh RBI of the day. Two innings later he homered again to drive in a pair, and he concluded with a couple of singles for his final three RBIs. Mark Whiten also wore a Cards uniform on September 7, 1993, when, in the second game of a doubleheader, he tied Bottomley by driving in twelve runs. Unlike Sunny Jim, "Hittin' Whiten" didn't stoop to pick up pennies—no singles, doubles, or triples for him, just four emphatic home runs, which made him only the twelfth player in history to accomplish that feat.

CHAPTER NINE

All-Star Games

This modest tie clasp was given to members of the American League All-Star team of 1936, the first American League team to lose such a game (they had taken the first three contests). The tradition of handsome, modest, masculine baseball jewelry like this tiepin has disappeared. (Of course, wearing ties has nearly disappeared from the major leagues, too.)

The key plays of the 1936 All-Star Game involved a rookie in right field for the American League. With a man on first in the second inning, Gabby Hartnett socked a line drive to right off Lefty Grove. Joe DiMaggio tried to make a shoestring catch but failed, and Hartnett wound up at third. He scored on a single, and the National League had a 2–0 lead. In the fifth, after an Augie Galan homer had tacked on another tally for the Nationals, DiMaggio bobbled a single by Billy Herman, advancing him to second, from where he scored an unearned run. The 4–0 lead was too much for the Americans, even though they roared back with three in the top of the seventh. They had the bases loaded with two out when a screaming line drive was snagged by shortstop Leo Durocher. The man who hit the liner was none other than "Joltin' Joe," who had plenty of reasons to forget his All-Star debut.

——★——

It was the greatest moment of a sensational career—he said so himself—and this is the ball that sealed it: Ted Williams's two-out three-run homer in the bottom of the ninth off Claude Passeau of the Cubs to win the 1941 All-Star Game in Detroit for the Americans. And he showed it—the usually aloof Williams clapped his hands in boyish glee as he saw the ball clear the fence and jumped with delight as he rounded first. It looked as though Arky Vaughan was about to win the hero's laurels for the National League, as he swatted two two-run homers, one in the seventh and one in the eighth (becoming the first man to hit two homers in a single All-Star Game), giving the National League a 5–3 lead as the last of the ninth began. But two singles and a walk and a near game-ending double play got one run home, and Teddy Ballgame did the rest.

The 1941 season was the highlight of Ted's career for more than that one swing; it was the year he batted .406, making him the last major leaguer to cross that magical line. He also hit thirty-seven homers to lead the American League and topped the league in runs scored and walks as well with an astonishing .551 on-base percentage (the highest ever) and a .735 slugging average (tenth best). Williams didn't win the Most Valuable Player Award, however, as writers were swayed by Joe DiMaggio's flashier record of hitting safely in fifty-six consecutive games. Oh, well . . . both would be back for more.

Hitting was Ted Williams's passion. And he pursued that passion ferociously, relentlessly. People have called him brash, egocentric, and driven, but like him or not, he is the genuine article. "A man has to have goals," he said. "And that was mine, to have people say, 'There goes Ted Williams, the greatest hitter who ever lived.'"

Could Ruth have been any better? Maybe—but Williams faced tougher pitching than The Babe did, and his career spanned such innovations as integration, night baseball, relief specialists, and the dreaded slider—not to mention such interruptions as two stints of military service that cost him four to five years of his prime. Whatever statistical noodling one does on the subject of "Who was the greatest hitter of all time?" there are only two reasonable answers. Ruth has the all-time highest slugging percentage, while Williams is second; Williams the best on-base average, and Ruth is next. In years to come, new stars may complicate the issue, but any way you look at it, this is a small, tough group to crack.

Williams's famous batting chart, constructed by Major League Baseball Productions for its children's program, *The Baseball Bunch*, shows what he would hit on every possible ball in the strike zone. No false modesty was required; he knew. And Ted didn't swing at many that weren't in the zone. He led the league eight times in free passes. Some say it was a function of his superb eyesight (which also helped make him a successful fighter pilot), but, like umpire Bill Klem, Williams himself never thought eyesight counted for much; the real reason for his unwillingness to swing at a bad pitch was that he knew an expandable strike zone would keep him from being a great hitter. An early minor-league batting instructor of his was no less than Rogers Hornsby, who offered the advice Ted took to heart: "Always get a good pitch to hit." He was also instructed by white-haired Hugh Duffy, the man who in 1894 achieved the highest batting average ever, .440.

On display here is the bat with which he hit home run number 500 of his eventual 521. The uniform is from 1942, when he won the first of his two Triple Crowns and the last year he would play until returning from the war in 1946. The previous year, when he hit .406, he became the last man to break the .400 mark. George Brett came close with .390 in 1980, and Tony Gwynn with .394 in 1994. *Close.* Ted was close in 1941, coming into a last-day doubleheader with the Philadelphia Athletics. In fact, he was so close, at .39955, that he could have sat out and eased into the record books with a rounded-off mark of .400. But that wasn't his style. He went 4 for 5, including a homer, in the first game, and 2 for 3 in the second.

Among the modern glories of the Baseball Hall of Fame are two wooden sculptures by Armand La Montagne of North Scituate, Rhode Island, one of Babe Ruth, on display elsewhere in this volume, the other of Ted Williams. Astonishingly realistic, the Williams sculpture captures for eternity the uncoiled energy of the stance that made "The Kid" a legend.

This is the cap that Bo Jackson wore during the 1989 All-Star Game, for which he received more votes than any other American League player that year. He started off with a bang. His fine running catch in the top of the first thwarted a National League rally. Then he slugged the first pitch he saw for a homer. In the second inning he beat out a slow roller to drive in the run that gave the American Leaguers the lead for good. He also stole a base (the first player since Willie Mays to homer and swipe a sack in the same All-Star Game). And he was voted the game's MVP.

Bo Jackson barely knew how to play baseball when he signed with the Kansas City Royals in 1986. He'd played some at Auburn, where he was an All-American football player, but baseball was pretty much a lark to him. He was a pure, natural athlete, and he was dedicated enough to learn his craft, the first man to play professional football and Major League Baseball in the same season in dozens of years. It was very clear to everyone that despite his rough edges on the field he was something quite special. The ball jumped off his bat with a distinctive crack, one that Kansas City scout and longtime baseball man Buck O'Neil said he had heard only a few times in his life, first with Babe Ruth, next with Josh Gibson, and finally Bo Jackson. I have not seen as many games as Buck (who has?), but with me Bo holds the distinction of having made the greatest throw I ever saw, from the left-field wall to home plate on the fly to nail a runner who should have been able to score standing up.

But like Herb Score, whose terrifying injury on a line drive to his face effectively ended his career, Jackson's career would never fulfill the promise it briefly displayed. A football injury led to hip replacement surgery. He actually returned, playing major league ball for the Chicago White Sox with an artificial hip, and hit one of the longest homers ever in the Kingdome, but his natural talent and enthusiasm weren't enough to overcome the injury. He retired from baseball after the 1994 season.

——★——

The All-Star Game has become more than just a showcase of baseball's stars in midsummer. It has become a showcase for the city and ballpark where it is held and for Major League Baseball in general. Now every All-Star Game is accompanied by a Fan Fest that attracts thousands for baseball displays and vendors and reminds one of the carnival atmosphere in which many professional baseball games were staged before the turn of the century— amid steeplechase rides, carousels, and shoot-the-chutes. Cities with new parks to show off (and thereby promote the influx of tourist dollars) eagerly jockey to be named the upcoming site (instead of just taking turns, as baseball did for decades). The Home Run Contest on the day before the game often provides more excitement than the game itself. But, as you can see from this selection of All-Star Game tickets, the passes to the games have been unusually good looking for a long time. Don't you love the grim visage of Commissioner Landis flanked by the cutout heads of Ford Frick and Will Harridge on the 1936 game ticket? Do you think Landis's head was really that much bigger than those of the league presidents?

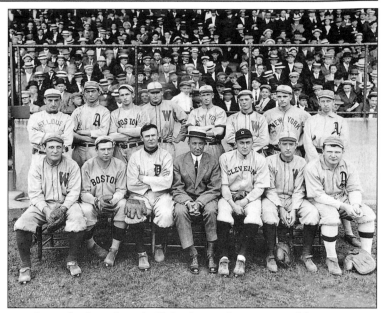

It had to be the loftiest example of clutch pitching in history. With the 1908 pennant in the nail-biting stage, in a three-team race among Chicago, Cleveland, and Detroit, Chicago's Ed Walsh, who was to win forty games that season, threw a four-hitter, allowing just one run, unearned, while striking out fifteen. But Addie Joss of Cleveland—known as "The Human Hairpin" because of his narrow build—was even better, fashioning a perfect game. In addition to being a fine moundsman—he allowed fewer base runners per nine innings than any pitcher in major league history—Joss was an honest and upright man, held in high esteem by everyone who knew him. But his body let him down. He took ill in the off season before 1911 and died just before the season started of tubercular meningitis, just thirty-one years old.

His funeral, presided over by Billy Sunday, the ballplayer-turned-evangelist, drew a huge crowd. His Cleveland teammates were scheduled to play their opening game the day of Joss's funeral. Expecting they would be fined or fired, they nonetheless headed for the services. Their solidarity has been called the very beginnings of the players' labor movement. It turns out their ownership was a little more enlightened and even scheduled a benefit game between Cleveland and an American League All-Star team to raise money for Joss's widow (this was long before baseball had anything resembling pensions). Ty Cobb, who donated an additional fifty dollars of his own money to the fund (as much as the whole Yankee team gave) is wearing a Cleveland uniform because his Tiger gear missed the train. For the record, here are the men in the picture from left to right, starting with the front row: Germany Schaefer, Tris Speaker, Sam Crawford, Jimmy McAleer, Ty Cobb, Gabby Street, Paddy Livingston; *back row*, Bobby Wallace, Frank Baker, Joe Wood, Walter Johnson, Hal Chase, Clyde Milan, Russ Ford, Eddie Collins. Not a bad group, eh?

Though unofficial, it was the first major-league All-Star Game.

These days All-Star Game players wear their own club's uniforms. That's the way the fans like it, and this photograph tells why—the uninspired road garb of the National League for its 1933 debut (this happens to be the uniform of outfielder Chick Hafey). The All-Star Game had been a brainstorm of *Chicago Tribune* sports editor Arch Ward, a way of lifting the spirits of Chicago and baseball out of the Depression doldrums while copromoting the national pastime with the Century of Progress Exhibition running concurrently down by the lake. Ward's idea turned out to be a hugely popular success and later that summer inspired an equally successful Negro League companion piece, the East-West Game.

Both All-Star Games owed a nod to such predecessors as the Joss Benefit Game of 1911, the mid-season All-Star contest in the Class D Hudson River League in 1903, and the granddaddy of them all, the Fashion Race Course games of 1858. Benefit games for the families of dead players had long been common in cricket, and they easily made the

transition here. In the last half century, however, the Players Association pension fund has made such public charities unnecessary. Organizations such as the Baseball Assistance Team attend to private charitable contributions for players and their families who may be down on their luck.

★

In its first year, the All-Star Game was a name bearing so little cachet that the official scorecard didn't even mention the name of the event on its cover. It wasn't until two years later, for the 1935 summer classic, that the name "All-Star" made it to the cover, only to vanish again in 1936, 1939, and 1942.

Recent program/scorecards have cost not ten cents but fifty times that amount and more, with fine feature pieces, full-color photography, bound-in and die-cut special effects, and even a computer chip that, when squeezed, played "Take Me Out to the Ball Game." The All-Star Game has become a big-time event with a big-time budget and national media coverage. Everything about the game is better, except that the animosity between the leagues, once real, no longer exists as players move easily from one league to the other over the course of their careers. Where once the All-Star Game was played for bragging rights, today the outcome is no more meaningful than that of a grapefruit- or cactus-league game.

★

These miniature beauties are prized as collectibles because, unlike baseball cards, which are mass produced and whose values are susceptible to fashions and player desirability, they have the traditional characteristics that drive all markets in tangible goods, from gemstones to fine art to stamps and coins. Given some minor variation in condition, a press pin is scarce by virtue of its controlled distribution. No

beat writer given one of these for covering the game is likely to toss it aside. In fact, for veteran scribes a collection of press pins accumulated over a lifetime is something of an heirloom, one of the few fringe benefits of a career in which the hours are long and the pay meager. Nobody becomes a baseball writer for any reason other than the one that drives grown men to play it and to hang on in the game as long as they can: love.

CHAPTER TEN

World Series

Before the World Series ring became the common reward to members of the winning team, items such as watches and medallions were more typical. This watch, given to the 1928 Yanks (for the second of their two straight sweeps in Series appearances), is an All-American gem. There's the ball, and the bats, but there's also the flag escutcheon with its thirteen stars and the ascendant American eagle. America was the world's champion in the decade after World War I; the Yankees were America's champion and, by patriotic extension, the world's.

In 1927 Babe and the boys had taken just four games to knock off the Pirates, but it was hardly a slugfest; only two homers— both by Ruth—were hit. In 1928 it was different; Gehrig pounded four himself, Ruth added three (all in the final game), and the Yanks outscored the Cardinals, 27–10. Babe hit .625 for the Series and scored nine runs, but Gehrig was the batting star, with an amazing 1.727 slugging average and nine RBIs in the four games. The Cards walked him six times, too.

It didn't matter. The already large Ruth legend swelled even more when he invented "the healing homer." He had sent two autographed balls during the Series to a seriously ill eleven-year-old, Johnny Sylvester, and "promised" a home run. When the Babe belted three, the tale holds that Johnny made a miraculous recovery.

———★———

With delicious serendipity, this 1912 World Series press pin, commemorating a New York–Boston contest for the ages, arrived at the Hall of Fame in 1986, the next time these two cities met in the World Series. You can tell the pin originated in New York: the teeny catcher cowers behind the giant batsman, which mirrored John McGraw's expectations. But events overtook expectations, as they so often do in baseball and real life, and the Red Sox emerged victorious in a spectacular finale.

The words faintly embossed in the ribbon read: "World's Series/Brush Stadium/Polo Grounds/New York, 1912." In our minds the staccato recitation of bare facts follows: Smoky Joe Wood, Christy Mathewson, and the eternally forlorn Freds, Merkle and Snodgrass. No World Series has ever been more full of on-field heroics and blunders and off-field weirdness. For one thing, the Series was scheduled for best of seven, but because of a darkness-inspired tie in Game 2, it took eight games. This triggered some problems in the Boston ticket office that would cascade onto the field.

The Red Sox were up three games to two when they returned to Fenway Park for Game 6 (actually the seventh played). But an enterprising clerk in the ticket office had sold the seats designated for the rabid throng of Sox fans, the Royal Rooters. Furious that they couldn't get in, the Rooters stormed the field, knocking down the outfield fence just before the game was to start, and paraded around loudly. The game was delayed, and Sox starter Smoky Joe Wood (34–5 during the regular season) cooled off. As a result, the Giants ripped him for six runs in the first inning on their way to winning the game, 11–4, and tying the Series.

Then came the final game, with heroic Christy Mathewson dueling journeyman Hugh Bedient. The Giants were holding on to a 1–0 lead in the seventh when the pinch hitter for Bedient doubled in the tying run. Wood came in to relieve. When Tris Speaker juggled a single in the top of the tenth, the Giants took the lead as baseball's all-time goat, Fred Merkle—he of the 1908 pennant-losing blunder—drove in the run. He was only three outs away from

shedding his horns at last, and the Giants were only three outs away from validating their press-pin stature.

The first batter in the last of the inning, Clyde Engle, lofted an easy fly toward the usually sure-handed Fred Snodgrass in center field. But Snodgrass inexplicably muffed it. On the next play he nearly redeemed himself when he made a super catch and almost doubled up Engle. The next batter took ball four, and Speaker came to the plate. Matty induced a low foul pop-up between first and home.

What happened next is shrouded in mystery. For some reason, first baseman Merkle didn't move toward the ball. Catcher Chief Meyers did all he could to reach it, but to no avail. Some said Mathewson made the wrong call, hollering for the Chief to take charge. Others say Speaker himself shouted, "Chief! Chief!" For whatever reason, the ball fell for just a strike. Speaker, given his reprieve, took advantage, lining a single to right to tie the game. Two batters later a sacrifice fly gave the Red Sox the championship. Never again—until 1986, that is—did another man emerge to vie with Merkle and Snodgrass for goat honors. And not until 1997 did another team come from behind in the ninth or extra innings to win the final game of a World Series.

———— ★ ————

Ballplayers and entertainers have always had a lot in common. Both expect and enjoy the limelight; both are separated from the rest of us by the adulation and money we pour on them. Sometimes in their separation from the rest of society they reach out to each other in matrimony: Rube Marquard and Blossom Seeley, Joe DiMaggio and Marilyn Monroe. In the 1880s John Montgomery Ward was one of the most famous ballplayers around. And Miss Helen Dauvray was a noted actress. The two hit it off and were married during the post-season championships of 1887, the fourth such "World's Series" between the American Association and National League champs.

An avid fan and self-promotional genius, Miss

Dauvray felt that the winners should receive something more than just recognition. She encouraged the owners of the two teams to put up money for a gorgeous trophy named after herself, and she put up her own money to create pins for each of the winners. This pin belonged to slugging Sam Thompson of the National League "Detroits," who defeated the St. Louis Browns ten games to five.

That's right. Baseball was experimenting with formats for the postseason extravaganza; that year's idea was a doozy: a fifteen-game World Series, played in eleven parks in ten different cities. They started and ended at Sportsman's Park in St. Louis. But after the Browns took Game 1, Detroit went to work, winning seven of the next eight. By the time they got back to St. Louis, the Detroits had a whopping ten-games-to-four lead. No wonder only 659 folks showed up for the October 26 finale, and they were grateful when the game was called after six innings because of cold weather.

—★—

The Hall Championship Cup of 1888 was devised to imitate the success of Helen Dauvray's initiative of the year before. This ungainly urn was presented to the New York Giants on the evening of October 26, along with the Dauvray Cup, for they had clinched their 1888 championship victory over St. Louis the day before. A handful of die-hard St. Louis fans were treated to meaningless Games 9 and 10, but Giant shortstop John Ward went home after the decisive Game 8.

Ward and his wife, Helen Dauvray, separated and reconciled several times in the years to come—becoming staples of the society pages as well as the sports section—because of Ward's opposition to her resuming her acting career. Ultimately, they divorced (the marriage of Helen's sister to Ward's teammate Tim Keefe endured), and the Dauvray Cup disappeared for decades.

The ostensible differentiation between the Dauvray Cup and the Hall Cup was that the Hall was awarded to the National League champion, while the Dauvray went to the world champion. Some silversmith may have created an American Association championship prize, but this awaits further research.

—★—

When the players broke ranks with the owners in 1890 to form their own league, the "World's Series" was a casualty. Albert Spalding and the moneyed men of the National League were able to break the Players League (and very nearly professional baseball altogether), and this success gave them the idea that they could eliminate the competition of the "beer and whiskey" league, the American Association, as well.

After one year the National League owners succeeded and the twelve-team National League (expanded to include four of the better American Association teams) was the only major league. The fans didn't take to the idea; major league attendance was down by 825,000 over the previous season, an incredible one-year decline of nearly 30 percent. The moguls tried to boost interest by splitting the season and pitting the two half-season winners in a postseason championship. Second-half winner Cleveland played first-half champs Boston in the best-of-nine series and didn't win a game.

Just as in the 1981 season, when baseball tried to mitigate the damage of the fifty-two-day strike in midseason by dividing the season in two, the whole thing left fans yawning. In 1893 the Pirates (who got their nickname because of the dubious way they obtained Louis Bierbauer, a player who had jumped to the Players League) finished a close second, but there was no chance to redeem themselves in a postseason series. So Pirate president William Temple suggested a championship series between the first- and second-place teams. In 1894 the Temple Cup Series began; it lasted just four years. The players, who weren't getting much money for the deal, didn't care for it. Neither did the fans: where 22,000 of them had attended a Temple Cup game in its first year, only 700 showed up for the dismal conclusion four years later.

Here's a historic document, all right. The only National League team not devastated by defections to the upstart American League in the first three years of the century was the Pittsburgh Pirates. Some say this is because Buc owner Barney Dreyfuss was such an honest and fair fellow that his players were exceptionally loyal (the story goes that Honus Wagner turned down $10,000 in cash to jump); others say that league president Ban Johnson and the American League owners figured that a strong team in Pittsburgh meant weaker opposition in the five cities where the leagues met head-to-head (New York, Boston, Philadelphia, St. Louis, and Chicago).

The two leagues made peace in 1903, but feelings were still pretty raw when at the end of that season Dreyfuss and Boston owner Henry Killilea cooked up a deal to pit their league champions in a best-of-nine postseason series. Note that this was an arrangement between two teams, not two leagues. The National Commission, baseball's ruling body before the advent of the commissioner system, did not mandate a World Series until 1905, after owner John Brush and manager John McGraw had declined to pit their victorious Giants against the American League champs in 1904.

A highlight of this document is the handwritten clause "4-1/2" stipulating that no player would be eligible for the Series who was not on the team's roster as of September 1. (In four of the previous century's Fall Classics, teams fielded players who had not appeared in any regular-season game for the club!) It was a canny way to prevent the opposition from stocking up on "rented" players, and it has been part of the Series covenant ever since.

———★———

This scarred and bedraggled artifact was thrown by Pittsburgh's Deacon Phillippe as the first pitch of the 1903 World Series. In the next inning, Cy Young threw it to Ginger Beaumont, who registered the first hit. Four innings, ten Pittsburgh hits, and six Pittsburgh runs later, the ball looked like this. Phillippe won Games 1, 3, and 4; he lost Games 7 and 8. All five efforts were complete games. He had to bear the load because the Pirate pitching staff had been decimated by injury and, in the case of sixteen-game winner Ed Doheny, mental illness.

So, despite a superior team on paper, the Pirates and Honus Wagner lost to the upstart Boston Pilgrims, five games to three, thus beginning the grand tradition of World Series upsets.

This souvenir scorecard from 1903 World Series Game 2 features Boston barkeep Mike " 'Nuf Ced" McGreevey (the typesetter here employs variant spellings). Compared to the proprietor of the Third Base Saloon ("the last stop before Home"), Boston and Pittsburgh managers Jimmy Collins and Fred Clarke were nonentities—on this card.

As head of Boston's Royal Rooters and ultimate authority on all things baseball (hence his definitive nickname), McGreevey was a legend in his town. The Rooters traveled to Pittsburgh for the away games and caused the Pirates no end of trouble with their loud cheering, particularly the way they altered the words to a popular song to get Pittsburgh's goat. Instead of singing "Tessie, why do you treat me badly," they hollered, "Honus, why do you hit so badly" and the like. Sixty years later Pirate third baseman Tommy Leach, when asked how the favored Pirates could have lost to the Pilgrims, groused about "that damn song."

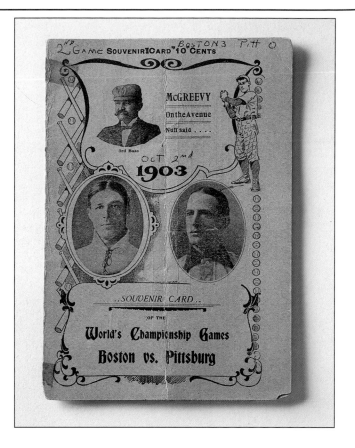

It's incredible that this insignificant slip of paper—the turnstile receipt for the first game of the 1903 Series—should have survived. Hiding behind this scribbled slip is a surprising story. Pirates owner Barney Dreyfuss, pleased at his team's effort despite their loss, chipped in his share of the Series moneys to the players' pot. As a result, the losing Pirates took home $1,316 each for their participation, the victorious Pilgrims just $1,182.

Attendance at World Series games has long been equal to stadium seating capacity. For the World Series of 1903, many of the 16,242 in attendance stood behind ropes in the outfield, an area termed the "bull pen." It is this enclosed area, a staple of ballparks since their beginnings in the 1860s, that gave rise to the domain of relief pitchers—not, as is often reported, the Bull Durham tobacco signs in the outfields of the 1910 era.

Wow. Talk about memories encapsulated on nine little pieces of cardboard. What would you give to have been at these games? The fifth game of the 1956 Series, when the quirky, barely average Yankee pitcher Don Larsen retired all twenty-seven Dodgers to face him on ninety-seven pitches. Game 5 of the 1969 World Series, in which the underdog New York Mets defeated the Baltimore Orioles to complete their climb from laughingstock to world champions. Game 4 of the 1919 Series, when Eddie Cicotte of the Black Sox tossed the game away on purpose. The final game in 1973, the second of Oakland's three consecutive championships in the 1970s (and, incidentally, Willie Mays's last time in uniform as a player). Game 7 of 1960, ended by Bill Mazeroski's ninth-inning homer, was one of the most thrilling, hand-me-the-nitro-pills games

ever played (and, incidentally, Casey Stengel's last game as Yankee manager).

There's a reminder, too, of the 1993 Series in which Joe Carter's home run against the Phillies joined him forever in baseball history with Mazeroski. There's the 1946 Series, the only one that Ted Williams ever played in, and the 1950 affair that was Robin Roberts's only chance for a ring; both were disappointed. And there's the game that a younger generation will remember simply as "Game 6," when the 1975 Red Sox rallied on a three-run pinch-hit homer by unlikely hero Bernie Carbo to tie the game with two outs in the last of the eighth, and ultimately prevailed as Carlton Fisk waved his long fly fair to win the game in the twelfth. Defining moments all, generational mileposts, embodied in these mere stubs.

———★———

The 1991 Series was full of pressure. Both the Twins and the Braves had been last in their respective divisions the year before. Neither team had the ability to break through, it seemed. Minnesota easily took Game 1 and Atlanta blew open Game 5, but every other game was decided by the thinnest of margins—one run. Game 3 went twelve innings.

nings. Game 6 went eleven because Kirby Puckett made a game-saving catch in the third and then homered to win it. Game 7 went ten.

The Series was memorable, and Jack Morris's shutout in Game 7 was remarkable, but, as usual, the Series thrust forward an improbable hero. It is this ball, lobbed to left field for the Twins' winning hit in the overtime frame, that guaranteed obscure pinch hitter Gene Larkin a little piece of immortality in the Baseball Hall of Fame.

———★———

This mitt doesn't seem to have much magic about it. It could have belonged to your uncle George. It looks like a glove that's made its share of catches, the glove of a hard worker, a journeyman.

For one day in 1947 the man who wore this glove was the toast of Brooklyn and the world. His name was Al Gionfriddo. Al had been a sometime out-

fielder for the Pirates during World War II. On May 3, 1947, the Pirates paid the Dodgers $100,000 and got five players. The Dodgers got, as a throw-in, Mr. Gionfriddo. He hit a measly .175 with the Dodgers in limited duty, but he earned his paycheck on October 5.

It was Game 6 of the World Series in Yankee Stadium, the first ever televised. The Dodgers were desperately trying to hang on. Down three games to two, they had just overcome a 5–4 Yankee lead with four runs in the top of the sixth. Gionfriddo came in to play left for defensive purposes. Sometimes the manager is a genius. The Yanks put two men on, and with two out Joe DiMaggio came to bat. He swung that sweet swing of his and lined a ball deep into left field, toward the bull pen. The Dodger lead looked short-lived. But Gionfriddo made a long run and snatched the ball out of the air just before it hit the 415-foot sign. The kinescopes show the usually stolid DiMaggio uncharacteristically kicking the dirt as he rounded second. The Dodgers lived to play another game. (Which they lost, of course, but that's a story of its own.)

Two days earlier Gionfriddo had taken part in an-

other all-time Series highlight. Yankee right-hander Bill Bevens held a 2–1 lead in the bottom of the ninth inning, and he hadn't given up a hit. He proceeded to record two outs, but he also put two men on via walks (including pinch runner Gionfriddo). With a World Series no-hitter and a 3–1 Yank lead in the Series hanging in the balance, Cookie Lavagetto (another former Pirate) smacked a double to snatch Bevens's claim on immortality and top the Yankees, 3–2.

Amazingly, after October 1947 none of these men—Bevens, Lavagetto, and Gionfriddo, all at the very center of a great World Series between two great teams—ever played another inning of major-league ball.

——★——

This tableau embraces four men and shows how, in baseball, whole careers can be whittled down to an instant. Ralph "Babe" Pinelli had played 774 games as an infielder in the majors, but he earned his greatest fame as an umpire. For twenty-two years he was a dependable and fair National League arbiter. The ball-strike indicator shown here was his, and it records the count prior to his final call behind the plate, on October 8, 1956, Game 5 of the World Series. The glove belongs to the Yankee catcher in that game, Hall of Famer Yogi Berra. The cap belongs to the pitcher Don Larsen, and after that final pitch he grabbed Berra in a huge Berra-hug and tottered off the field in joy and amazement.

The call was strike three on Dodger pinch hitter

Dale Mitchell, the last pitch he faced in a distinguished baseball career. It was also the last pitch Pinelli called behind home plate. Most important, it was the pitch that landed Larsen a place in baseball history. Never before or since has there been a feat to equal it: a World Series perfecto—no runs, no hits, no one allowed on base. (Never before or since, either, has a member of the press asked a more fatuous postgame question: "Don, was this the best game you ever pitched?")

As a (former) Brooklyn Dodger fan, I must say that each time I look at the film of that call, the ball looks a little higher and a little farther outside. But rational people would most likely file such perceptions under "sour grapes."

The World Series can create surprising heroes. Bill Mazeroski wasn't a bad hitter for a second baseman, but he was arguably the greatest infield gloveman of all time. No one holds more individual fielding records. In a way, Maz is the Babe Ruth of defense.

His greatest moment, however, came with the bat, when he did something that not even Ruth ever did—win a World Series with one swing of the bat. Maz's Pirates, huge underdogs coming into the 1960 World Series, had been trounced by the Yankees in three of the games, by scores of 16–3, 10–0, and 12–0. But the Bucs eked out three victories of their own, forcing a seventh game. With the score tied at 9–9 in the bottom of the ninth, Mazeroski sent Forbes Field into a frenzy with his leadoff homer against Ralph Terry. It was the first time a Series

ended with a home run and is still the only seventh-game Series-ending smash.

An odd detail that sticks in the minds of those who saw the game is that Maz would never have come to bat in that inning and Hal Smith would be the man of Pittsburgh legend if Mickey Mantle hadn't run backward in the top half of the ninth. The Pirates had come from a 7–4 deficit in the last of the eighth to score five runs, the last three coming on a Smith homer (the pitch after the Yankees, and most of the people in Forbes Field, thought he had been struck out). The Yanks battled back in the top of the ninth. With one out, a run in, and a man on third, Mantle led off first base. Yogi Berra chopped a high hopper down the first-base line that Buc first sacker Rocky Nelson gloved. He easily stepped on first, then raised his arm to throw to second for the tag play on Mantle (by tagging the bag Nelson had eliminated the force at second), but Mantle had reversed directions in an incredible display of baseball instinct and dived back to first safely. The tying run scored, and a customary October event—a Yankee victory—seemed a foregone conclusion.

And then along came Maz.

★

This dazzling array of World Series press pins is dominated by the one issued by the Philadelphia Athletics to the working press for the 1914 World Series. Only in this pin is the team's logo linked to that of the scribes' fraternity, the Base Ball Writers' Association of America (BBWAA; yes, baseball was spelled "base ball" back then).

The link between players and press (the "knights of the keyboard," Ted Williams derisively called them) has corroded through the

years. Once chummy, the relationship has turned downright hostile. It's hard to believe now, but there was a time when the reporters who traveled with a team were considered part of the family.

The owners saw to it that the writers had plenty of food and drink, and the writers did their best to protect the players from ugly rumors and scandals and to promote the healthful game of baseball.

Even in the early, palmy days, however, the writers were sometimes reminded of what the magnates really thought of them. For instance, when big games drew show-business celebrities and political dignitaries to the ballpark and quality seats were at a premium, writers were frequently bounced from the press box and left to find a place in the grandstand. Prior to the 1908 Giant-Cub play-off for the pennant (necessitated by the "Merkle Boner" game), correspondent Hugh Fullerton ascended to the press box only to find actor Louis Mann, a buddy of Giants manager John McGraw, in his accustomed press-box seat. Fullerton simply plopped down in Mann's lap and dictated 5,000 words on the game from his shared perch.

During the 1908 World Series, Cub ownership moved the writers to the last row of the grandstand. Even worse, in Detroit during that Series, they were forced to climb a rickety ladder to sit on the roof. The fact that it was raining and/or snowing much of the time didn't improve their spirits. Before the next game the writers banded together to form the BBWAA.

CHAPTER ELEVEN

The Art Gallery

This handsome painting, *Little Base Ball Player* by J. G. (John George) Brown (1831–1913), is a highly sentimental depiction of boyhood of the sort common in the moral tales of the Tract Society and the uplifting adventures of *Ragged Dick* and other Horatio Alger novels of pluck and luck. The painter, Brown, like sportswriter Henry Chadwick, was born and raised in England but, once having made his mark on this side of the Atlantic, devoted his entire professional life to cataloging and affirming "the American way." Beginning his art studies at the National Academy of Design in 1853, after starting out as a glass cutter, Brown was a commercial success as a painter throughout his long career.

American art critics soon began to dismiss his sanitized depictions of urban gamins and bucolic lads, but Brown remained popular on these shores and abroad, winning a prize at the Universal Exposition in Paris of 1889, which celebrated the centennial of the French Revolution.

For the baseball fan, a point of historic interest in this rosy little oil painting is the naive, natural, untutored style of catching a ball. At the presumed time of the action (date of execution 1860), the how-to manuals were instructing would-be baseball players to position their hands like a clamshell, hinged at the heels, to await the ball.

---★---

A glorious painting by J. F. Kernan, commissioned for *Baseball Magazine* and autographed by the subject, posed in an atypically happy mood. Grover Cleveland Alexander ("Old Pete") may have been the greatest right-handed pitcher in National League history, posting 373 wins, but he had tough luck from the very beginning. In his very first professional season he tried to break up a double play and took the shortstop's throw square in the noggin. He was unconscious for two days. The episode may have contributed to the epilepsy he suffered from for years afterward. In World War I he suffered from shell shock, which severely damaged his hearing and intensified his seizures. Epilepsy was later deemed treatable with phenobarbital, but Alexander, like other sufferers, self-medicated with a more readily available sedative, alcohol.

It's amazing how good a pitcher he was, given the tortures he suffered. In his first major league season, 1911, he won twenty-eight games, including a twelve-inning, one-hit, 1–0 shutout against Cy Young. It was one of the seven shutouts he posted that year. Throwing a "heavy" ball, blanking the opposition became his forte. He led the league seven times in whitewashes. His record of ninety career shutouts tops all National League hurlers. In 1915 he threw twelve shutouts and topped that the next year with sixteen, a figure made even more astounding because his home park was Baker Bowl, which is

the definition of a "bandbox" ballpark.

In 1915 he began a series of three consecutive thirty-win seasons and led his team, the Phillies, to their first World Series. His most dramatic Series appearance, however, came with the St. Louis Cardinals in 1926. Discarded by the Cubs in midseason, the thirty-nine-year-old Alexander beat the Yanks of Ruth and Gehrig with complete-game performances in Games 2 and 6, then returned in Game 7 with the bases loaded and the tying run on third to fan Tony Lazzeri and seal the win for the Cards. But the years were hard on Alexander. At age forty-three, when he could no longer pitch at the major-league level, Alex joined the barnstorming House of David team and lesser attractions. Destitute, he sunk lower and lower. Near the end he joined the troupe at Hubert's Flea Circus & Museum, in New York's Times Square, answering baseball questions for patrons bored by the geek show.

The sad story of Alexander the Great was memorialized two years after his 1950 death in a Hollywood feature called *The Winning Team*, starring Ronald Reagan. Trivia buffs note that this is the only instance of an actor who would become president playing a ballplayer named for a president.

Dick Perez has painted the portraits of Baseball Hall of Famers since 1981. One glance at this image and you know why. In Perez's sculptural style of painting, Landis might as well be looking down on us from Mount Rushmore rather than Kenesaw Mountain, the site of a Civil War battle in which his father lost a leg and from which the son gained a distinctive name. Perez's gift is that he has captured not only the craggy visage but also the blazing idealism of the man who saved baseball at a crucial moment in its history.

Landis will always be remembered as the tough guy who banned the Black Sox and suspended Babe Ruth, but most people don't recall that he was one of the game's greatest fans. From his place on the judicial bench he once admonished a long-winded plaintiff to keep things short, stating, "Matty and Three-Finger are going at it over at the ballyard today." In January 1915, the height of the Federal League war, he heard an antitrust case brought by the Feds against organized baseball. By sitting on the case for over a year without issuing a verdict, the great trustbuster foiled Federal League hopes for an injunction and ensured another red-ink bath that pushed the Feds to settle with organized baseball and shut down their rival operation. When scandal rocked baseball in September 1920, as news of the fixed World Series of 1919 finally spilled out, the owners remembered the judge who had befriended them once before and offered him a virtually unrestricted governance of the game.

Landis was a showboat judge, whose flamboyant rulings were often overturned on appeal. He was no visionary on the question of race. But Kenesaw

Mountain Landis possessed a moral weathervane; he did not rule by consensus, and he did not give a damn what anyone thought of him or his rulings. The fans felt secure that when faced with any situation in which the best interests of the game were at issue, he stood up for *them*.

—★—

The kinetic painting style of LeRoy Neiman, so exciting and apt for the sizzling 1960s and '70s, never found a more appropriate subject than Juan Marichal, a kinetic artist on the mound, where for sixteen splendid seasons he was poetry in motion. This is baseball in grand perspective: the whole ballpark is swept up in the oversize delivery of "The Dominican Dandy." Marichal threw his last pitch in earnest in 1975, leaving younger fans who view this painting to wonder: How did anyone hit this guy? Marichal was not only one of the toughest pitchers during the 1960s but one of the greatest of all time. In 1965 and 1966, opponents' on-base averages (not batting averages) were .240 and .230, the fifth and sixth best marks by a pitcher in this century. He used no windup, but his high leg kick and baffling array of pitches were delivered from several different angles. Amazingly, and despite his ever-varying release point, he possessed splendid control (1.82 walks per nine innings).

Juan's first start in the majors was a one-hit shutout; the next time out he allowed only four hits. He won twenty-one games or more six times—including twenty-five twice and twenty-six once—and led the league in complete games and shutouts twice each. So why didn't he ever win a Cy Young Award? The answer has two words: Koufax and Gibson. When Marichal was brilliant, the other two were mythic. But Juan had his share of legendary accomplishments. In 1963 he and Warren Spahn hooked up in a sixteen-inning game in which both pitchers went all the way, in which the only run was provided by a Willie Mays homer. In the 1960s Marichal won 191 games, 27 more than runner-up Bob Gibson.

—★—

How do you get to the Hall of Fame? Practice, practice, practice—or, in the case of Joe Palooka in this comic storyboard, get in the car and drive.

But seriously, folks, getting to the Hall of Fame isn't so hard, it's getting into it, as an inductee, that's tough. "A victim of soikumstance," Joe Palooka's pal Jerry Leemy finds out the hard way just how tough it is.

Ham Fisher was the creator of the *Joe Palooka* comic strip in 1928. He later employed a talented assistant named Al Capp, who made his own name with *Li'l Abner*. M. Leff drew the *Palooka* strip in the 1950s. How did this comic strip make it into the Hall of Fame when Leemy couldn't? Ask Leemy.

Almost invariably, this lithograph by Nathaniel Currier and James Merritt Ives is reproduced with a caption identifying it as a tableau of the Knickerbockers cavorting on the Elysian Fields about 1845. In fact, the litho dates from 1866 (the same year as another depiction of the site, by Bachman, shown in Chapter 4), and while the play grounds are indeed the Fields of Elysium, Hoboken-style, the Knickerbockers are nowhere to be seen. The First Grand Match for the Championship of the United States is the subject, and it was played between the Atlantics of Brooklyn and the Mutuals of New York, on August 3, 1865. The Mutuals are in the field, the Atlantics at bat and such celebrated visages as those of Dickey Pearce and Joe Start are realistically drawn. See if you can spot Henry Chadwick!

The crowd, reported at 15,000 to 20,000, is barely hinted at, and the rain that halted the contest in the sixth inning is forever off in the distance. When the clouds burst at five-thirty, after an hour and forty-five minutes of play (today's game is too slow, eh?), the Atlantics led the Mutuals 13–12. The Mutes had two men on base, but play could not be resumed. The Atlantics also won the second game of the series, later that month, 40–28, and by going on to finish undefeated in all its contests with first-class opposition became baseball's first "national champion."

Note that the first baseman and third baseman stand right on their bases because the rules at that time permitted the "fair-foul" hit, in which a skilled bunter could angle his bat so that a ball could bounce once in fair territory, skitter off into foul ground, and be a valid hit. The second baseman's position is harder to explain, but the vast hole between first and second is what prompted Chadwick to suggest, first, that batters hit the ball on the ground in that direction, and second, that a "right shortstop" be added to the complement in the field—a tenth man. By the time anyone got around to testing Chad's idea, in the mid-seventies, eliminating the fair-foul hit seemed the wiser course.

Currier & Ives printed lithographs only in black and white and employed a legion of colorists to tint the pictures by hand. Smaller editions of this print sold for fifteen to twenty-five cents upon original publication and were made available for ten cents with a subscription to the *New York Clipper*, the main sporting paper at the time. A 20″ × 30″ print like this would have cost three dollars in 1866—half a week's pay for a workingman, but nothing like the $30,000 or more it might fetch at auction today. This litho is one of the earliest acquisitions by the Baseball Hall of Fame, a gift from the Steven C. Clark collection, and went on display in 1936 along with the Doubleday Baseball at the municipal building across the street from where the Hall was to be erected in 1939.

—★—

Patented by K. Muller & J. Deacon in 1865, these bronzes—a pitcher and a batter, less than a foot in height—were offered for sale in the classified-ad section of the *New York Clipper*. Today they are museum pieces, housed in the Whitney Collections of Sporting Art at Yale University as well as in the archive of the Baseball Hall of Fame and Museum. What makes treasures of inexpensive mass art like the Currier & Ives litho or these bronzes? It is not merely that someone thought to keep them for future generations or that they fortuitously survived—emerging as great rarities—but also why the objects were prized in their time and what they say to ours. Come to think of it, that's not a bad description of what this virtual tour is about.

This remarkable 1867 lithograph by J. L. Magee, *The Second Great Match Game for the Championship*, is a treasure trove of history and a marvel of detail. It gives us a real flavor of being right there, right then. It depicts the game of October 22, 1866, between the Athletic Club of Philadelphia and the Atlantics of Brooklyn, played at the ball grounds at Fifteenth and Columbia in North Philadelphia.

A previous attempt to pit these teams against each other had proved disastrous. The proprietors

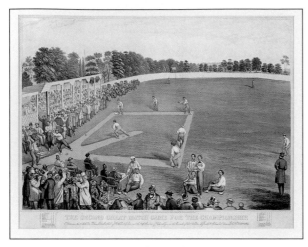

of the Athletic grounds had sold 8,000 seats at twenty-five cents each, but a near stampede to see the game resulted in a crowd of 30,000, which surrounded and constricted the playing area to such an extent that midway in the bottom of the first inning, the game was halted. A return match at Brooklyn's Capitoline Grounds proceeded without disruption, and the Atlantics won, 27–17.

For the "second great match game" (not counting the abortive first attempt), Philadelphia's policemen were out in force and the proprietors of the park charged one dollar admission, the most ever up to that time and still a high price half a century later. The Athletics delighted their fans by winning, 31–12, as the game was halted by thundershowers in the eighth inning. For the A's, Al Reach scored six runs, Wes Fisler five. Lipman Pike, the first Jewish professional ballplayer, made four outs that day, but he had slugged seven homers in a game earlier in the season. A potentially thrilling rubber match between the clubs was canceled because of a dispute over the division of the gate receipts; the Atlantics thus retained their championship.

Above each player is a small number that corresponds to his position in the key printed below the image. So we have McBride batting and Kleinfelder taking off from first (is there a hit-and-run play going on?), with Mills catching and Pratt on the mound. On deck is Reach. The handsome Pike is seated at the far right. Standing next to him (left to right) are Wilkins and Fisler. Dockney is sitting between them. Sensenderfer is seated by the scorer's table, where Gaskill is standing. Could they be asking that the scorer change a ruling? Unlikely—keeping score is the "father of baseball" himself, Henry Chadwick.

And there's more going on here than the game. Delightfully, Magee depicts gambling slips being exchanged, a pickpocket caught in the act, a vendor whose tray is about to topple, and a slew of tipplers. Note the round enameled-iron plates at home and the pitcher's point. These were fixed to the ground by their formidable attached center spike. Surprisingly, not a single example of these plates, which were regulation issue until 1872, is known to have survived.

———★———

This is not a cheery depiction of baseball. Depression-era mining towns like this one in western Pennsylvania, racked by unemployment and violence related to the unionization struggle, may seem an unpromising subject for a painter. But art comes from everywhere and is not announced by its pedigree; rather, it announces itself. Mervin Jules, who painted *Mine Baseball* in 1937, has said, "I was collecting studies among the bootleg mines in western Pennsylvania and saw a group of miners on a slag field playing baseball late in the day. They cast long shadows, and it all fascinated me." Long shadows indeed, and scant relief, but a splendid painting nonetheless.

Polychromed-wood cigar-store figures are among the most highly prized examples of nineteenth-century folk art, whether attributed to noted wood sculptors such as Samuel A. Robb or to unknown hands, such as the sculptor of "Joe Wood." This life-size statue was on display in the former basement exhibit space of the museum prior to 1980. Since then it has been well tended in the archive, for it is the oldest such baseball figure known, dating from 1867. The man who donated "Joe Wood" to the Hall on July 15, 1939, was Frank Rutz, Rochester's self-proclaimed number one baseball fan and for more than thirty years the marshal of that city's annual Opening Day baseball parade.

Rutz had attended the dedication ceremonies for the Hall of Fame (the "Cavalcade of Baseball," the celebration was called) one month earlier and had been moved to share his treasure with the whole baseball world. The ditty on the brass plaque affixed to the base tells the story best (spelling and punctuation verbatim):

Seven decades Joe Wood in Rochester stood
and boosted the National Game
He did all he could, so its fitting he should
have a niche in this Hall of Fame

—★—

Imagine art like this arriving in your mailbox every month. *Baseball Magazine* was a fan's dream come true. Great stories, inside dope, player profiles, and dazzling covers like this one. Artists such as Gerrit E. Beneker and J. F. Kernan created cover designs that changed not only their subject each month but even the graphic treatment of the logo, which was painted fresh every issue in the early years. No magazine would stand for such a thing today, when the marketing mantra of "brand awareness" homogenizes and pasteurizes inventiveness.

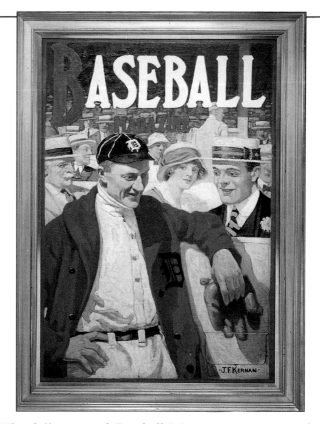

The full story of *Baseball Magazine* appears in the next chapter.

The Cobb portrait by J. F. Kernan appears through the courtesy of Mac and Angela Grimmer of Washington, D.C.

This shimmering bronze is one of the greatest works of art in the Baseball Hall of Fame and Museum. California-born sculptor Douglas Tilden (1860–1935) created a life-size plaster of the *Baseball Player* (sometimes called *Ball Player,* also *The National Game*) during a stay in Paris in 1889, and it won him admission to the Paris Salon, which gave him an award the following year for *Tired Boxer.* The plaster was sand-cast into a monumental bronze, greater than life-size.

Upon its arrival in America in 1890, the bronze statue was purchased for $1,700 by William E. Brown of the Southern Pacific Railroad, who donated it to the city of San Francisco. It was placed in Golden Gate Park on July 8, 1891, and there it stands today. Tiffany's of New York commissioned replicas from Tilden in that same year, and these were cast by the Gruet foundry of Paris. The Hall of Fame's statuette (thirty-one and three-quarters inches high), acquired in 1958, is one of the three table-model versions known to exist today.

A twenty-one-inch model has recently been discovered as well. It was created by Tilden in Paris and cast at the Gruet Foundry. The discovery of the plaster model of this smaller version in a storage crate in San Francisco in 1988 has led to a recent edition of bronzes.

Totally deaf and mute since the age of four following a bout of scarlet fever, Tilden went on to a long and notable career as a sculptor, with such other massive statuary compositions as *Bear Hunt*, *Mechanics*, and *Football Players*, as well as *Tired Boxer*, all still on view in the San Francisco area. But his most lasting legacy may be not his sculpture, splendid as it is, but his lifelong activism on behalf of the deaf, particularly his early advocacy of signing in preference to oralism.

———★———

Baseball is a lot like life, only more so. We play it or watch it in real time, but we ring variations on it in a dimly conscious fugue state, intertwining the intrinsic order of the game with the randomness that makes it a lifelong delight. *Fugue of the Pepper Players* by David G. Baldwin nudges us off center, from watching the players engage in the familiar pregame pepper ritual to tracking the movements of the ball, the limbs, the air.

And you thought the Baseball Hall of Fame was about the history and tradition of the game. Well, you were right, but history begins where the present ends, and the Museum's great collections contain modern and abstract works as well as older representational art. What makes this large mixed-media canvas doubly interesting as a treasure of the Hall is that its creator used to be a relief pitcher for the Washington Senators, Milwaukee Brewers, and Chicago White Sox. Dave Baldwin was notable for his submarine delivery, especially baffling to right-handed batters. In his first full year in the big leagues, 1967, he appeared in fifty-eight games, saving twelve, with an ERA of 1.70.

I was surprised and delighted to find Baldwin's painting in the Hall of Fame collection because our paths had crossed some twenty years ago, when I was interviewing and corresponding with hundreds of men who had pitched in relief from the 1920s on. Asked what the principal reason for his success as a reliever was, Baldwin said at the time, "An unorthodox delivery, more than anything else. My style contrasted sharply with any pitcher I would replace."

That certainly describes the path of David G. Baldwin from relief pitcher to serious full-time artist. Along the way, he stopped to earn a Ph.D., with a research specialty of ecological genetics, and to make a career in the mining and defense industries. His unorthodox approach to art is evident here, but also in the titles of some of his other paintings: *The Goddess of Historical Pranks*, *Jitterbug of the Prophets*, and *The Mockingbird Sings to the Relief Pitcher*.

FUGUE FOR THE PEPPER PLAYERS   DGBaldwin

CHAPTER TWELVE

Movies, Music, and Media

It was a bit of an overstatement for *Sporting Life* to claim it "made baseball popular," but this little pin tells quite a story. Francis C. Richter founded the paper in 1883 after working for several Philadelphia newspapers as everything from copyboy to managing editor. While at *The Public Ledger* in the early 1880s, he created a sports department, with features and columns in addition to game scores and reports. These features were long established in such New York weeklies as *The Spirit of the Times* and *The New York Clipper*, but they were new to daily newspapers. Richter's success with this concept emboldened him in 1883 to create *Sporting Life: Devoted to Base Ball, Trap Shooting, and General Sports*.

The weekly newspaper certainly did have a major impact on spreading the gospel, in large measure because of Richter's deep knowledge of the game and his keen sense of how sport and business needed to interact if baseball were to become a profession worth pursuing. He was a real moral force in base-

ball, opposed equally to the oligopolistic actions of National League owners and the profanity and pugilism of the ballplayers. In 1900 he came very close to establishing a rival league, the "second American Association." As an example of his idealism, here's the headline and incredibly long subhead to the issue of May 28, 1910:

RELIGION OF BASEBALL
*Our National Sport Founded Upon the Same
Principles as Underlie All True Religion and All
Other Essentials to Moral and Physical Welfare
and to Rightful Conduct in This Life.*

From its inception into the second decade of the twentieth century, *Sporting Life* was the real baseball authority. The games, the personalities, the controversies of the day were covered in detail, and Richter took unpopular stands if he thought they were right.

———★———

In the early years of the nineteenth century, our English cousins mocked our relentless pursuit of the dollar, our puritanical and hypocritical ways, and our preference for the tavern to the turf. In *America and the Americans*, W. E. Baxter wrote of the spindle-limbed urban bachelor culture: "to roll balls in a ten pin alley by gaslight or to drive a fast trotting horse in a light wagon along a very bad and dusty road, seems the Alpha and Omega of sport in the United States."

In the South, however, horse racing and breeding—"the turf"—was of consuming interest. In 1819 John Stuart Skinner of Baltimore gave America its first periodical with a sporting section, *The American Farmer*, which debuted a "Sporting Olio" column on January 21, 1825. This proved so popular that Skinner sold the weekly to launch a monthly, *The American Turf Register and Sporting Magazine*, in 1829. Ten years later that publication moved to New York, where it came under the editorship of the aptly named William Trotter Porter.

And here our baseball tale begins. In 1831 Porter, at twenty-two, started a New York weekly called *The Spirit of the Times*, a racy "Chronicle of the Turf, Agriculture, Field Sports, Literature, and the Stage." It became extremely popular, with a circulation exceeding 40,000; in December 1844 he folded *The American Turf Register* to focus on *The Spirit*. Porter did not immediately include baseball in his sports coverage, for he was president of the New York Cricket Club, an organization he started in 1842 to attract American players rather than the British expatriates who had formed the St. George Cricket Club (whose professional was Samuel Wright, father of Harry and George).

The New York *Daily News* and the *Herald* began to report on baseball matches in 1845; by 1853 William Cauldwell of the *Mercury* joined in, and in 1854 so did Porter, finally. Two years later he left the old *Spirit* and joined with George Wilkes to form a new publication, *Porter's Spirit of the Times*. When Porter died in 1858, Wilkes continued alone, though in 1859 he reattached his paper to the old *Spirit* and renamed it *Wilkes' Spirit of the Times*, an example of which is before you in the accompanying collage. An amazingly durable publication, it remained in print continuously until 1902, although its baseball content began to diminish by the late 1860s, when competitive baseball periodicals were sprouting up everywhere.

Henry Chadwick, the only writer ever to earn a plaque in the Baseball Hall of Fame alongside the players, executives, and other pioneers, launched *The Base Ball Players' Chronicle* on June 6, 1867. It ran for about a year, renamed as *The American Chronicle of Sports and Pastimes* midway. *The New England Base Ballist*, shown here, made its debut on August 6, 1868, with ballplayer Mort Rogers as its copublisher and baseball editor. Rogers played for the Resolutes of Brooklyn from 1861 until 1867, when he moved to Boston and donned the uniform of the Lowells. Rogers's *Base Ballist* ran its course by year's end, only to relaunch ten days later as *The National Chronicle: Journal of American Sports and Amusements*, adding features on cricket and "the new Canadian game of Lacrosse." This paper lasted longer, printing its final issue on June 18, 1870. Rogers, a pioneering baseball entrepreneur, went on to publish the game's first pictorial scorecards (an example is depicted in this volume), which were sold at Boston's South End Grounds before Red Stocking games in 1871.

The Sporting News was first published by the Spink family of St. Louis on March 17, 1886, and has been published weekly ever since then (excepting the issue for May 30, 1946, owing to a rail strike). It thrived as a baseball-only paper, calling itself the "bible of baseball." In 1917, Colonel Tillinghast Huston, co-owner of the Yankees, suggested to Taylor Spink, the *News*'s owner, that he send copies to the boys fighting in Europe to remind them what they were at war to protect. Spink reduced his rate and convinced Ban Johnson to pick up the freight costs of shipping 150,000 copies "over there" every week, a coup that forced the closure of the rival *Sporting Life*. Though no longer a baseball-only paper and owned by Times Mirror since 1966, *The Sporting News* remains a formidable voice in baseball.

Also on view is a *Sporting Life* press credential for Ren Mulford of Cincinnati for the year 1912, signed by Richter, and a card issued by the Base Ball Writers' Association of America in 1913 to

F. C. Lane of *Baseball Magazine*. The baseball reporters' fraternity was formed in 1908 to combat the writers' mistreatment by club owners, who provided no pressbox (and, often enough, no seats) for the men assigned to cover the game.

An early BBWAA pin may be found at the lower right of the composition. The association's logo has not changed in all the years since its inception, but its roots lie deeper still, in the field and turf of Skinner and Porter, in the missionary zeal of Rogers and Chadwick, in the dedication and endurance of Richter and Spink.

—★—

The yellow-back dime novels of Erastus Beadle (who began his publishing trade in Cooperstown) were famous for allegedly corrupting youth with their tales of wild abandon, bare-legged lassies, mustachioed villains, and rampant gunplay. The famous series began with *Malaeska: The Indian Wife of the White Hunter* in September 1860, flourished (like baseball) during the Civil War, and died in the 1870s. It inspired such imitators as Robert M. DeWitt and George P. Munro to make millions from their ten-cent libraries, just as Beadle had. But the dime novels that were loved by the millions were also deplored by "right-thinking individuals." So in the 1880s such purveyors of "wholesome" literary fare as Robert Bonner and Street & Smith made their fortunes one nickel at a time, with such characters as Buffalo Bill (stories by Ned Buntline in *The New York Ledger*) and Nick Carter (literally thousands of stories by a slew of writers, with such thrilling opening sentences as "We will have the money, or she shall die!").

Displayed here are five evocative examples of the five-cent story paper, all from a ten-year period at the turn of the century and all from the publishing firm of Street & Smith. The *Tip-Top Weekly* of 1904 features Frank Merriwell of Yale, the immortal creation of Gilbert Patten; Frank was already in his ninth year as a national icon of manly virtue and, upon his imminent graduation, was to be replaced by his younger brother Dick, who proved long-lived but not nearly as successful. The *Golden Hours* of July 7, 1900, presented a gorgeous tableau of a dreadful baseball team, the New York Giants, with whom Christy Mathewson, Merriwell in the flesh, would make his debut ten days later.

The New York Five Cent Library of 1894 featured three successive issues devoted to famous ballplayers, all written by "Billy Boxer, the famous referee," in real life the writer Frank J. Earll. A fourth baseball title in that year's series, *Amos Rusie: Prince of Pitchers*, was serialized over five issues later that summer. Based on his performance that season, Rusie was worth the space: he won thirty-six games for the Giants, with an ERA that was two and a half runs below the league average. William Henry "Yale" Murphy, on the other hand, enjoyed a career as short as his 5'3" stature. The combination of "toy" cuteness, a Yale degree, and New York exposure, however, made him a heroic subject for a while.

Captain Billy Nash of the Boston Red Stockings is little remembered today, but he was the best-fielding third baseman of his era, and he had the right moral stuff, too, to earn inclusion in this virtuous though fanciful series of biographies. King Kelly, on the other hand, was no moral beacon for youths or adults, and his playing career had ended the year before. He died on November 8, 1894, not half a year from the publication of *King Kelly, the Famous Catcher.*

In the golden age of magazines, the period 1900–1920, the newsstands were bedecked with general-interest and literary publications. The weeklies included such fare as *The Saturday Evening Post*, *Collier's*, *Frank Leslie's Popular Magazine*, and *Harper's*; the monthlies boasted, among others, *Atlantic*, *Munsey's*, *McClure's Magazine*, and *Century Illustrated Monthly Magazine*. Competition for rack space was fierce, as was the competition for the eye (and pocketbook) of the browser; the fees that top writers routinely received in 1920 exceed those available today, when the dollar buys so much less, and artists whose work graced magazine covers, like James Montgomery Flagg, Edward Penfield, Maxfield Parrish, and J. C. Leyendecker, became truly wealthy.

But first-class cover art had never been viewed as a necessary competitive edge for an all-sports publication until the advent of *Baseball Magazine*. In December 1907 veteran Boston sportswriter Jacob Morse issued a prospectus on behalf of The Baseball Magazine Company for the creation of a new, deluxe, all-baseball monthly the likes of which had never before been contemplated. Its articles would run as long as interest held, sometimes to 10,000 words; its writers would be the best the sport had to offer; and the eye appeal of the covers would compete on the newsstand with the best general-interest publications, not to mention the specialty monthlies. Morse had written *Sphere and Ash*, a history of the game, back in 1888 and had even managed the Boston Union Association club in 1884.

Through its first decade or so, *Baseball Magazine* proved both an artistic and a commercial success, reaching six-figure circulations that would make a modern special-interest publisher envious. Here are three particularly grand examples of the painterly elegance that was the publication's trademark at the time. The middle cover was painted by Gerrit E. Beneker, the other two by J. F. Kernan. The background is an original oil on board for yet another *Baseball Magazine* cover. By the 1920s the covers had turned rather dull in aesthetic terms—red borders around a player photograph. This heralded not only the cost cutting that characterized the magazine industry as a whole at the dawn of the new age of radio, but also a growing perception that on the newsstand and throughout the sports/entertainment industry, it was stars, not sensibility, that sold. More's the pity for the culture, perhaps, but in sports as in theater, the play's the thing, and so are the players.

—★—

Won in the Ninth. Now that's a title to set the heart racing! Ring Lardner declared that it ruined the literary tastes of an entire generation, but its readers certainly loved baseball all the more for sharing Christy Mathewson's thrilling adventures and imagining themselves pitching in a pinch. This 1910 book was the first of a series to be known as the "Matty books"; later exemplars of Matty's stilted prose (actually, his ghostwriter's) are *First Base Faulkner*, *Second Base Sloan*, *Catcher Craig*, and *Pitcher Pollock*. Subtlety was lost on boys avid for detail and for echoes of the big leagues, so the ballplayers in *Won in the Ninth* included such barely camouflaged characters as awkward-looking shortstop Hans Hagner, slick-fielding double-play specialist Johnny Everson, and nimble first sacker Hal Case. Newspaperman John Wheeler, who covered the Giants on a daily basis, was Matty's ghost for the series.

Baseball books for boys, with their strong graphics and sturdy bindings, enjoyed their golden

age in the 1910s and 1920s, as the nickel papers and dime novels had dominated earlier years. But ghosted stories of the diamond such as Frank Chance's *The Bride and the Pennant* (penned by none other than Ring Lardner) went back as far as King Kelly's *Play Ball* of 1888. And the genre of baseball stories for boys really took off with Noah Brooks, a celebrated journalist whose book *The Fairport Nine* was serialized in *St. Nicholas* magazine in 1880 and issued in hardcover by Scribners that same year. (A lesser known title, William Everett's *Changing Base*, had been published in 1868, taking the prize as the first baseball novel.) On display here is Brooks's 1884 book *Our Base Ball Club and How It Won the Championship*, dedicated to the Chicago Base Ball Club (gaudily depicted on the back cover) and containing an introduction by Albert Spalding himself.

All the same, the most coveted books for young baseball fans were the series titles of Edward Stratemeyer, the man of a thousand pen names, who wrote as Lester Chadwick, Captain Ralph Bonehill, Elmer Dawson, Arthur M. Winfield, and a true plethora of other subterfuges. *Batting to Win* (1911) was a Stratemeyer book, credited to Lester Chadwick, famous "author" of the Baseball Joe series—*Baseball Joe on the Giants*; *Baseball Joe on the School Nine*; *Baseball Joe, Saving the League*; even *Baseball Joe, Club Owner*; and ten other volumes. (Another Stratemeyer nom de plume you might recognize—Franklin W. Dixon, chronicler of the Hardy Boys.)

The splendidly simple typography on the cover of *The Big League* (1911), a collection of baseball stories, signaled that this was a book for an older audience—young adult and adult. Its author was Charles Van Loan, wildly popular in his day for his stories in *The Saturday Evening Post* and for such later collections as *Score by Innings*. It was Van Loan who persuaded the *Post* editors to reconsider their initial rejection of Lardner's Jack Keefe stories, which came to be collected as *You Know Me Al* (1916), in my view the greatest of all baseball fiction. Also depicted in the collage is the clever glossary of baseball lingo discussed in Chapter 14 of this volume, Thomas W. Lawson's *The Krank: His Language and What It Means*. Here you get an idea of how very tiny this horsehide-covered book really is.

And, finally, we have a ringer—not fiction, not funny, not quaint. It is simply the first hardcover book whose subject (among its coverage of other sports) is baseball: the game of its day, including rosters, team profiles, and game scores. *The Book of American Pastimes* was compiled in 1866 by Charles A. Peverelly, a veteran writer for the New York *Daily News* who covered the up-and-coming game of baseball until his eyes began to fail and he could no longer see at a distance. At that point he published this book and started a yachting monthly.

— ★ —

Not all press pins are shiny confections with enamel inlay and silk ribbons. That's a rather weary and wistful Indian shown on this penny-celluloid pin from the 1920 World Series. Maybe the chief was still in grief over the sudden death of shortstop Ray Chapman, who had succumbed after being hit in the head by a Carl Mays pitch on August 17 of that year. At the time the Indians were locked in a bristling pennant race with the Yankees and White Sox (the Black Sox team—they just hadn't been caught yet). But minor leaguer Joe Sewell stepped in and hit .329, and the Indians took the flag. Cleveland was responsible for a number of World Series firsts in the highly memorable fifth game that year. Jim Bagby became the first pitcher to homer in a World Series contest; Elmer Smith hit the first Series grand slam, and Bill Wambsganss turned the first (and only) unassisted triple play in the postseason.

Baseball players were big stars with nationwide reputations in the first decade of the twentieth century. But unlike today's ballplayers, who make enough money to support a typical family reunion all year round, the old-timers had to work in the off season, generally in menial jobs, to bolster their income. And if they were coming off an especially good year, they had to capitalize on their good fortune before it turned on them. In 1912 Rube Marquard of the New York Giants performed the astonishing feat of winning nineteen consecutive games. No one has touched that record since (though Carl Hubbell won twenty-four straight over two seasons). Marquard and his wife, actress Blossom Seeley, took to the vaudeville stage, where they performed a skit about the winning streak and sang "The Marquard Glide," which featured such immortal lyrics as "Stood up through all the knocks/Had it on those

'Red Sox'/You can bet all your rocks/On Reuben! Reuben!" Rube did capture his two starts against Boston in the World Series that year, though the Red Sox won in eight games.

Rube wasn't the only ballplayer who trod the boards. Joe Tinker, Frank Chance (Johnny Evers was too crabby to join them), Rabbit Maranville, Mike Donlin, John McGraw, Rube Waddell (who's surprised?), and even Christy Mathewson performed skits. Doc White and George Moriarty wrote baseball songs. Marty McHale, "the Irish Thrush," proved a better baritone than he did a baseball pitcher. Larry Doyle played the villain in a melodrama, and Johnny Kling put on billiard exhibitions. The vaudeville tours also gave folks who didn't live in the ten big-league cities a chance to get close to their heroes.

★

J. R. Blodgett, of the Niagara Base Ball Club, wrote a tune called "The Base Ball Polka" in 1858, the first reference to the game in published sheet music. Today when we think of polka we call up visions of Lawrence Welk and champagne bubbles or lederhosen-clad beer-barrel boys with accordions. But in the 1840s and 1850s in the United States and Europe, the polka was king. First performed in Prague in 1837, this Bohemian folk dance migrated to Paris in 1840; by 1845 it was the rage in England, the United States, and even India. Everything was named after it (polka puddings, polka hats, polka fishing lures, and, of course, polka-dot patterns) the classic one being blue circles on a white ground, previously called "spotted cotton" rather than "polka dots"—in hopes of skimming some of the popularity of the dance step.

In 1860 Mr. J. H. Kalbfleisch composed the "Live Oak Polka" to honor the valiant Live Oak nine of Rochester, New York. It's the first sheet music featuring baseball art and the second baseball ditty composed in polka form, a further attempt to link

the new, hopeful fad of baseball to the universal approval of the polka. Rochester (and all of Geneseo County, in fact) was a hotbed of the sport before the Civil War. Rochester has had a professional-league team since 1877 and even had a big-league team, the Hop Bitters (guess what their owner did for a living), in the American Association in 1890.

Is baseball still "America's game"? To wiseguys who propose that the NFL or the NBA or golf or snowboarding has pushed baseball aside, you might respond, "Oh, yeah? Tell me another sport that has its own song!"

"Take Me Out to the Ball Game" has indeed become the national pastime's national anthem. We sing it together as we stretch our legs during the seventh inning of every game and, if the home team is winning, with more fervor and feeling than we usually bring to "The Star-Spangled Banner." The mundane ditty was improbably created in 1908 by composer Albert von Tilzer and lyricist Jack Norworth, neither of whom had ever seen a big-league game. Norworth went on to pen 2,500 other songs, including "Shine On, Harvest Moon," but, to his amazement, "Take Me Out" became his signature song. With the exceptions of "The Star-Spangled Banner" and "Happy Birthday," it has probably been sung more often and by more people than any American song.

The Hall of Fame possesses Norworth's original penciled composition, dashed off in the half hour it took him to travel by train the length of Manhattan. He was inspired by a straphanger's placard suggesting that riders consider taking in a ball game at the Polo Grounds. After von Tilzer added music, Norworth tried out the song in his act at Brooklyn's Amphion Theater. It flopped, and the vaudevillian stuffed it back in his trunk. Three months later he was booked as the ninth act at Hammerstein's Victoria Theater. Imagine his surprise when several performers who strode the boards before him incorporated his "flop" into their acts. Before the year was out, Edwin Meeker had recorded it on an Edison cylinder, eventually others pressed it on discs, and the sheet music became a national best-seller. If you went to the nickelodeon or vaudeville house in those days, a between-act specialty was a magic-lantern show of song slides depicting a day at the ballpark, to which the audience enthusiastically sang Norworth's gem. Here is the first verse, far less familiar than the chorus:

Katie Casey was baseball mad,
Had the fever and had it bad.
Just to root for the hometown crew,
Ev'ry sou, Katie blew.
On a Saturday, her young beau
Called to see if she'd like to go,
To see a show
But Miss Kate said, "No,
I'll tell you what you can do:

And here's the chorus, in case you're just in from Mars:

Take me out to the ball game,
Take me out to the crowd,
Buy me some peanuts and cracker jack,
I don't care if I never get back,
Let me root, root, root for the home team,
If they don't win it's a shame.
For it's one, two, three strikes you're out,
At the old ball game.

"Take Me Out to the Ball Game" was written as a waltz, but over the years since 1908 it has seen more variations than its authors could ever have imagined. Rock, jazz, gospel, country—how many different versions did Ken Burns have in his film, anyway? Norworth rewrote "Take Me Out" in 1936, introducing "Nelly Kelly" as the song's heroine, some say to honor a Ziegfeld Follies favorite, others say to clean up some wrenched rhythms in the original. Frank Sinatra and Gene Kelly starred in a movie bearing the song's title in 1949. In the following year an unlikely quartet of Phil Rizzuto, Roy Campanella, Tommy Henrich, and Ralph Branca teamed with Mitch Miller and the Sandpipers to produce the yellow-vinyl version shown here. Everyone thinks he can sing well enough to record this song: pitcher Buzz Capra and the Atlanta Braves, National League umpire Joe West, and, of course, the late Harry Caray, who commanded the Wrigley Tabernacle Choir.

—★—

This is the jacket Robert Redford wore when he played Roy Hobbs, the thirty-five-year-old rookie from nowhere, in the 1984 film *The Natural*, which has become a litmus test for baseball savants and film critics. Either it was horrible, a comic-book parody of Bernard Malamud's excellent 1952 novel, or it was grand and mythopoetic, a tour de force by director Barry Levinson that was vastly superior to the book on which it was based.

The Natural was not a movie about baseball, the critics charged. Overly simplistic, they said, it was instead an allegory about the eternal battle between good and evil, between our past and our future, between what could have been and what is. (Sounds like baseball to me.) The film was chock full of allusions to baseball players and events—Babe Ruth, Jim Creighton, Eddie Waitkus—and to classic legends—Faust, King Arthur, the serpent in the Garden, Prometheus. It gave us a dazzlingly visual ending—the famous homer into the light stanchion that explodes into a brilliant fireworks display. *Bull Durham* and *Field of Dreams* touched new sets of nerves about baseball, life, love, and myth, but for me, *The Natural* is the long ball of baseball movies.

—★—

One baseball movie that didn't disappoint was *Pride of the Yankees* (1942), the bittersweet story of Lou Gehrig. With Gary Cooper as the quiet "Iron Horse," the film garnered nine Oscar nominations. Real players who had played with Gehrig portrayed themselves in the film, including Babe Ruth, Bill Dickey, and Mark Koenig. This postmodernist artifact, in which art imitates life imitating art, is more phony than Roy Hobbs's jacket. It is a scrapbook of "Gehrig's" life assembled for the film, combining actual newspaper articles with fake ones, real photos with doctored photos, showing Cooper/Gehrig in his Columbia University uniform, stretching for grounders and reaching for a liner. The producers hired Lefty O'Doul to instruct Cooper in baseball action, but the problem was that Cooper was right-handed. So when he bats in the finished

product, it is a film reversal of the actual event; Cooper batted righty and ran to third base.

In a further twist, the Hall of Fame also has the real scrapbook on which the fake one was based.

———★———

"The Big Leagues' Big Love Story!" "The True and Truly Wonderful Story of Grover Cleveland Alexander and the Blue-Eyed Girl Who Was His Inspiration!"

Can you tell that maybe Alexander's wife was the technical adviser to *The Winning Team*, the 1952 film about her recently deceased hubby? Ronald Reagan could never have fanned Tony Lazzeri with the bases loaded in Game 7 of the 1926 World Series if Doris Day hadn't told him to start Tony off with an inside fastball, then throw two curves away.

The Kid from Left Field (1953) starred hoofer Dan Dailey and Anne Bancroft ("And here's to you, Mrs. Robinson . . . Where have you gone, Joe DiMaggio?") in the story of a young boy who becomes manager of a big-league team. It was remade in 1979 with Gary Coleman, to no better effect. Dailey had also played Dizzy Dean in *The Pride of St. Louis* (1952), a failed attempt to capitalize on the resonance of *Pride of the Yankees*, already ten years old. What did Lou Gehrig and Dizzy Dean have in common, anyway?

———★———

A League of Their Own was based on the real All-American Girls Professional Baseball League (AAGPBL) whose story we told in Chapter 5.

A lightweight feature for morning talk shows in the early 1980s, the AAGPBL would have retreated back into the anonymity of sociological theses had it not been for director Penny Marshall and actors Tom Hanks, Geena Davis, Madonna, Lori Petty, and Rosie O'Donnell. The film, released in 1992, was a huge hit and brought renewed attention to the women's league. As a feminist rallying cause, *League* reversed the classic paradigm in which art imitates life; Geena Davis imitating life puts an additional spin on the ball.

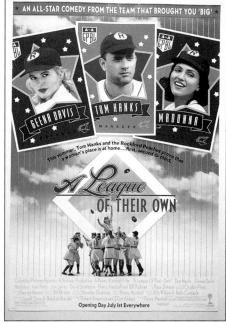

A League of Their Own rekindled interest in the AAGPBL and its stars, many of whom are still alive,

giving them a well-deserved second chance at honor and fame. But the film's impact extended further than that. The Women in Baseball exhibit is now one of the most popular at the Hall. As to the whole question of whether a woman could play Major League Baseball, reasonable people, myself included, believe that a female equivalent to Jackie Robinson will break the gender line in the next generation.

——★——

Motion pictures were first exhibited in 1894 (*Fred Ott's Sneeze*), the year the Temple Cup Series was first played and the year before Babe Ruth was born. But it didn't take long for filmmakers to realize what baseball had to offer. The first baseball film was a workout by the Newark Base Ball Club in 1898; a dramatization of baseball's ultimate story, *Casey at the Bat*, followed in 1899. By 1909 film cameras were whirring at the World Series, and that year the first baseball dramatic film was released: *His Last Game*, a movie that somehow combined cowboys, Indians, and baseball. Ty Cobb, Lou Gehrig, Babe Ruth, Hal Chase, and

Home Run Baker have had film roles, as did boxing champ Jack Johnson—as a baseball player.

These cans are full of baseball history, a random sampling of the assorted riches to be found in the National Baseball Hall of Fame Library and Archive, all available to scholars and fans by appointment. Here you see a Yankee trip to Japan, highlights of the 1948 All-Star Game, some of Bob Wolff's "Dugout Chatter," even the original Hall of Fame Induction Ceremony of June 12, 1939. The audiovisual facilities of the Library are newly expanded and provide fertile ground for baseball archaeologists.

——★——

Like life, baseball is more about losing than winning. All the same, in art we exalt the heroic, sometimes the ordinary, but never—well, hardly ever—do we find a ballad or portrait or bust that celebrates failure. The glorious exception is Ernest Lawrence Thayer's "Casey at the Bat."

Thayer was born into a well-to-do family in Lawrence, Massachusetts, where his father owned a mill. He studied philosophy at Harvard, graduated magna cum laude, and served as editor of the *Lampoon*, whose business manager for a time was William Randolph Hearst. After expulsion from Harvard, Hearst was given the editorship of the newspaper his father had just purchased, the *San Francisco Examiner*. Hearst invited Thayer to contribute a humor column, which he did, under the name "Phin," for the better part of two years. On June 3, 1888, *The Examiner* published Phin's final effort, the rollicking ballad soon to be known across the land.

Yet "Casey at the Bat" might have vanished without a trace except that novelist Archibald Clavering Gunter clipped it from the paper and kept it with him on his next trip east. On the night of August 15, 1888, at Wallack's Theatre in New York, he was backstage before a performance of *Prince Methusalem*, given as a "complimentary testimonial" to the New York Giants and visiting Chicago White Stockings. One of the stars of the comic opera was DeWolf Hopper, a regular at-

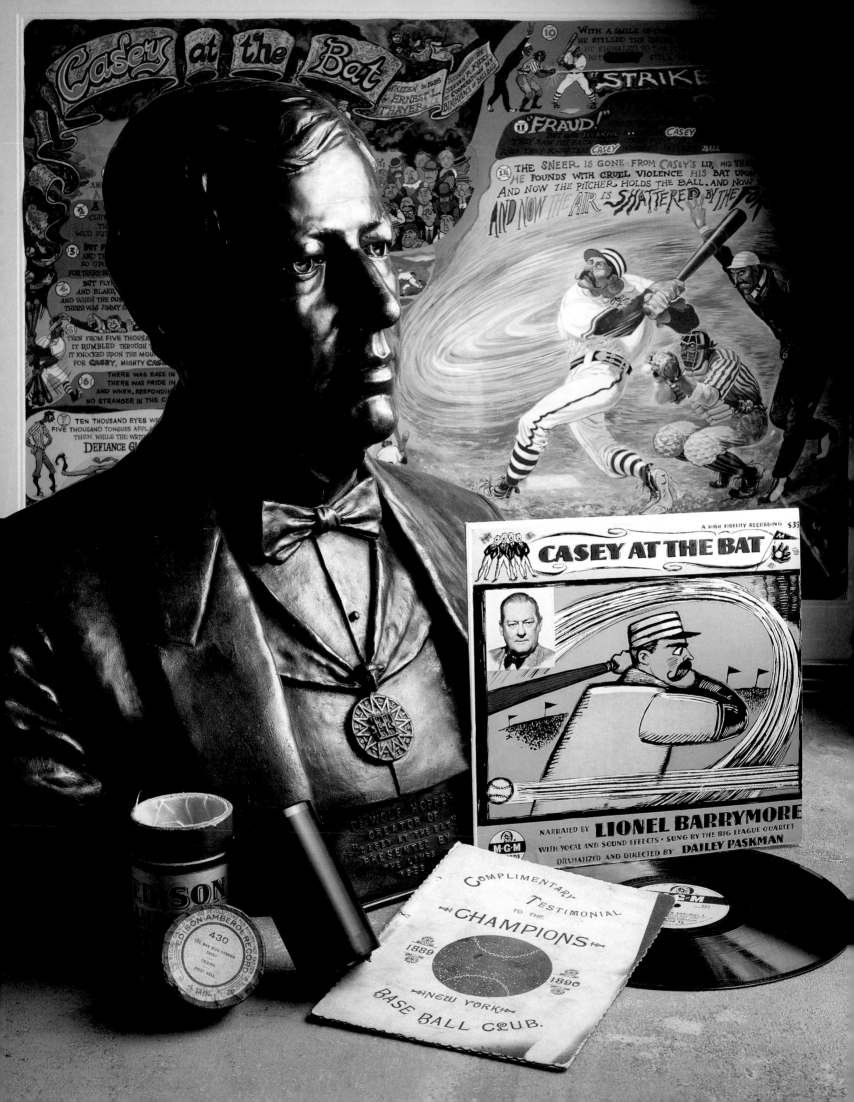

tendee at the Polo Grounds who wanted some diversion with a baseball theme to spice up the evening's entertainment. Gunter gave Hopper the poem, Hopper proved a quick study, and between acts of the comic opera he recited "Casey at the Bat."

The audience loved it, particularly the ballplayers. ("At 'the multitude was awed,' " Hopper later recalled, "I remember seeing Buck Ewing's gallant mustachios give a single nervous twitch.") Hopper kept on reciting it, by his estimate some 10,000 times over the next four decades. The mock-epic stentorian style of Hopper's five-minute-and-forty-second recitation was a delicious match for the classical march of the story (a talking film of him in action survives and is quite a hoot). Hopper's bust, on display at the National Baseball Hall of Fame Library, was donated by Frank Crumit of the Lambs Club, New York's theatrical fraternity.

By 1889 King Kelly was taking to the boards to recite the poem (naturally renamed "Kelly at the Bat"), and many thought the poem had been written not only for him but also about him. No poet came forth to dismiss such notions. Thayer was so shy and retiring that he kept quiet while everyone but your uncle Henry claimed to be the author of the poem or, like onetime Phillies pitcher Dan Casey, its inspiration.

Defenders of Thayer stepped up only as he neared death in 1940. Defenders of Casey's honor, however, sprang up much earlier, with happy-ending sequels and further adventures ranging from "Casey's Revenge" to "Casey—Twenty Years After" (also known as "The Volunteer") and "The Man Who Fanned Casey," here shown in an Edison cylinder recording by Hopper's musical-comedy partner Digby Bell. None is as pleasing as the original.

There have been parodies (Ray Bradbury wrote "Ahab at the Helm"), recitations accompanied by music (the sonorous Lionel Barrymore, the enthusiastic Tug McGraw), a movie with Wallace Beery, a cartoon epic from Disney, a ballet, and in 1953, an opera, William Schuman's *The Mighty Casey,* revived by Cooperstown's Glimmerglass Opera in 1989. A massive bronze statue by sculptor Mark Lundeen graces the reception area of the Library. And in Steven Kidd's psychedelic illustration from the 1960s, which forms the backdrop to this collage, Casey shows that it's hip to be square. Casey will continue to strike out and render Mudville joyless, but we live in a favored land indeed to take pride in so flawed a hero.

—★—

Take me out to the ball game—by satellite dish, by fiber-optic video backhaul, by microwave pager, by Internet cybercast. These are the digital media of today and tomorrow; telepathy cannot be far in the distance. But here, set against the centennial flag that flew at the Baseball Hall of Fame's dedication on June 12, 1939, are their analogue forebears, the mechanical marvels

that brought baseball reports into the age of the Jetsons: the clacking typewriter, the clicking tele-graph, the clunky microphone. These were the tools of the pioneers, the men who transformed base-ball from an occasional summer outing or a sometime special event into a nation's pastime.

The calling card at the right is that of the game's first great writer and relentless promoter, "Father" Henry Chadwick, who melded the language of business and the turf to create a statistics-laden reportorial style whose influence is still clear today. The telegraph was vital in linking baseball to its fans ever since the undefeated Red Stockings' transcontinental tour of 1869. Each inning's score and, for games of national importance, every play, was relayed over the wires by Morse code to Western Union tickers in newspaper offices. For World Series or other special games, fans would gather by the hundreds to see the plays posted in public places. The typewriter belonged to none other than Grantland Rice, whose final sheet of foolscap was still in the typewriter when it was pre-sented to the Hall of Fame following the great man's death in 1954. The NBC microphone was used by Graham McNamee to broadcast World Series games beginning in the 1920s.

Each year a baseball writer is honored by the Hall of Fame with the J. G. Taylor Spink Award, named for the last member of the Spink family to own the venerable *Sporting News*. Here is the award given to Walter Wellesley "Red" Smith, the man who succeeded Grantland Rice in the status of "dean of baseball writers." The corresponding honor for broadcasters is the Ford C. Frick Award. The award displayed here belonged to another redhead named Walter, Red Barber. His southern twang, singularly perfect for the borough of Brooklyn, found its perfect confederate in Mel Allen; combining to broadcast New York Yankees games, the two were the first recipients of the Frick Award in 1978.

CHAPTER THIRTEEN

Baseball Cards, Games, and Memorabilia

The first businesses to exploit baseball players to promote their products were tobacco companies. It seems strange now to see advertisements featuring such Hall of Famers as George Wright, King Kelly, and Hoss Radbourn endorsing Red Stocking Cigars, but those were the days when smoking was an unalloyed pleasure. Cigarette companies like Allen & Ginter's ("Straight Cuts"), or Buchner ("Gold Coin"), or Goodwin ("Old Judge," "Gypsy Queen") included cards of baseball players in their packs as early as 1886. The largest card set ever issued—numbering over 2,300 separate images—was a photographic series produced by the Goodwin Company for its Old Judge brand in the late 1880s.

This spectacular chromolithographed 1888 premium is called the Goodwin Round Album and featured the most popular players of the day in eight cards with anywhere from one to four stars per page: Anson, Kelly, and Comiskey each occupy a page of their own. The black-background card shows the Goodwin tobacco products—Old Judge, Tennis Buffs, and Boudoir cigarettes, among others. The page shown here has some of the New York National League team, such as manager Jim Mutrie, third baseman Art Whitney, and pitcher Ledell Titcomb, who was graced with the splendid alias of "Cannonball." The "mascot" was a young boy; in years to come the fashion in good-luck charms ran to street urchins like Detroit's "L'il Rastus," dwarfs like the A's Louis Van Zelst, and gently demented souls like Charles "Victory" Faust. Definitely not politically correct.

Baseball cards continued to be identified with tobacco products into the 1910s, when confections like Colgan's Chips and Cracker Jack got into the act. Gum cards were next, and they ruled the hobby from the 1930s to the 1980s (Goudey, Fleer, Topps). Finally, a court decision broke Topps's virtual thirty-year monopoly on trading cards by permitting Donruss to distribute trading cards *without* gum. The go-go decade of card collecting was in gear, as other companies joined the industry (Score, Pacific, Upper Deck, a reinvigorated Fleer). Cards were not just for kids anymore; for the first time since the days of the tobacco cards, grown-up collectors spent big bucks to recapture their youth or, with often unhappy results, to invest for their own kids' futures.

———★———

The more things change, the more they stay the same: "Cool stuff" you get for "free" if you buy the product often enough to collect the requisite proofs of purchase. It's hard to tell from the illustration if the catcher's chest protector was of any real quality, but you can bet plenty of aspiring Mickey Cochranes chowed down on their puffed cereals to get it. The umpire watch fob may still be seen at collector shows—amazing what people will keep if it's connected with baseball—and *Babe Ruth's Big Book of Baseball* is fairly common, too.

I confess that I like this sort of thing—mass art, commercial graphics, ephemeral claptrap—better than most of what collectors prize, such as autographs, jewelry, and trading cards. The typography

and graphics and color palette root the piece in time in a unique way. With this Quaker Oats store-window placard, however, the clue to the date comes from the absence of a graphic on the Babe's cap. This was the winter of 1934–1935, when he had been cut loose by the Yankees but had yet to don his Boston Braves gear.

It took Babe Ruth to turn advertising endorsements into big money (not counting the salary-cap evasion by which Boston in 1887 paid King Kelly $2,000 in salary and another $3,000 for use of his photograph). Until Ruth came along, the players accepted the small checks they got for using their likenesses and names as found money, enough to buy a nice dinner or a round or two of drinks. Babe had been selling his byline to articles written by others for five bucks a pop. Christy Walsh, a publicist and theatrical agent who founded a sporting news syndicate, told the Babe he could land him $500 for each. Babe signed, and before long Walsh took over all of Ruth's finances. The payoffs were huge; Babe, who never smoked cigarettes, gladly said that he did, in print, for $5,000, more than most major leaguers made all year long.

———★———

What is the first baseball card? Learned knights of the cardboard may dispute my judgment, but I believe it is this battered view of the Atlantics of Brooklyn team of 1868, distributed free by Peck & Snyder Sporting Goods to their customers. Featuring such luminaries as Joe Start, Dickey Pearce, John Chapman, and Bob Ferguson, the Atlantics were champions of the baseball world that year, as they had previously been in 1864, 1865, and 1866. In fact, the Library of Congress collections contain a small photograph of the 1865 team with a printed mount, and the Baseball Hall of Fame has another small photograph of the Unions of Morrisania of 1866 (on view in Chapter 14). But both are better described as *cartes de visite,* or calling cards, commissioned by the teams themselves for distribution to their close followers. What makes this 1868 card of "The Atlantic Nine" a true baseball card is its wide distribution to the public as a "trade card," with its clear intent to promote the sale of products in some real trade, namely sporting goods. (I say "real" because today the sale of the cards themselves is a real trade, but it was not always so. Even in the 1940s and 1950s card manufacturers like Topps, Bowman, and Fleer used the cards to help sell the bubblegum, not the other way around.)

Trade cards, generally of the comic illustrative sort, continued to be the form the baseball card would take until the mid-1880s, when the age of the baseball hero was dawning and chromolithographed cards of individual players came into being as promotional inserts in packs of small cigars. Before long cigarette manufacturers, too, jumped on the bandwagon and issued colored cards pro-

moting such evocative brands as Gypsy Queen, Buchner Gold Coin, Old Judge, Dogs Head, Mayo Cut Plug, Allen & Ginter's, Duke of Durham, Newsboy, and other cheap smokes of an era gone by. The incredibly extensive Old Judge set—512 players, each in multiple poses—was not a printed set but consisted entirely of sepia-toned photographs. Even a century later collectors continue to find previously undocumented cards in this set, cataloged as N172 and now numbering well over 2,000 distinct images.

Old Judge cards could be collected and redeemed for handsome larger premiums, referred to as "cabinet cards" (cataloged as N173). John Ward of the New York Giants is shown here in a Newsboy cabinet card, "Jumbo Jim" McCormick in a Buchner Gold Coin of 1887, and "Deacon Jim" McGuire in an Old Judge regular issue of 1887. McGuire wound up playing in twenty-six major-league seasons, suiting up for his final game on May 18, 1912, at age forty-eight *and* getting a hit. In that memorable game he was the catcher for the Detroit Tigers because their regular team was on strike, in support of Ty Cobb, who had been suspended by the league for attacking a heckler in the stands. (The toothless Tigers filled their lineup with recruits from the Philadelphia sandlots such as pitcher Aloysius Travers and lost to the A's 24–2.) Thus the abstemious McGuire presents an interesting transition to the golden age of baseball cards, arrayed on a following page.

— ★ —

These images from 1909–1941 are not realistic, they are romantic—and that is the essence of being a baseball fan. We preserve for ourselves the illusion that we could be down there on the field alongside our heroes (or, through totemic worship, in place of them). These cards are magical tokens, permitting us to shuttle back and forth between fantasy and reality with utter safety; it's just a game, after all.

Against a backdrop of Hobe Ferris leaping to snare a high throw about 1905, cardboard stars vie for the affections of two generations of baseball fans. Now that photographs of our favorites have long since ceased to be a novelty, wouldn't it be wonderful to see painted cards again? Dick Perez created the long-running series of Diamond Stars for the Donruss company from 1981 onward, but wouldn't it be swell to see Ken Griffey depicted in the style of Sport Kings Gum hero Ty Cobb? Or Barry Larkin in the manner of Big League Chewing Gum's Ossie Bluege? Or Larry Walker in a slim gold-bordered card like the T205 of Clark Griffith? Best of all would be a return to oversize baseball cards like the famous issues available through the Turkey Red brand of cigarettes (T3), here shown in the example of Frank "Home Run" Baker.

In the first decade of this golden age of baseball cards, candy manufacturers competed with cigarette companies for the hearts and minds of American youth. Let the names of the candy-card sponsors roll off the tongue, and savor them: Nadja Caramels . . . Mello Mints . . . Colgan's Violet Chips . . . Zeenuts . . . Texas Tommies . . . Juju Drums . . . Cracker Jack. The great candy set was issued by the American Caramel Company from 1909 to 1911, and its most valuable rarity is the card of Mike Mitchell of Cincinnati.

The American Tobacco Company, a huge trust of interlocking manufacturers, issued not only the above-mentioned Turkey Reds but also the classic T206 set of cards (1909–1911), the giant of tobacco issues and the set that includes the hobby's most valuable card, the Honus Wagner. Listen to the roll call of just a few of the T206 producers: Sweet Caporal . . . Piedmont . . . Old Mill . . .

Polar Bear . . . Hindu . . . Tolstoi . . . Cycle . . . American Beauty . . . Ty Cobb (yes, he was a subject of the front of the card and, in a handful of cases, the sponsoring tobacconist on the back).

In 1911 the trust added the Mecca folder series to its burgeoning roster of baseball hits, here depicted in the Gabby Street card, which, when folded up, reveals battery mate Walter Johnson sharing a pair of legs with his catcher. In that same year the trust issued its classic T205 set (Gold Borders), of which the Griffith card is an example. In the following year there were the Hassan triple folders (cleverly reproduced in the 1990s by Upper Deck with modern players). A Ramly card of 1911 is visible at the upper right of the composition.

By the 1920s the popularity of the cards among youngsters prompted the tobacco companies to back out of the baseball-card business, and candy and ice-cream manufacturers had the field to themselves, issuing such shabby yet appealing issues as the garishly colored strip cards and Frojoy's grainy photo reproductions. The 1930s marked the end of the candy-caramel period and the beginning of the bubblegum phase, which lasted into the 1980s. The Goudey set of 1933 is the classic gum-card issue, here represented by Bluege, but the most prized card is that of the retired Nap Lajoie, issued in limited numbers. That set was followed by another in 1934 featuring the "Lou Gehrig Says" subset of baseball tips. The four-player card of Pirates Paul Waner, brother Lloyd, Guy Bush, and Waite Hoyt had a piece of a much larger puzzle on the back. In the hobby this set has come to be known as the "4-in-1."

—★—

These are the cards that forever linked my generation with our baseball idols. Author Luke Salisbury called them "cardboard madeleines," à la Proust. Even today, on the dark side of midlife, I cannot hold a 1952 Topps card like the Robin Roberts card shown here without feeling, in a sensual way, the heat of a Bronx sidewalk, the thrill of fanning the cards to see "who I got," the taste of a Mission orange soda, the smell and peculiar feel of the pink slab of bubblegum, and the thrill of flipping my hard-earned prizes toward the wall of our apartment house, hoping to win my pal's Jackie Robinson card.

I learned how to read by studying the backs of those baseball cards, but I suspect my story isn't that unusual. Baseball cards were tickets permitting entry into neighborhood society and the larger American culture for many other immigrant boys, too. The other, more important arena for which these cards proved a ticket of admission was the world of my own imagination; what a marvel of compactness these cards were—the visage of a hero, the chronicle of his heroics, perhaps a tidbit of odd information or an amusing cartoon, a team logo, an autograph—and all on a piece of cardboard you could hold in your hand! I have sometimes thought the curriculum vitae of millions of American men, the trail of their occupational records, might start not with that first job out of high school or college, but here, in a loving gaze at a baseball card on a sidewalk on a hot summer afternoon.

The Second World War shut down the baseball-card industry, but it came back strong in 1948 when the Leaf Company issued a set of 168 cards (see Dick Wakefield's card). Here, displayed on the Brooklyn flag that flew at Briggs Stadium, are other representative cards of the most popular companies. We have the 1951 Bowman set, a classic painted set here represented by Richie Ashburn, that long-overlooked center field star of the Mays-Mantle-Snider era. We have the remarkable

Bowman set of 1955, which pictured players inside a TV screen, thus commemorating the stormy marriage between baseball and television broadcasting. (Dig that line "Color TV" on the brass plate!) Bowman was fading as a brand, unable to sign the up-and-coming stars to contracts, and this quirky set proved the company's last. Aside from historical sets from Fleer and regional issues for wieners or ice cream or gasoline, Topps issued wonderful cards during its more than two decades of dominance, but the hobby of card collecting didn't skyrocket until new brands brought innovation and competition.

Here we see a Donruss card from 1981 featuring Reggie Jackson, the first complete set since the early 1950s not to bear the name of Topps—and not to include gum. Today's cards are applying new technologies: impressive gold stamping and 3–D designs and die-cutting abound; hologram cards, which, held to the light just so, depict the player in action for three and a half seconds; a card with an actual speck of dirt from Cal Ripken's infield; and, most amazingly, a set of cards that have the smell of that old, brittle bubblegum that blessed wrappers of our youth.

— ★ —

Stars can sell things, as entrepreneurs found through theatrical performers' endorsements before the Civil War. Here we have Ty Cobb the Snarling Spitfire as Fashion Dandy, 1914. In this happy idea for a promotion, the Tiger is identified with the product and its promoter: "Mr. Tyrus Cobb, keen in clothes-buying, a Royal Tailorite, of course." Mr. Cobb was pretty keen in stock buying, too, retiring from the Tigers as a millionaire through his investments in Coca-Cola and General Motors.

Mild-mannered Walter Johnson, a national treasure like the Capitol, is simply "Mr. Walter Johnson, World's Greatest Pitcher, Royally wardrobed."

The gentlemanly Christy Mathewson received this inane caption: "The immortal Christy Mathewson votes the Royal Ticket." It may have been a golden age of baseball, but not for copywriters. I'm old-fashioned in most things, but give me "Bo Knows Baseball."

— ★ —

I love baseball in the summer, when it sizzles. I love baseball in the fall. I love baseball in the night time, under arc lights. I love board games best of all.

You understand, I'm not speaking for myself. But increasingly, there are such baseball fans, seemingly straight out of the dice-baseball heaven-hell of Robert Coover's *Universal Baseball Association, J. Henry Waugh, Proprietor.* Baseball is indeed best played outdoors, in the sunshine. Next best is under the lights, but still outdoors. Baseball in a domed stadium is a very different experience of the game, still weirdly cool. But sometimes it rains, and that's when fantasy baseball may indeed be the best of all.

Today "Rotisserie-style" baseball keeps fans involved in leagues, swapping players, competing for prizes. I believe the seeds of Rotisserie were planted in 1884 by Thomas W. Lawson's game Base Ball with Cards, shown here. This 1884 card game has lovely if disquieting graphics, but you can't blame Lawson for the menace that future generations would find in that bodiless, four-ball, four-armed swastika.

Lawson sold candy on trains in the Boston area as a boy, saved his money, and invented a card game that he sold himself, on the trains and at the ballparks. This is that game. Played by four players, two on each side, its object was "to secure as many tricks, or runs, as possible and by skilful [*sic*] combinations to destroy the value of opponent's cards." The game was successful, and in 1885 Lawson arranged a tournament of the National League clubs, with prizes he posted himself

("$1,600 in gold and handsome trophies"). Unlike Rotisserie, however, in which a player contents himself with statistical stand-ins for the players on his team, the Base Ball with Cards tournament was played by real members of the National League teams deploying fantasy elements. The St. Louis Maroons defeated the Boston Red Stockings on their first eastern swing, but in September they lost to the Chicago White Stockings, who had such scientific card players as Ned Williamson, a crack whist player, and Fred Pfeffer, an expert at faro. Chicago thus won the right to play the Philadelphia Phillies for the championship, but the results of that match are lost to history.

The success of Lawson's invention inspired a rival game known as Parlor Baseball, played with 125 cards "representing all the features of baseball." What was interesting about this rival game was that its inventor was Jake Aydelott, a big-league pitcher with Indianapolis and Philadelphia. Fantasy and reality were one in baseball's Garden of Eden.

Simulated baseball table games go back to 1868 and another amusement called Parlor Base-Ball, a mechanical game in which a bat attached to a coiled spring met a penny pitched toward the plate. It, too, was invented by a pitcher, Francis C. Sebring of the Empire Base Ball Club. Today's pinball games are not very much different in concept nor is the metal gameboard depicted here, labeled "Strike 3." The other mechanical game shown, The Great American Game, is on the way to simulating baseball in the manner of Ethan Allen's landmark game of 1941, All-Star Baseball, but it must have been a real snooze to play.

Celluloid dreams, electroplate trophies. Who could have known that by issuing this bat-and-button trinket in 1960 the Pittsburgh Pirates, ultimately world champions, had propitiated the baseball gods? Or that the unwittingly lame-duck Brooklyn rooters, with a similar offering in 1957, had offended them? What wisdom and loss are bound up in this little button!

I don't know what accounts for the melancholy that drips from this assemblage. Maybe it's that funereally dignified Baltimore Orioles pin of 1894, with McGraw and Kelley and Keeler and Robinson trapped like butterflies under glass. Or maybe it's just personal, that damned 1957 Brooklyn pin, which I owned when it was new and so was I, when it never would have occurred to me that my beloved Dodgers would willingly leave me any more than any other member of my family would.

———— ★ ————

The ownership of the New York Giants was never famous for overpaying its players. A man who became one of the club's presidents, John T. Brush, even proposed a salary structure based upon years of service that sparked the Players League revolt of 1890. But Brush and his followers realized that they were, after all, situated in the media capital of the world. So they made sure their most loyal, influential, and celebrated fans were particularly well treated, as this collection of sterling silver passes from the years 1898 to 1930 indicates.

The 1898 pass went from the despised owner Andrew J. Freedman to John B. Foster, editor of the American Publishing Company, the publishing arm of sporting-goods magnate Albert Spalding's company. Designed by famous artists such as Charles Dana Gibson, the passes ranged from the elegant (pencil and holder, 1914) to the whimsical (the winking man in the bowler, 1929) to the celebrated (Gibson's three hopeful fans, bases full, originally published in 1904 but here rendered in silver for the 1930 season). There is a greeter's "glad hand" for 1926, a fence with a knothole for 1924, a key to the stadium for 1921, and on.

The point is, things haven't changed much in all the years since Broadway stars and stock-market whizzes and cardsharps thought the Polo Grounds was the place to see and be seen. Clubs still lavish gifts on those whose personal celebrity or "connections" add to the team's mystique.

The art against which the passes are displayed is a monochrome issue (there was a colored one, too) of Henry Sandham's view of the Polo Grounds during the 1894 Temple Cup series.

CHAPTER FOURTEEN

National Baseball Hall of Fame Library and Archive

Two documents that wrench the soul. The poignant letter from Lou Gehrig to his wife, Eleanor, was uncovered in her estate around 1990. Gehrig wrote to her on hotel letterhead from Detroit on May 2, 1939, after the game between the Yankees and Tigers for which he had benched himself after 2,130 consecutive appearances. Lou had played in the first eight games of the 1939 season, but he knew that he was swinging feebly (four singles, no extra-base hits) and was immobile at first base. And one may infer from the letter's second paragraph that Eleanor, too, knew that something was dreadfully wrong.

Because the manuscript has become faint through the years, here is a transcript of that portion of the letter that has been released for publication, in accordance with the provisions of the estate.

> My sweetheart—and please God grant that we may be ever such—for what the hell else matters—That thing yesterday I believe and hope was the turning point in my life for the future as far as taking life too seriously is concerned. It was inevitable, although I dreaded the day, and my thoughts were with you constantly—How would this affect you and that was the only question and the most important thought underlying everything. I broke just

before the game because of thoughts of you. Not because I didn't know you are the bravest kind of partner, but because my inferiority grabbed me and

> made me wonder and ponder if I could possibly prove myself worthy of you—As for me, the road may come to a dead end here, but why should it?— Seems like our backs are to the wall now, but there usually comes a way out. Where, and what, I know not, but who can tell that it might not lead right out to greater things?—Time will tell—
>
> As for our suggestion of farewell tour and farewell day Joe [McCarthy, Yankees manager] had a different but sensible idea—He said there wasn't any body [sic] more deserving of the remaining salary—and he wasn't afraid of Ed [Barrow, Yankees president], but with this new setup that ques-

tion might arise, and if we planned a farewell day to record, newspapermen would interpret it as the absolute finish and that might cause quite a squabble among all the new directors, whereas if we said just a temporary rest and lay off—to come back in warmer weather, there could hardly be any doubt—I couldn't tell all this over the phone because Bill [Dickey?] was . . .

Six weeks later, the day after the Hall of Fame dedication, Lou Gehrig entered the Mayo Clinic in Rochester, Minnesota, for a battery of tests. The terse letter shown here is written to address Gehrig's occupational future and may be worded in such a way as to address the concerns Lou raised in his letter to Eleanor. It is the official end to Lou Gehrig's career as baseball player—and maybe the first time anyone who was not a doctor saw the words "amyotrophic lateral sclerosis." Today known as ALS, or Lou Gehrig's disease, it continues to ravage the nervous systems and sap the strength of adults in their prime. But Lou and Eleanor's public acknowledgment of his condition and their enduring support of efforts to find a cure, even after their deaths, provide one of the game's greatest stories.

———— ★ ————

King Kelly was the first baseball star to milk his fame for all it was worth. Product endorsements, personality licensing, theatrical appearances, Kelly pioneered them all. With *Play Ball: Stories of the Diamond Ball Field*, he launched what has become a staple of baseball literature, the celebrity biography. Published by Emery & Hughes of Boston, this forty-six-page paperback (here shown in archival board covers) is highly entertaining if not demonstrably factual. The stories

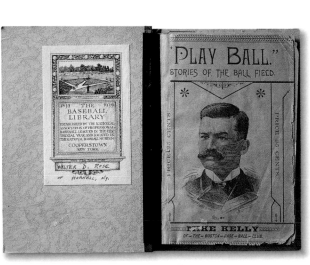

about Kelly are legion, and like the ones attaching to Rube Waddell, that other great mythic figure of early baseball, if they're not true, well, they ought to have been. History is more than the mere recitation of fact. Scrupulous fact checkers may successfully repudiate this story or that one, but they can't attach feet of clay to Kelly's idol because he did such a good job of that himself, drinking himself to death before he reached forty.

———— ★ ————

Nothing has so linked the fan and the game's history as the scorecard. We make our own special notes, creating our own play-by-play chronicle of the game. We can then keep it forever and relive those moments with a specificity of detail (and a unique subjectivism) beyond that of the box score. Ever see anyone keeping score at a football or hockey game?

Mortimer Rogers was a skilled amateur player with the Lowells of Boston in the 1860s, but his claim to fame was his pioneering entrepreneurship. In 1869 he published *The New England Chronicle*, a baseball weekly. In 1871, the inaugural year of the game's first professional league, the National Association, Rogers published a handsome series of score-cards featuring the faces of ballplayers. Printed scorecards date back as far back as 1865, but the Rogers card was the first pictorial specimen. In 1871 the halftone printing process had not yet been invented, so for each of these scorecards a paper photograph had to be attached to the cardboard. A different player would be featured for each game, in a studio portrait by Boston's celebrated J. W. Black. Several fine examples have survived, and the National Baseball Hall of Fame Library has its share.

Note that this picture is of the "Tom Thumb" shortstop Davey Force (5'4" and 130 pounds), the man who in his gypsy wanderings created the National League. Shown here as a member of the Washington Olympics of 1871, he played with five clubs in the five-year life of the National Association. He starred in 1874 with the Chicago White Stockings, one of whose owners, William Hulbert, wanted to get him signed up early for the following season so he wouldn't jump to another team. But by putting him under contract in September 1874, Chicago technically violated National Association

rules on early signings (the association was a cooperative league, with free player movement between seasons). Force was declared a free agent and signed for more money with the Philadelphia Athletics. The outraged Hulbert felt that the western clubs had yet again been treated as second-class members in the National Association, and that he had lost the Force case because of favoritism shown to Philadelphia interests. In revenge, he raided the Athletics of their top player, Cap Anson, and Boston of its top four, again flouting the rule against early signings. But this time Hulbert didn't care because the National Association was dying, and in 1876 he would take his White Stockings to the top of the new National League.

— ★ —

In baseball literature, this little book—sixty-four pages, size two inches by two-and-a-half inches, and "bound in the skin of a baseball"—may be the rarest of the rare. The Library of Congress has a copy, and so does the National Baseball Hall of Fame Library. I am aware of no other. Each right-hand page contains humorous definitions, and each left-hand page offers an amusing four-line poem and a silhouetted illustration in the crude style of the cover art. Printed in 1888 by Rand & Avery of Boston and sold to the public for twenty-five cents, *The Krank: His Language and What It Means* is a humorous glossary of baseball terms. Many of these are extremely picturesque to modern ears (a strikeout is "cutting a hole in space," "smashing the wind," or "compressing the atmosphere"). Others are fascinating for their etymological clues. What we today call a "pop fly," for instance, is defined and depicted as a *pot fly*—the household insect that traces lazy circles over a steaming pot in the kitchen. The book begins:

The Krank is a heterogeneous compound of flesh, bone, and base-ball, mostly base-ball. He came into existence along back in the early seventies. He came to stay.

The Krank is purly American. He is found in no other country.

The Krank is of the masculine gender. The female of the tribe is known to science as a Kranklet.

The Krank has reached a high state of cultivation. The Kranklet is at present only partly developed.

The Krank has a shell, into which he crawls in the month of November. He does not emerge from it until April. While in his shell his only article of food is stray newspaper articles on deals. During the Krank season, from April to November, he subsists on air, and waxes strong.

"Krank" surely derives from the German word for "sick" as well as the British dialect meaning of "cranky," which is "feeble-minded." Baseball devotees at the turn of the century were also called "bugs," thus casting another aspersion on those who were simply mad about the game. Baseball's specialized language is so wonderful.

Thomas William Lawson became a "candy butcher" on the New England trains, which meant that he sold candy, tobacco, and newspapers in the aisles. He was a rabid baseball fan—even before that term replaced the older "krank"—to such an extent that in 1884 he took the profits of his candy business and poured them into a baseball-card game of his own invention (see Chapter 13).

Next was a stint on Wall Street during which he became seriously wealthy through stock-market manipulation. He became a full-fledged financier of the Amalgamated Copper Company, one of the trusts that enraged Teddy Roosevelt and Judge Landis. In 1904 and 1905 Lawson confessed to his stock-market swindling and bared the whole Wall Street mess in a famous book called *Frenzied Finance*, which was first published serially in *Everybody's* magazine. Then he became a novelist, writing *Friday the Thirteenth* for publication by Doubleday in 1907, and after that a satirist under the pseudonym Thomas W. Roastem.

Quite a career. And until now, you had never heard of this baseball Leonardo.

*B*aseball as Viewed by a Muffin is not written from the point of view of a biscuit. Even though baseball started getting serious in the 1860s, there were still a lot of people who wanted to play the game just for fun, as generations before them had done. As a result many baseball clubs, which, you must remember, were organized primarily for fraternal rather than competitive reasons, divided themselves between the good players and the irregulars, known as "muffins" (they "muffed" the ball more often than they caught it). So a club might

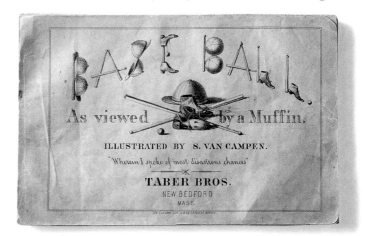

field a "first nine," composed of crack players, and a "muffin nine," made up of out-of-shape, middle-aged supporters who would play a game against the opponents' muffins after the regular contest had concluded.

Baseball as Viewed by a Muffin, the game's first illustrated book, was created by S. Van Campen in 1867. It was all about the laughs that resulted from muffinlike play, including a bobbled grounder, an outfield collision, and the catcher getting hit in the head by a thrown bat. The humor of baseball played badly has always been an integral part of our enjoyment of it. There is a direct line from "muffin" to today's "bloopers" videos.

The archness of baseball reporting in the early days seems particularly delicious today, when sports coverage is dominated by inane locker-room quotes. With each cartoon drawing (they are large, one to the page), Van Campen supplied a classical quotation ("A hit, a very palpable hit!").

The cover quote, "Wherein I spoke of most disastrous chances," is from Shakespeare's *Othello*. Another interesting element on the cover is the "tulip" or lemon-peel-stitched panels of the baseball. As we recall, the figure-eight style of today, employing only two panels of horsehide or cowhide, was probably invented by Ellis Drake in the late 1860s and rapidly became the standard.

——★——

The envelope reads: "not to be opened till after the death of Sam Rice. [signed] Paul S. Kerr." Oh, if that doesn't pique your interest, you're reading the wrong book.

A baseball controversy settled from beyond the grave—surely one of the oddest letters in the Hall's collection. In the eighth inning of Game 3 of the 1925 World Series, in Washington, the Senators held a 4–3 lead over the Pirates. But with two outs, Pirate catcher Earl Smith slugged a ball into deep right center. Right fielder Sam Rice ran for it, leapt, and tumbled into the temporary bleachers. He didn't reappear for at least ten seconds, but he held the ball for all to see. Umpire Cy Rigler called Smith out; the Pirates went bonkers. How could anyone tell whether Rice had caught the ball? A fan could have handed it to him.

The play might have remained controversial had the Pirates not won the Series. Forty years later Sam Rice decided to set the record straight. He composed this letter on July 27, 1965, during Induction Weekend in Cooperstown, and gave it to Paul S. Kerr, then the president of the Baseball Hall of Fame, with instructions that it not be opened until after his death. Rice had been inducted into the Hall in 1963 for his twenty years of stellar play, nineteen of them with Washington. When Sam met his Maker on October 13, 1974, the controversy could be settled at last (what follows is a verbatim transcription):

> It was a cold and windy day. The right field bleachers were crowded with people in overcoats and wrapped in blankets, the ball was a line drive headed for the bleachers towards right center. I turned slightly to my right and had the ball in view all the way, going at top speed, and about 15 feet from bleachers jumped as high as I could and back handed and the ball hit the center of pocket in glove (I had a death grip on it). I hit the ground about 5 feet from a barrier about 4 feet high in front of bleacher with all the brakes on but couldn't stop so my feet hit the barrier about a foot from top and I toppled over on my stomach into first row of bleachers. I hit my adams apple on something which sort of knocked me out for a few seconds but [Earl] McNeely arrived about that time and grabbed me by the shirt and pulled me out. I remember trotting back towards the infield still carrying the ball for about half way and then tossed it towards the pitchers mound. (How I have wished many times that I had kept it.)

> At no time did I lose possession of the ball.

>   "Sam" Rice

> P.S. After this was announced at the dinner last night I approached Bill McKechnie (one of the finest men I have ever known in Baseball) and I said Bill, you were the Mgr of Pittsburgh at that time, what do you think will be in the letter. His answer was, Sam there was never any doubt in my mind but what you caught the ball. I thanked him as much as to say you were right.

Rice, curiously, retired with 2,987 hits. He didn't see any great value in hanging on to get number 3,000. In later years he was often asked why he retired so close to the magic number. "You must remember," he'd explain, "there wasn't much emphasis on three thousand hits when I quit. And to tell the truth, I didn't know how many hits I had."

——★——

Of all the baseball photographs ever taken, this for me is the greatest—not because it depicts an epic moment in the game's history nor because it shows a great player. It is simply beautiful. Auguste Rodin and Douglas Tilden would see the sculptural mass of this tableau and weep for their inability to capture it as well as this photograph.

Hack Wilson was a physical phenomenon. He stood just 5′6″, scarcely taller than Freddie Patek. He wore a size 5½ shoe. But he weighed at least 190 pounds and had an eighteen-inch neck. And when he hit the ball, the horsehide screamed in pain. He was power personified. Wilson's fifty-six homers in 1930 are still the most ever in the National League; his 190 RBIs that year are more than anyone's, ever. Playing in the friendly confines of Wrigley Field in an era of great sluggers, he topped the National League in homers four times (three in a row) and RBIs twice. But Hack had huge appetites for more than just runs batted in; his drinking got him into problems with all his managers. Once a manager tried to give him a lesson. "If I put a worm in a glass of water, it swims around. If I put it in a glass of

whiskey, it dies. What does that tell you?" the manager asked. Wilson allegedly replied, "If you drink whiskey you'll never get worms."

———★———

Until late in his career, Babe Ruth spent his off season barnstorming. When Lou Gehrig became a star with the Yankees, the two traveled as leaders of "The Bustin' Babes" and "The Larrupin' Lous." Ruth traveled the countryside, putting on a show for people in small towns who had never seen professional baseball. And he made a sizable amount of money doing it.

Once it got him into hot water with Commissioner Landis. After the 1921 World Series Ruth

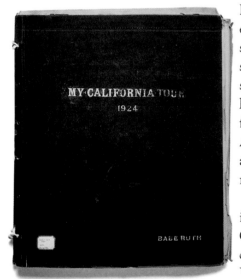

and Bob Meusel headed out for a tour but were told by Landis they could not. The commissioner felt that World Series players touring so soon after the Series diminished the value of the postseason championship. He suspended the two for thirty-nine days at the beginning of the 1922 season. Ruth was defiant. "Who the hell does Landis think he is?" he said. But the commissioner was bigger than the game's biggest star, and the Babe sat down. Landis judiciously changed the rule the next year.

This is actually the 1924 California tour scrapbook of Babe Ruth, who was so often the subject of others' scrapbooks. It holds many wonderful photographs and window cards for upcoming games in addition to the expected clippings. But one has to wonder. Do you think Babe came back to his hotel early each night so he could paste the latest news reports and tour mementos into this book?

———★———

This is a celebrated early team, the Unions of Morrisania, of interest for such players as George Wright, shortstop par excellence; Doug Birdsall, who went on to play professionally with George for Boston in the National Association; and Charlie Pabor, longtime pitcher and outfielder with

the most inexplicable of all baseball nicknames: "The Old Woman with the Red Cap."

Shown here is the 1866 group that brought honor to Morrisania and laid the ground for the next year's national champions, despite the defection of Wright to the Washington Nationals. The *carte de visite* is the basis of the gloriously painted photograph that reposed in the archives for generations and now, after painstaking restoration, is available for viewing in the National Baseball Hall of Fame Library. Shown here along with the team views is a simple ticket of admission to the ball game, showing that Ladies' Day had been dreamed up before the generally accepted inception in 1883, when Tony Mullane the handsome "Apollo of the Box," lured the ladies to games. Even in the 1860s gentlemen appreciated the tone lent by the fair sex, whether in the stands or sipping cool libations in the retiring tent.

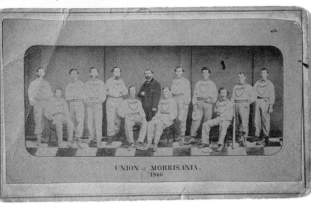

Where is Morrisania, anyway? In former times it was a municipality in Westchester County, which ran north to Eighth Street, now 165th Street, and south to Harlem Bridge. How do I know that? Well, I'm not 150 years old. In an interesting modern spin on antiquarian baseball, I found it on the Internet, of all places, where I discovered in the annals of the Library of Congress an interview that a WPA worker conducted on August 18, 1938, with an old resident of Morrisania, Mr. T. Emery Sutton, of 430 East 160th Street in the Bronx. Like a ghost voice that cannot die because it's trapped in cyberspace, Mr. Sutton speaks to us today of

Morrisania in the 1860s with an offhand specificity that no modern writer could hope to equal:

The Unions, as the team was called, played their games at the Triangle, on a lot behind Fisher's coal yard, at what is now 163rd street. About 1868 or 1869 they moved to Tremont and Arthur avenues, and there built the first enclosed baseball grounds. The first game played was for the championship between the Unions and the Brooklyn Mutuals [known as the New York Mutuals to historians today, they in fact played their home games in Brooklyn]. The home team won. The price of admission was 25 cents; and I had the distinction of taking in the very first quarter. Ed. Wright was the cashier; I was only a boy at the time. There was no grand stand, only board seats.

The great baseball leagues had not yet been organized, and the only prize awarded a winning club was the ball with which the game had been played. We used to silver these balls and keep them as trophies. They were kept in a large case in Louis Comb's establishment, Morrisania Hall. Thomas E. Sutton was the first president, and Henry J. Ford the first vice-president of the Union Baseball Club.

Our team made trips through the country, as do the big league teams today. Funds to defray expenses were donated by the townspeople, each one of them subscribing according to his inclination, and financial ability. The players used to be gone for two or three weeks at a time. Among the members of the Union team were C. Payne, D. Bickett, A. Abrams, B. Hourigan, T. Beals, and the great George Wright whose brother afterwards managed the Athletics [brother Harry managed the Boston team, not the Athletics of Philadelphia] when the leagues were organized.

The past lives.

———★———

Check out the great names on the scorecards from the early 1870s, the Boston Red Stockings against the Athletics of Philadelphia. Reach, McBride, Anson for Philly, Al Spalding, Ross Barnes, and the Wright brothers for Boston! And look at the peculiar scoring system offered in the Chicago half of the other scorecard, from 1877: A, B, C, and H represent four bases; F is for a catch on the fly; D is for a catch on the bound; LD for a foul bound catch; LF for a foul ball caught on the fly; K, PO, and A are as today; RO is for run-out between bases; and a dot represents a run. The grand old game has changed a bit after all.

And from Mort Rogers's first pictorial scorecards to the chromolithographed beauties shown here was but a matter of a decade. With all the printing, publishing, and communications advances of the present age, has any generation produced such splendid color imagery as the 1880s and '90s?

— ★ —

These faded score sheets are typical of the treasures housed in the National Baseball Hall of Fame Library and Archive and the awesome task confronting that institution in trying to preserve baseball's past for future generations. Writers and fans know the story pretty well—how Johnny Vander Meer, an erratic left-hander for the Cincinnati Reds, captured lightning in a bottle on two successive starts in 1938. They know that new Reds manager Bill McKechnie worked with Vander Meer to improve his mechanics and thus his control and how Vander Meer responded. Not only did he win fifteen games for the Reds to keep them in the pennant race most of the season, but on June 11 against Boston in Cincinnati and on June 15 against the Dodgers at Ebbets Field, Cincinnati's enigma became the most puzzling pitcher in baseball history. He threw consecutive no-hitters, the only time the feat has ever been accomplished at the major league level (though it's happened a couple of times in the minors, and Marty McHale, later of the Red Sox, threw three straight no-nos for the University of Maine in 1910).

CHAPTER FIFTEEN

The Hidden Hall of Fame

—★—

They used to call "kranks" or "bugs" those of us who followed the game (or our team) with loving devotion. Where the term "fan" came from has long been in dispute (like so many of the terms peculiar to our national game, such as "fungo" or "chin music"). The explanation I buy is that Ted Sullivan, manager of the St. Louis Browns in 1883, referred to the crowd as a bunch of fanatics, which he shortened to "fan." Some learned etymologists have pointed to a 1785 dictionary that refers to those of the class who followed sports, particularly boxing, as "the fancy," which also got abbreviated to "the fance," and then "fans."

This diminutive metal pin, found in the Hall's archives, suggests another possibility. Could the name have come from the tools the attendees used to cool themselves on hot summer afternoons? (Another item popular in the 1910s was a cardboard fan with the likeness of a star player on one side, sold in the stands as "A Fan for A Fan.") Imagine looking upon a crowd of several thousand people all fanning themselves—might you not refer to the congregants themselves as fans, just as the original operators of typewriters were themselves named for their instruments? (Only later were they called typists.) Or maybe the name comes from the incessant chatter and debate by which true baseball devotees are known.

In just the second year of its existence, 1877, the National League faced a threat. Ball teams from seventeen different cities had joined the International Association of Professional Base Ball Players, a loose confederation of "cooperative" nines—that is, the players ran the teams as well as the league and divided gate receipts rather than work as employees for fixed wages. The association, headed by a player as its president, Hall of Famer Candy Cummings, was nothing like the National League in organizational structure; in fact, it strongly resembled the National Association that had died after the 1875 season. Only seven teams paid the ten-dollar fee to play for the championship, while the remainder became associate members and played exhibitions against full league members, who played each other whenever profits seemed likely. By the end of the season only five of the seven clubs had played out their schedules. The Tecumseh team, of London, Ontario, was named champions.

Today the International Association (IA) of 1877 is thought of as baseball's first minor league, but in fact it was a full-fledged rival, with its best teams as good or better than the National League's second tier. The IA developed such future National League stars as Pud Galvin, John Ward, George Gore, Fred Dunlap, and Joe Hornung, the original owner of this Tecumseh pin. As good as they were, the Tecumsehs were refused National League membership because their hometown, with just 25,000 residents, failed to meet the minimum population requirements. A hundred years later, an Ontarian city finally was accepted into the majors when Toronto got the expansion Blue Jays.

—★—

It wasn't the thousands of balls that this mitt snagged successfully that make it a significant historical artifact—it's the one it didn't. This is the glove of Mickey Owen, who has earned a place alongside Fred Snodgrass, Bill Buckner, Fred Merkle, Lonnie Smith, and Tony Fernandez. Owen had been a steady defensive catcher for the St. Louis Cardinals in the late 1930s. When the Dodgers traded for him in December of 1940, he became their regular backstop. In 1941 the Dodgers won their first pennant in twenty-one long seasons. Despite the overhanging cloud of war in Europe and the Far East, 1941 was a marvelous year in some other ways, too—Ted Williams hit .406 and Joe DiMaggio jolted hits in fifty-six straight games.

The Dodgers went up against the vaunted Yankees in the World Series, and they were doing just fine. They split the first two games and lost the third, but they had a 4–3 lead with two out in the top of the ninth of Game 4. It looked as though the Series would be tied, but here's where Mickey comes in. With two strikes on batter Tommy Henrich, Owen called for pitcher Hugh Casey's curve. He expected the quick, sharp slider-style curve. Casey threw a big, Blyleven-style bender instead (though rumor persists that Casey loaded up a wet one for the fatal pitch). Henrich

swung and missed, but the balled zipped past Owen and Henrich scampered safely to first. Then the Yank thunder roared: a single, a double, a walk, and another double, and when the third out was finally made the Yanks had a 7–4 lead. The Dodgers lost that day and the next one, too, and the Series was over.

Some people said the Dodgers were cursed by Owen's third-strike mishap. They wouldn't make another Series appearance until 1947, and they lost that one, too. And the ones in 1949 and 1952 and 1953. And when they missed making it to the Series in 1950 and 1951, it was by the slimmest of margins—heartbreaking losses in the opposition's final at-bat, with knockout blows delivered by Dick Sisler of the Phils and Bobby Thomson of the Giants.

—★—

At first in the 1930s Brooklyn fans referred to their Dodgers as "Dem Bums" with a mixture of frustration and disgust, as Wilbert Robinson's "Daffiness Boys" evolved into Casey Stengel's bad clubs of mid-decade. But as the team's fortunes improved, its mascot hung on; the Bum took on a strangely lovable air. As drawn by Willard Mullin, he became a badge of honor for the citizens of Brooklyn, summing up not only the disdain shown the Dodgers by the rest of baseball, but in particular the disrespect  shown Brooklyn by its neighbor across the East River. For this inspired creation and a lifetime of memorable caricatures, Mullin was acclaimed in 1971 as the sports cartoonist of the century by his peers. The Bum's most celebrated appearance was on the back page of the tabloid New York *Daily News* the day after Brooklyn defeated the Yankees in the 1955 World Series. His beaming visage was surmounted by the headline WHO'S A BUM?

Not exactly a specimen of the batmakers' art, this decal-bedecked club looks, at first glance, like a sales promotion for a tattoo parlor. Louisville Slugger dreamed up these decal trophy bats about 1910, but the idea lost favor when star signatures

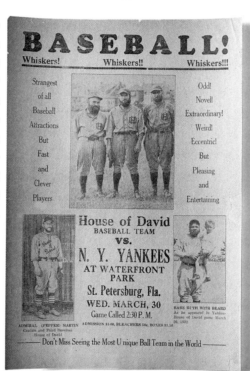

were burned into the bats, making it possible to use a hero's model bat without fear of scraping off his likeness. Visible are Cobb ("The Georgia Peach") and Eddie Collins; wrapped onto the other side of the bat are Tris Speaker and Harry Davis.

Never heard of Harry Davis? It's interesting to learn which players were regarded as stars in their own time yet have faded from view in ours. (If you look at the Hall of Fame voting for the early years, you find such intriguing names as Herman Long, Boston shortstop in the 1890s, who polled more votes in 1936 than King Kelly or Amos Rusie or twenty other men who subsequently made it into the Hall of Fame. But I digress.) Home Run Harry Davis was the man who handed over the classic nickname to teammate Frank Baker in 1911. Davis was the first man to lead his league in homers four years in a row. Only two men have surpassed that: Kiner and Ruth.

---★---

Strangest of All Baseball Attractions! Well, maybe not. In 1883–1884 the craze for all things baseball spawned not only a new professional league (the Union Association) and the World Series (Providence Grays against the New York Mets) and night baseball (at Fort Wayne, Indiana), but also a proliferation of eccentric nines matched in what were called "novelty games." There was an all-Chinese nine (the John Lang team), a "Colored Girl" team from Chester, Pennsylvania, called the Dolly Vardens; the fat man's team, the Jumbos, who played against the lean men, the Shadows. The most distinctive games of the season matched the Snorkey Club of Philadelphia (named for the crippled hero of the famous melodrama *Under the Gaslight*), whose players each lacked an arm or a hand, against the Hoppers of Washington—all one-legged or on crutches. Not a pretty picture, for sure, but certainly poignant and a mirror of that brutal age: most of the crippled players on both teams had been railroad workers.

The bearded barnstormers of the House of David nine were devised as a moneymaking promotion for the House of David or Branch Davidian colony at Benton Harbor, Michigan, around 1910. They were disciples of Benjamin Purnell, an Ohio farmer who in 1903 had a vision in which he was proclaimed the Sixth Son of the House of David, with a mission to unite the Lost Tribes of Israel before Judgment Day. He and his fellow colonists swore off sex, smoking, drinking, and shaving.

Once on the baseball field, however, the only thing that was hidebound was the baseball itself. The House of David men were indeed "Fast and Clever Players," as the broadside indicates, renowned especially for their Harlem Globetrotter–like pepper games. And they were not averse to welcoming an occasional ringer like Babe Ruth or Pepper Martin.

Jesse Tannehill may be the best pitcher you never heard of. Six times a twenty-game winner, this little left-hander pitched for the Pirates of Honus Wagner and Fred Clarke for six years on both sides of the century's turn, then jumped to the New York Highlanders of the new American League for the 1903 season, missing out on a World Series appearance. Then he joined Cy Young with the Boston Americans.

This morning jacket, from his Boston Pilgrims team of 1907, was the dressy outerwear players favored before the heavy cardigan sweater became the standard for warm-ups and bench sitting. These jackets were sufficiently showy for field exercises and ceremonies before games, but, more important, they were what the players wore to go to the game. There were no clubhouse dressing rooms in most parks of the era, so the team had to dress at the hotel and ride horse-drawn carriages (or, later, trolleys) to the ballpark. This is what they wore to keep their uniforms clean, themselves warm, and their fans enamored of them. No wonder every street urchin hoped to grow up to become a ballplayer. Then as now, it was a treat to see a baseball hero on the street, but with flashy threads like these, I'll bet it was better then.

———— ★ ————

"I ain't superstitious, but a black cat's crossing my trail." It's easy to imagine bluesman Willie Dixon singing this, but it's also a line John McGraw might have penned on the eve of the 1905 World Series. He was about to square off against Connie Mack's Philadelphia Athletics, who had proudly adopted the epithet White Elephants, hurled at them by McGraw during the war with the National League in 1902. In Mack's own words, from his 1950 autobiography:

In 1902 the Baltimore Club forfeited its franchise in the newly formed American League. Its spot was filled by the New York Highlanders, "the acorn from which sprung the mighty Yankee oak." The astute John McGraw took advantage of the opportunity and jumped from the crumbling Orioles to the New York Giants, a leap to fame and fortune. When the sportswriters gathered around McGraw to fire a barrage of questions, one of the questions was, "What do you think of the Philadelphia A's?"

"White elephants!" quickly retorted Mr. Mc-Graw. "Mr. B. F. Shibe has a white elephant on his hands."

When peace was declared in 1903 and the first modern World Series was played, it was Boston, the American League representative, that emerged victorious. After killing the World Series in 1904 by refusing to insist that the National League pennant-winning Giants play the defending champion Boston Red Sox, his league ordered McGraw to play in 1905. When his opponent turned out to be Mack's White Elephants, the superstitious McGraw decided he would take the upper hand by going black against white.

This black Giant jersey was worn by Hooks Wiltse, a pitcher who had a fine year in 1905 (15–6) but didn't get into the World Series because

Christy Mathewson tossed three shutouts and Joe McGinnity one in the Giants' five-game victory. Hooks may have been given his nickname for his fine curve, or for his misshapen nose, or maybe just because he was left-handed and thus, in that age of superstition, twisty, serpentine (his brother, also a big-league lefty, was nicknamed "Snake"), even sinister (the Latin for left is *sinistra*).

Hooks was a man destined for bad luck, McGraw's wiles notwithstanding. On July 4, 1908, in the first game of a twin bill with the Phillies, Hooks took a perfect game into the ninth inning and retired the first two batters. The last man up figured to be a pinch hitter for the pitcher, George McQuillan, but he, too, had failed to give up a run, so he came up to bat. Strike one. Strike two. Then poor Wiltse tried to get cute and threw an 0–2 hook to McQuil-

lan . . . and hit him, erasing his perfect game. Although the Giants won the game in the tenth and Hooks retained his no-hitter, it was cold comfort.

When the Giants next returned to the World Series, in 1911, McGraw revived the black uniforms, but the charm was off, as his team lost to the A's in six games. Wiltse made two relief appearances and was clobbered. In the rematch of the clubs in the 1913 World Series, the Giants wore white yet lost in five. But Black Cat Wiltse, fading out as a pitcher, played a vital part in their only victory. Forced into action as a first baseman in the late innings of Game 2 because of an injury to Fred Merkle (talk about a bad-luck charm!), Hooks made back-to-back excellent throws home in the last of the ninth to twice nail the potential winning run. The Giants won in ten innings.

— ★ —

Imagine a combination of the pugnacity and tenacity of Pete Rose, the speed and acrobatic ability of Ozzie Smith, and the audacity and volubility of Deion Sanders. Now put a handlebar mustache on the player, transport him back to the four-time league champion St. Louis Browns of the 1880s, and call him Arlie Latham.

Although other players sported better stats and better dispositions, Latham came to the ballpark to beat you. He was a speedster (in 1888 he totaled 129 steals), but he stole most of his bases through daring and disregard for his body, belly-flopping for the bag and reaching out a hand or barreling into the base, kicking up a dust storm and kicking over the

Earth." His private life was as tumultuous as that on the field: his first wife attempted suicide, and his second wife divorced him, charging "perversion, assault, desertion, and infidelity."

In 1909 John McGraw, who had played against Latham in the 1890s and knew how he could disrupt the opposing pitcher's concentration, hired him as baseball's first full-time coach (Arlie had coached part-time with Cincinnati in 1900). From his box at first base, Latham would dance around, enrage the pitcher, steal signs from the catcher, and lead the fans in cheers and jeers. More constructively, perhaps, he also instructed the Giants in the art of base stealing. In 1909, incredibly, one of these steals belonged to Latham himself, who at age forty-nine was acti-

baseman. He was also something of a clown and thus a fan favorite. In a game in 1882 he scored the winning run by turning a somersault over the catcher and landing on the plate. He was famous for profanely badgering the opposition and hectoring his own players, thus earning him the enmity of both and the nickname "The Freshest Man on

vated for four games in September. When Arlie grew too old to play or coach, he stayed on with the Giants as a press-box attendant, and he remained with the Giants in an official capacity until his dying day. His baseball career spanned an incredible seventy-six years.

— ★ —

Urban "Red" Faber pitched himself into the big leagues by showing his stuff around the world.

Faber was purchased from Dubuque by the Pirates the day after pitching the first perfect game in minor-league history, on August 18, 1910. Unfortunately, however, he hurt his arm throwing too many curves before getting a chance to play for Pittsburgh. Instead he was forced to stay in the minors, where he developed a spitball, which became his dominant delivery. The White Sox eventually signed Faber, but he was already twenty-five years old. He was on their roster when the Sox and Giants were beginning their 1913 world tour by playing games throughout the west. Several players backed out of the international portion of the tour, preferring to stay in the U.S. McGraw was short of pitchers, so Chicago manager Nixey Callahan suggested that Faber, who was supposed to end his participation in the tour in Seattle, pitch for the Giants. He was so impressive in venues like Shanghai, Manila, Hong Kong, and Cairo that McGraw tried to buy him. Callahan refused, and Faber's big-league career began. This is Faber's tour sweater, a beautiful button front that would make a great reissue.

In the 1917 World Series, he gave McGraw further reason to wish he had been able to purchase him as he won three games and helped Chicago capture the title. When the Sox returned to the Fall Classic in 1919, it was without Faber, who contracted a bad case of the flu (at a time when this was a matter of life and death, not simply a call for a rest). His catcher, Ray Schalk, always said that if Faber had been healthy, there would have been no Black Sox Scandal.

——★——

Where's the Nike Swoosh? These venerable high-tops sped around the bases for 321 steals on the feet of outfielder Jack "Red" Murray. In the 1911 World Series the unfortunate Murray became red-faced as he learned the meaning of the adage "You can't steal first base." One of the team's leading hitters during the regular season, he went 0 for 21 in the Giants' six-game defeat by the A's. There went Murray's chances of a shoe-endorsement deal.

Low-cut shoes had begun to take over in the previous decade. Murray's fashion statement was a traditional one, born in the 1860s when players strapped spikes to their street shoes and wrapped elastic around their pants legs to prevent baseline mishaps. The 1870s brought lighter shoes, two-toned combinations of canvas and leather that looked like the Keds and P-F Flyers sneakers of the 1930s. But these gave way to basic black ankle boots by the 1880s, which looked not very different from Murray's. With Ty Cobb slashing around the bases in low-cuts around 1910, everyone else wanted to wear them, too. But black remained the only color anyone dared to wear until Charlie Finley's Kansas City A's of the 1960s brought us white shoes (and an orange baseball, and a bunny that delivered baseballs from beneath home plate, and other equally fabulous innovations). Red or blue shoes, matching a color in the team's uniform, became common in the 1980s. Now, just as we begin to brace for the next revolution, high-top shoes are making a comeback.

Harry Hooper was a surprising but splendid choice of the Veterans Committee in 1971, nearly fifty years after he had played his last game of major-league ball. It was in the summer of 1971, when he came to Cooperstown for the induction ceremonies, that he donated this gorgeously pristine red mackinaw and cap.

Hooper was known for his defensive skill as much as his hitting ability. He formed one third of what some experts feel is still the greatest outfield of all time—the Speaker-Lewis-Hooper trio of the 1910–1915 Red Sox. Tris Speaker was one of the top hitters of all time, Duffy Lewis was the master of the fifteen-foot incline in left field known as Duffy's Cliff, and Hooper was a quick leadoff man with extra-base-hit power. But it was as a defensive unit that the three outpaced all who had come before. Speaker played so shallow a center field that he got involved in rundown plays and made several unassisted double plays. Lewis posted double-digit assist totals every one of the eight years he played in Boston. Hooper's assist total in right field reached as high as 29 and averaged over twenty for his entire career.

Hooper's greatest catch occurred in the last game of the legendary World Series of 1912. The visiting Giants had a 1–0 lead in the top of the fifth when Larry Doyle ripped a line shot into deep right center field. Hooper chased it back to the temporary fence, reached up, and had the ball pop out of his mitt as his hip struck the low fence; instinctively, he snatched the ball with his bare hand and tumbled into the joyous mass of fandom.

— ★ —

Jim Gentile was given the nickname "Diamond Jim" by Roy Campanella when the young slugger was a farmhand in the Dodger system. The problem was that the Dodgers already had a pretty fair first baseman named Gil Hodges. Gentile had belted 208 homers in seven minor-league seasons and one major-league season in Brooklyn when he was purchased by Baltimore before the 1960 season. He hit .292 with twenty-one homers and ninety-eight RBIs that year, but teammate Ron Hansen was named Rookie of the Year. The following year was Gentile's season in the sun. Feasting on the diluted pitching created by American League expansion, he hit 46 homers and drove in 141 runs. That was the year Roger Maris hit 61 home runs and added the RBI crown by collecting one more than Gentile. Thirty-five years later, a researcher discovered that Maris was mistakenly credited with an RBI for a run that scored on an error; Major League Baseball will have to wrestle with this issue, and Gentile may yet get a share of the RBI crown.

Gentile also slugged five grand slams in 1961, which tied Ernie Banks for the record until Don Mattingly passed it in 1986. Two of those grand slams took place in the first two innings of a game on May 9. This is the bat that struck those blows.

— ★ —

Tim Raines, Omar Moreno, Willie Wilson, Vince Coleman, Kenny Lofton, Brett Butler, Otis Nixon, and Lance Johnson are just a few of the speedy leadoff men of our generation. Each has walked the proverbial mile in this man's shoes.

When Maury Wills stole fifty bases in 1960 it

was the highest total in the National League in thirty-seven years. Although Luis Aparicio and Chicago's Go-Go Sox of the 1950s had built their offense around speed, they were slow to exert influence, even in their own league. Baseball remained a base-to-base game dominated by sluggers. Willie Mays and Hank Aaron were fast enough to steal, but they seldom bothered. Maury Wills changed all that. The Dodger team he joined for the pennant drive of 1959 was old and slow, its offense carried by such last-hurrah Brooklynites as Duke Snider, Gil Hodges, Jim Gilliam, and Carl Furillo. The Dodgers won the championship in 1959, but to stay at the top in the next decade would require a dedication to pitching, defense, and, in the absence of real power, speed.

By mid-decade Wills had changed the way the game was played in both leagues, more than any man had since Babe Ruth in the 1920s. Maury's 104 steals in 1962 broke the record Ty Cobb had set in the dead-ball year of 1915 (that season Braggo Roth led the American League with seven homers!). Wills led the National League in stealing six straight years; three times his Dodgers won the pennant, another time they lost in a play-off. The Dodger version of the home run was for Wills to reach first base, steal second, advance to third on a ground ball, and score on a sacrifice fly. His accomplishments ushered in the great baseball era of the 1970s and 1980s, when power returned to the game but, this time, speed stayed. Lou Brock broke Wills's record, then Rickey Henderson broke that, and both passed Cobb on the lifetime list as well. The good old days were great, but baseball has never been played better than it has been since Maury Wills came along.

—★—

This polite letter from baseball's greatest hero is made poignant by our knowledge that he had said his farewell to baseball the day before, and that he had only two months left to live. Ruth wrote this letter to general manager George Weiss to acknowledge the silver anniversary celebration of Yankee Stadium, during which he wore number 3 for the last time. (Incredibly, the number had not previously been retired; rookie outfielder Cliff Mapes had been wearing it that very season.) Ruth was weak from the radiation treatments for his throat cancer; as he paused in the dugout before entering into that cauldron of sound one last time, he was quivering with cold. On the spur of the moment he accepted the bat proffered by Cleveland pitcher Bob Lemon. He leaned on it as a prop while he accepted the rolling cheers from the crowd. Nat Fein's famous photograph of the event, taken from behind Ruth, makes the Babe look rather noble; it was a kind camera angle, for the fact was, his withered face looked terrible. It was beyond belief that this giant of a man, who exuded invincibility, had dwindled to such a state by age fifty-three.

Within two weeks the Babe had checked into a cancer center at Memorial Hospital. His film biography, starring William Bendix, opened on July 25. Ruth and his wife went to the premiere, but could manage to sit through only half of it. He died on the sixteenth of August.

—★—

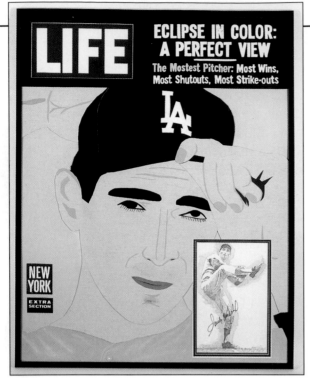

Why are the painting and sculpture of baseball so satisfying when its fiction and film so often are not? I think it's because the game is itself a sublimation of mythic conflict and as such cannot easily sustain another layer of legend or story imposed upon it. Our baseball heroes are not real people in our eyes—they are icons of the game themselves, no less than their baseball cards. The crossed paths of the "A" and "L" on Sandy Koufax's cap could signify the game's curious intersection of Art and Life. Murray Tinkelman's witty homage is not only to Sandy Koufax but also to Andy Warhol, Hokusai, and Hiroshige. "Eclipse in Color," the lead story on this issue of *Life*, could serve as a description of the portrait of Koufax and his effect on batters.

———★———

Bud Abbott and Lou Costello, who had been a comic duo since 1931, visited the Baseball Hall of Fame in 1956. They presented the institution with this gold record and plaque, as well as a transcription of their routine. When I published this classic in *The Armchair Book of Baseball* in 1985, I prefaced it by writing:

> This classic assault on sense and syntax is generally associated with Abbott and Costello, who, having performed it in the 1945 film *Naughty Nineties*, are

presumed to have written it. They didn't. Who did? Naturally.

I went on to say that the skit was of anonymous authorship, as were some 2,000 other stock burlesque bits in Abbott and Costello's repertoire. Only recently, however, I have learned that they aired "Who's on First?" as far back as 1938, when they performed it on Kate Smith's radio show, and that the skit had an author: Irving Gordon (1915–1996), a versatile fellow who also wrote Nat King Cole's 1951 hit song, "Unforgettable," as well as "Prelude to a Kiss" for Duke Ellington, "What Can I Tell My Heart?" for Bing Crosby, "Throw Mama from the Train" for Patti Page and, in a song title for Billie Holiday that puts one in mind of "Who's on First?," the strangely populated "Me, Myself and I."

Here's Gordon's unforgettable lineup:

> First Base: *Who*
> Second Base: *What*
> Third Base: *I Don't Know*
> Shortstop: *I Don't Care*
> Left Field: *Why*
> Center Field: *Because*
> Pitcher: *Tomorrow*
> Catcher: *Today*

Note that this team had always taken the field without anyone in right or to write. Now you can put Irving Gordon in. Naturally.

———★———

M*agic:* the sparrow of 1919 has been transformed, some forty years later, into a parakeet. What has not changed is the impish grin on Casey Stengel's face as he reenacts for the camera one of the most engaging scraps of baseball lore: Casey tips his cap, and a bird again flies out.

It first happened on a Sunday in 1919 at (where else?) Ebbets Field. Stengel, the original of Wilbert Robinson's Daffiness Boys, had been traded to Pittsburgh before the 1918 season, but spent most of that season and the start of the next in the military. Playing his first game back in his spiritual home, Casey was 0 for 3 and had just made a bad play in the outfield that gave Brooklyn the lead. When he came to bat the crowd made a lot of noise, some booing, some cheering derisively. He politely doffed his cap, and out came a sparrow. The crowd convulsed in laughter (and so did everyone on both teams). The *New York Sun* said, "Casey Stengel, the jolly right fielder of the Pirates, has pulled a lot of comedy in his life, but yesterday he got one off in Ebbets Field that wins the brown derby." If he had done it in the days of film or TV, we would have all seen it a million times by now. But this large photo residing in the archive, of unknown provenance, is all we've got. For me, it's more than enough—it's the best way to remember Casey.

ABOUT THE AUTHOR

JOHN THORN wrote his first baseball book twenty-five years ago. Since then he has written and edited a great many more, among them *The Hidden Game of Baseball*, *The Game for All America*, and *The Armchair Books of Baseball*. With statistician Pete Palmer he created the official encyclopedia of the game, *Total Baseball*, now in its fifth edition. He was senior creative consultant to the Ken Burns film *Baseball*.

John Thorn is the publisher of Total Sports, a cross-platform sports information company. He lives in Kingston, New York.